Essential
Internet

OTHER ECONOMIST BOOKS

Guide to Analysing Companies
Guide to Business Modelling
Guide to Economic Indicators
Guide to the European Union
Guide to Financial Markets
Guide to Management Ideas
Numbers Guide
Style Guide

Business Ethics
China's Stockmarket
Economics
E-Commerce
E-Trends
Globalisation
Measuring Business Performance
Successful Innovation
Successful Mergers
Wall Street

Dictionary of Business
Dictionary of Economics
International Dictionary of Finance

Essential Director
Essential Finance
Essential Investment

Pocket Asia
Pocket Europe in Figures
Pocket World in Figures

Essential

Internet

Sean Geer

ROO4.648

WITHDRAWN

THE ECONOMIST IN ASSOCIATION WITH
PROFILE BOOKS LTD

Published by Profile Books Ltd
58A Hatton Garden, London EC1N 8LX

Designed and typeset in EcoType by MacGuru Ltd
info@macguru.org.uk

Printed in Italy by Legoprint – S.p.a. – Lavis (TN)

A CIP catalogue record for this book is available
from the British Library

ISBN 1 86197 540 6

Contents

Introduction   vii

The essential internet   1

A to Z   15

Appendices
1 A brief history of the internet   245
2 Abbreviations   261
3 Recommended websites   265

Introduction

Instant gratification, said Carrie Fisher (an American actress best known for her role in *Star Wars*), takes too long. This sentiment underlies the astonishing rise and fall of that other high-tech fantasy, the dotcom boom. If it was once possible to get rich quickly by investing in internet companies, it was also possible to get poor just as quickly, which for a while obstructed a clear view of what this still new medium was really for.

That kind of instant gratification is hard to find in today's internet economy, at least from a commercial perspective. Hyperbole and hysteria have given way to a kind of common sense that is based on more conventional business ideas. But as more than 500m people around the world continue to discover, the internet is still the fastest and best way to get all sorts of things done. The purpose of this book is to help the reader understand how and why this is so, and why the internet remains one of the most important inventions of our time.

Many of the things that the internet is best at are now taken for granted by many of its users, in the same way that utilities such as water and electricity are. In most Western countries, internet traffic now outstrips that of the telephone networks, a clear indication that this vast network of wires and computers has become a vital part of the way in which people want to communicate. The ways in which it connects them together may not always be those envisaged by the internet gurus of the late 20th century, but it continues to provide an important platform for discussion, business and invention that has far-reaching implications for the world's societies.

Essential Internet explains the ways in which this is happening now, and how they might evolve in the future. In it you will find the technological terms explained, the viable (and the not-so-viable) business ideas analysed, the important parts of the internet's short history laid out and some of its startling statistics presented. It is designed as a companion for anyone who wants to make sense of this sometimes confusing but always fascinating medium. From bandwidth to burn rate, from mail rage to malware, it's here. And cross-references, highlighted in SMALL

CAPITALS, make it easy to find your way to related entries.

Business is still finding its feet on the internet. But as the smoke clears from the burn-out of thousands of companies, some of the ways in which the survivors and new players might build profitable and sustainable ventures online are becoming more evident. At the same time, the internet's ability to drive social and political change becomes daily more apparent. The more people that use it, and the more things that it is used for, the more useful it becomes. This simple fact has become if anything more obvious in these calmer times.

Sean Geer
March 2003

The essential internet

As revolutions go, the digital version triggered by the growth of the internet is in good company. Charles Dickens, writing about the prelude to a much earlier revolution in France, summed up the spirit of such things perfectly in the opening sentence of *A Tale of Two Cities*: "it was the age of foolishness, it was the epoch of belief, it was the epoch of incredulity". This will resonate strongly with anyone who has observed the extraordinary shifts in the internet landscape since the beginning of the 21st century. Retrospectively, it all seems like a bad joke: companies barely a year old filing for IPOs and becoming worth billions of dollars days later; teenage entrepreneurs with no track record in business raising hundreds of millions of dollars to start companies; and online retailers racking up huge losses while being valued more highly than long-established blue-chip companies. Driven by what seemed like boundless optimism to some and sheer greed to others, thousands of companies appeared to be on their way to fabulous futures in which the rules of business and economics had been turned on their heads by revolutionary technologies and a new kind of business vision. Now, that optimism seems misplaced at best, and criminally negligent in the worst cases. Half a decade after the madness began we are back where we started, in a world where profit matters and paying customers are once again the benchmark of a successful business. The internet companies that could not supply these are for the most part out of business, and a new kind of sanity prevails.

That, at least, is the theory. But a casual glance at the metrics of the internet show that things are anything but stable. The investment world may have turned its back on the vast constellation of cables and computers that make up the internet, at least for the time being. Yet in every other way this extraordinary medium continues to grow, both physically and conceptually. Every day it sprouts thousands of new tendrils as consumer demand for internet connections continues to rise. Demographically, the internet is reaching more kinds of people in more kinds of places, some of them highly unlikely ones. The number of websites is measured in tens of millions and the number of individual pages in multiple billions. All that has really changed is the perception of what the internet is actually for.

You have mail

The thing the internet is best at, and for which it is still most widely used, is communication. The ways in which is it used for this are evolving quite fast, but the fundamental principle remains the same: take a message of some kind, put an address on it and send it to its destination across the wires. These wires are completely agnostic. If something can be turned into a message of some kind (and most things can, thanks to the miracle of digital technology; legal documents and love letters, purchase orders and petitions are all treated with equanimity) it can be exchanged with someone else. It is this exchange of information, rather than the exchange of mere cash, that makes the internet an enduringly important phenomenon.

The most common kind of message sent in this way is still e-mail, the instrument that has persuaded hundreds of millions of people of the usefulness of the internet. E-mail breaks one of the fundamental barriers to global communication because of its asynchronous nature: unlike a telephone call, it makes no requirement for sender and recipient to communicate simultaneously, bringing instant freedom from the inconvenience of time zones or busy lines.

The number of messages sent by e-mail is staggering, even in the context of the dizzy numbers that characterise the internet. IDC, a research company, estimated that 31 billion e-mail messages were sent every day in 2002, 11 trillion or so over the year, a figure it expects to rise to 60 billion by 2006. Europemedia, a company specialising in new media research in Europe, reported that 70 billion e-mails were sent in Italy alone in 2002, about 1,200 for every citizen.

E-mail's appeal is not hard to understand, as anyone who has received a message from a forgotten friend or a distant relative will attest. Communication between individuals is now so common that it is taken for granted by most people; it is just there, in the same way that the postal service has been for decades, and it is always available even when you are not at home or at your desk. Free webmail services and the now ubiquitous internet cafes have combined to create a culture in which people are rarely far from an e-mailbox, and they use them enthusiastically. Microsoft's free Hotmail service alone now claims over 110m accounts worldwide, with similar offerings from Yahoo and others not far behind.

E-mail's relatives have also become extremely popular. Instant messaging, in particular, has caught the imagination of hundreds of millions of users around the world, enabling real-time communication of a kind that is beginning to find its way into finance houses, medical establishments and legal practices as well as people's living rooms. Not all of this communication is as intimate or as private as e-mail and instant messaging. One-to-one technologies have been around for several decades in one form or another, but the web has given people a one-to-many platform from which to share their thoughts daily with the online populace. Bill Clinton's 1996 observation that even his cat had its own home page now seems somewhat outdated. Today, what it really needs is a weblog, a simple diary-like web page in which thousands of people now routinely record their ideas. Weblogging exploded in 2002, as people flocked to a sort of digital soapbox which is now busily creating a new generation of enthusiastic (if not always inspirational or even interesting) social and political commentators.

These developments and others like them may or may not turn out to have lasting importance. But the things that people really find useful are still those that have been around for a good while, and their popularity shows no sign of abating. The continued evolution of search engines, in particular, is a logical response to the enormous demand for better ways of finding and filtering information, encompassing everything from the most trivial telephone number enquiry to the most demanding scientific research projects. If you want to find out where to get the cheapest flight from Alaska to Australia, the best place to buy French cheeses in Dublin or the nearest saxophone teacher to your home in Moscow, the web is the easiest and best place to do it. So reliable is the web at this that the tools for indexing and searching it have become household names and even verbs in their own right; "googling" is a well-established expression among web enthusiasts. For millions of people, the ability to find information on any conceivable subject (and some inconceivable ones too) makes the internet as indispensable a resource as water or telephony.

This thirst for electronic knowledge has forced some interesting changes among established information providers. Although enormous numbers of websites still support the information economy out of a sense of philanthropy and altruism, many are now forced to maintain their digital presence because of the impact on their existing brands and reputations if they fail to do so. Newspapers, entertainment companies, television stations and telecoms companies now support their online presence in the knowledge that it is unlikely to be directly profitable, simply because people will go somewhere else if they do not. This is why organisations such as the BBC continue to expand their global online products as they replace their old-fashioned distribution mechanisms. By maintaining high standards online, they can be reasonably sure that their audience will remain loyal, no matter how many other interesting places there are to go to; and with a happily captive audience, there is always the potential to build a business around it or sustain an existing one.

Not dotcom

Quite what else the internet is for is harder for many to appreciate. Some scepticism about its broader usefulness is hardly surprising in the wake of the dotcom debacle, but it is nonetheless interesting to note what people are not doing with the internet. At the height of the dotcom mania anything seemed possible, and if it was possible people did it. So pervasive was the idea that the internet represented the future of more or less everything that apparently sane individuals, and in some cases whole communities, abandoned their lives and identities to it. In early 2000 Mitch Maddox legally changed his name to DotComGuy and spent a year living online, buying everything he needed to survive by sponsoring e-commerce sites, a marketing experiment which some of its sponsors failed to survive long enough to see through to its conclusion. At around the same time, the town of Halfway in Oregon (population 345) was persuaded to change its name to Half.com, in support of an eponymous online retailer. The name persists on the town's website to this day, although the company has since been absorbed into the eBay portfolio.

Such behaviour is conspicuous by its absence in these more sober times. People are not only not changing their names; they are also not doing many of the other things that the net evangelists said they would be doing. The internet's almost limitless ability to link people together in apparently exciting new ways has proved to be an expensive illusion for thousands of companies which adopted a "because we can" mentality, only to discover that the prevailing mood among potential consumers was "actually, we don't want to". Instead of consulting doctors, lawyers and counsellors online, most people still choose to do things the old-fashioned way: turning up in someone's office and talking to them face-to-face, for example, rather than consulting them across video links or secure e-mail channels. Trust, it seems, has little to do with unbreakable encryption technologies and high-speed streaming media, and everything to do with social ritual and convention. At the same time, the fact that you can sell elephant manure online, as at least one company tried to do, does not mean that it is a good idea.

These inescapable facts had profound implications for many of the companies that tried to build businesses selling products or services to consumers and for the 5,000 or so internet companies that have closed or been acquired since the beginning of 2000, according to a 2003 survey by Webmergers, a mergers and acquisitions research company. If you want a lobster, the chances are that you want to buy it from a fishmonger that you know sells good, fresh ones rather than a website of unknown location and reputation. This may be one reason why the lobsters.com domain was available for sale at the time of writing. Some such sites continue to exist and may even do good business, but most of the profitable examples are adjuncts to an existing business, for which the addition of a website is just another channel to market rather than the only way in which it makes its living. Geography, it seems, is alive and kicking, despite predictions of its demise by the people whose businesses trumpeted its increasing irrelevance in a world connected by wires rather than roads.

The big brand

This "clicks-and-mortar" approach, once derided by the digerati as a stepping stone on the way to oblivion for old-fashioned companies with real-world assets, now seems to have real value. A survey of British internet users in 2001 showed that of the 20 most visited websites in the UK, 17 were linked to existing commercial brands, a trend that is replicated in many other places around the world. Some countries still display fierce loyalty to local offline brands; in France, for example, Fnac (a big seller of books, music, DVDs, games and electronic equipment) still inspires greater confidence online than American imports such as Amazon, and its domestic grocery giants do good business via their websites. But in general, even the most successful electronic retailers still accrue only a tiny percentage of their profits from online sales. Tesco.com, the online arm of one of the UK's biggest retailers, reported sales of over £10m a week at the end of 2002, representing orders from over 100,000 households, about 2% of the group's average weekly revenues, according to figures the company released earlier in that year.

If retail giants such as these are still struggling to make a strong impression on the web, the prospects for smaller companies with far fewer resources and limited brand power seem hopeless. It may once have been possible to attract investors to a new business even if your prospectus loudly proclaimed that your sales margins were actually negative – as buy.com, an American retailer, was able to in 1999 – but the success of such businesses depends on generating huge and repeatable sales volumes which might at least form the basis for profit at some time in the future, even if you currently sell dollar bills for 90 cents each. Most of the dotcom businesses failed to pass this test, instead burning cash at a rate far exceeding revenues. Despite gigantic investment in marketing and advertising, few companies have managed to build the steady stream of customers needed to make their business models work. Boo.com, one of the most celebrated of the dotcom failures, spent a staggering $42m in 1999 on television and print advertising for its fashion-retailing service in six countries, only to discover that its site's technical shortcomings were matched only by the indifference of potential customers to its proposition; the company's assets were sold for $2m in May 2000. Countless similar tales contributed to the implosion of the dotcom sector in 2000 and 2001, and today's e-commerce landscape is a far leaner and, to many eyes, much more attractive one.

It's the old economy, stupid

Not every company burned out in the dotcom supernova. The few companies that built businesses around large and sustainable numbers of customers are still in business, most notably Amazon and eBay. Amazon reported a net profit for the first time from its sales in the last quarter of 2001 and has many loyal customers; between the beginning of November and mid-December 2002, for example, it took nearly 48m orders. eBay, meanwhile, persuaded visitors to its auction sites to do business worth nearly $15 billion in 2002, slicing off enough commission from its sales to sustain its vigorous growth and acquisitions policy. Yahoo, one of the very few companies to build a successful business from a portal strategy, has had a leaner time, but it is in better shape than it was in early 2001, when it announced plans to lay off 12% of its workforce. Long reliant on advertising for most of its revenue, Yahoo combined some smart acquisitions of companies with paying customers, such as the HotJobs recruitment company, with a new strategy designed to make people pay for things such as classified advertising and e-mail services. The result is a more diverse business with multiple revenue streams that continues to post profits, despite a general decline in the advertising market that constitutes 60% of its revenue.

None of this guarantees the future of these companies or those like them. Amazon in particular must demonstrate that after billions of dollars of losses since its launch in 1995, it will provide a good return in future. But it seems that people are prepared to spend their money with players whose brands they trust. Every recent survey shows that consumer spending online is growing. People may not be buying many lobsters, but sales of items such as books, CDs, DVDs and electrical goods continue to grow. The Department of Commerce reported that online retail sales in the United States passed $45 billion in 2002. That figure, however, represents only 1.6% of the total retail spend, a stark illustration of exactly how significant retail e-business is.

Some sectors are growing much faster than others. Travel, in particular, is fulfilling the high expectations that were set long ago, neatly illustrating one of the internet's most persuasively useful attributes: its ability to aggregate and compare information sources. Buying airline or rail tickets online is not only quicker and more convenient than doing it in a cramped travel agent's office; it is more cost-effective too, because buyers can see for themselves what their options are. There are now many large and efficient online travel services that can not only display all available flights for a particular date and time, but also find you a hotel or a hire car at the other end. The Travel Industry Association of America estimates that around 64m Americans now research their travel options online and 39m of them actually paid for it in 2002.

B2B or not B2B?

The predictions made at the height of the dotcom mania for online business-to-business (B2B) trading may have been ridiculously optimistic, but in 2002 the US Census Bureau reported that B2B transactions accounted for 94% of all e-commerce sales in 2000, at a time when the rest of the market seemed to be in serious decline. The manufacturing sector alone accounted for shipments worth $777 billion for the year, with sales by wholesalers coming in a respectable second at $213 billion; these numbers put even the most optimistic estimates for retail sales into sharp perspective. Forrester, a research company, predicts that the value of online trade in European business goods and services will amount to €2.2 trillion in 2006. Most such estimates predict that the biggest volumes of business will be done in sectors such as electrical equipment, industrial machinery, oil, chemicals, metals and energy, where deals can be negotiated and items paid for electronically with minimal requirements for human intervention.

Once again, it is the ability of electronic networks to aggregate and compare products and prices that makes this possible, combined with the low costs of electronic transactions. But the ways in which this is happening now are not necessarily those originally envisaged by industry analysts and suppliers. Companies selling b2b procurement software, once the darlings of the stockmarkets, have had to change radically as the vertical markets they once served have proved to be too limiting to form the basis for profitable businesses. b2b exchanges, too, once touted as the glittering future of e-commerce, have been forced to re-examine their businesses. Chemdex, an American chemicals exchange, which once had a market capitalisation of $11 billion, shut down in 2000; its parent company has since shifted its focus to selling software that automates business processes. Part of the reason for such reversals is that suppliers of goods and services inevitably suffer in electronically mediated sales environments as price becomes the main differentiator and they are forced to cut their margins to the bone in order to compete. Electronic exchanges and marketplaces have subsequently been unable to generate the enormous volumes of trade needed to generate the commissions that make their businesses profitable and have been forced to retrench; only those offering deep knowledge of their industries are showing signs of thriving.

Speaking your language

One emerging source of hope for the b2b sector is in web services. Much has been promised for these by the technology industry's biggest players, most notably Microsoft, ibm and Sun. Web services allow software programs and services to be plugged together irrespective of their original source or format, thus allowing disparate networks to share information without the need for massive re-engineering of existing systems or expensive investment in new hardware and software. Because they are based on industry standards such as xml (Extensible Mark-up

Language, a relative of HTML designed for data exchange), in theory they allow any program that presents data in standard formats to speak to any other, thus solving one of the business world's most intractable and expensive problems.

Most of the early noise about web services involved consumer-based offerings on websites. But by far the biggest market for web services is in the business sector, where firms can realistically look forward to being able to share information that was previously impossible to distribute, both internally and with business partners. Jupiter, an American research company, reported that 82% of companies surveyed in 2002 were already using web services of one kind or another, most of them as part of pilot projects; and the web services market is inevitably being hyped as hard as its B2B predecessors.

Web services may or may not turn out to be the salvation of e-commerce, but they will at least tell us whether its proponents have learned anything from the harsh lessons of the last two years. Web services alone do not help to solve the problem of how to persuade consumers to pay for content or businesses to pay for services, something that both remain reluctant to do. People will buy all sorts of things on the internet – and, importantly, come back again – if you try to sell them something they really want, absolutely need or can easily use, as simply and conveniently as possible. Companies like Amazon have understood and used this to their advantage, with judicious use of technology, to give people few reasons to go elsewhere. By contrast, people will probably not do so if you require them to cross a cultural or commercial barrier without some hard evidence that it is worth their while, evidence that thousands of dotcoms failed to provide. Fortunately, the technical barrier that for some years dissuaded people from taking full advantage of new online products and services is at last beginning to diminish.

The byte fantastic

When the World Wide Web was born it might as well have been in another world altogether. The fastest modem owned by a member of the still tiny online community would, in theory, connect to another member's identical modem at a speed of 14,400 bits per second. This was enough to send text-only e-mail but totally ill-suited to anything more complicated. Internet service providers (ISPS) were more or less unheard of, and if you somehow managed to dial in to the central web server at CERN in Switzerland you would have found a handful of machines devoted to high-energy physics and the people who studied it. Today, although ISPS help us connect to the vast resource that the web represents, most people in the world still rely on modems a mere four times faster than their 1993 predecessors to help them surf and send e-mail. In the ten years since its arrival, the web has become not just immeasurably bigger but immeasurably richer too, as its simple text content has mutated into a complex blend of formatted text, graphics, animations and multimedia components such as sound and video.

Unsurprisingly, people want access to this, and ISPS have been happy to oblige them; at the end of 2002 well over 500m people were online, nearly all of them connected via one of many companies providing basic access to a wide range of internet services for a monthly fee. But despite the tremendous growth in the sophistication of the web and a correspondingly greater demand for access to it, the world's bandwidth providers have been slow in helping subscribers tap into it more effectively. The technology to do so has been available for several years in the form of cable and digital subscriber line (DSL) services, both of which offer much faster access to the net than the modems that still reside in people's PCs or on their desks. In some countries, these technologies have already become well established. In most, however, they remain luxury items, out of the reach of many subscribers because of high pricing and limited availability. The reluctance of telecoms companies to expand their high-speed networks has been one of the biggest barriers to the growth of potentially profitable digital services. As a result, the much-heralded bandwidth explosion that hyperbolic commentators foresaw as the most significant social development since the discovery of fire is only now beginning to materialise.

One reason for this reluctance is a general unwillingness on behalf of monopolistic telecoms companies to expand their precious networks for competitors to exploit. Another is the high cost of converting exchanges to exploit DSL technology or, in the case of cable companies, digging up enough roads to get cable to a big enough percentage of the population to make it worthwhile. But it is beginning to happen, and broadband technology is slowly seeping into the lives of families and businesses as its potential benefits become more accessible.

The fact that this is happening at all is miraculous, given the difficult position of many telecoms companies and the apparent unwillingness of governing bodies to help sort out the mess. Despite repeated statements of intent by governments keen to make names for their countries as progressive technological societies, few have been willing to do much about it themselves. Indeed, many have seen bandwidth merely as another revenue stream, as witnessed by the wireless bandwidth auctions in 2000, in which telecoms operators throughout Europe bid billions of dollars for licence fees. There are exceptions. South Korea, for example, now has the highest number of DSL subscribers in the world, outnumbering even the United States, thanks to enormous investment in infrastructure and widespread marketing support for the companies that build it and sell it. The United States, though, has a long-established cable culture that keeps it high on the list of best-connected nations. And while some countries struggle with the challenge of building their corners of the wireless internet, others such as Finland have been happily doing it for years.

A private function

Digital technology brings with it all sorts of possibilities to improve communications with citizens, as thousands of projects around the world have shown. Electronic voting and the ability to file online tax returns are now commonplace everywhere from Brazil to Belgium, and they bring with them the potential for huge increases in efficiency and precision. But governments everywhere face a huge problem in designing useful electronic interfaces with their citizens. In the UK, where even a small post office may offer several hundred kinds of transactions and services, any e-government system must eventually be able to deal with over 5 billion interactions with its citizens every year. The logistics of this are hard enough to manage in wealthy Western countries where private finance is often available to bolster public-sector projects. In countries with larger populations or those where internet technology is less widely available to the populace, the difficulties in managing electronic governmental projects become severe. Attempts to provide some sort of consistent approach to these problems are gathering momentum, however. The European Commission issued benchmark guidelines for its members in late 2002, and even in China, where only about 3% of citizens have access to the internet, state bureaus are online and offering some services.

It will be a long time before "joined-up government" is something that the world's voters and taxpayers take for granted. It is perhaps unsurprising that many governments have not received the idea of a connected society with unremitting enthusiasm, given their historical suspicion of technology that brings independent communication to their citizens. That suspicion has grown as they have begun to understand how little control they have over the things that people choose to communicate to each other. The same digital technology that promises to streamline interaction with citizens also provides new ways of concealing information, and quite a lot of people want to exploit this potential to secure their exchanges against prying eyes. Not all of this is for nefarious reasons. Privacy of this kind is, at an important level, one of e-commerce's defining characteristics; the ability for people to conduct transactions of whatever size securely and privately is a critical part of building confidence in an emerging electronic marketplace.

But governments are often wary of what they cannot control and they cannot control what they cannot see. Encryption technologies, in particular, allow people to render their conversations invisible to the most sophisticated snoopers and thus make regulators extremely nervous. Even before the events of September 11th 2001, most governments around the world had started to draft legislation governing access to these virtually unbreakable ciphers. Now armed with apparently hard evidence that the internet is indeed the playground for terrorists that they had long feared, they have been busily introducing legislation that gives them widespread powers to intercept communications between individuals in any number of ways and without accountability. The US Domestic Security Act 2003 and the UK Regulation of Investigatory Powers Act 2000 may be the two most high-profile examples, but their sentiments are being expressed by authorities as distant as New Zealand and South Africa.

Many campaigners and some politicians vigorously oppose these and other devices to restrict freedom of expression on the internet. So far, their opposition has been largely unnecessary. It turns out that the internet's uniquely democratic and flexible structure still defies most attempts to censor it, as the continued expansion of pornography sites amply demonstrates. Ironically, some efforts by the authorities to track down serious offenders have been helped rather than hindered by the web. Paedophiles, in particular, have found that their apparently untraceable web hideaways have served only to concentrate them all in one place, from where they can be identified en masse.

So the uneasy balance of power that has characterised the web's short history continues. If would-be regulators suddenly have more power over it, so too do the people who build and populate it, as dramatically exemplified by the spread of peer-to-peer (P2P) file-sharing networks widely used to distribute copyrighted music among millions of internet users. Defying both the industries that claim they are stealing intellectual property and the copyright legislation designed to support them, such as the much-criticised and often-defeated Digital Millennium Copyright Act, public-spirited hackers are attempting to maintain the freedom of the net and the spirit in which it was created. The open source movement gathers strength daily, wresting more power from software companies and handing it back to their users as programs are created and distributed for free. At the same time, less benign individuals are finding new ways to cause havoc online with a new generation of viruses and other malicious programs. Somewhere in between all this sit governments and businesses, both still fighting to find their place in the ever more diverse ecosystem that the internet is becoming. Whatever the doomsayers might claim in this post-dotcom world, the fun is really only just beginning.

A to Z

@

The symbol in E-MAIL addresses that separates the user's name from the DOMAIN name. Credit for its first use goes to Ray Tomlinson, an engineer at Bolt, Beranek and Newman, an ARPANET contractor. Tomlinson wrote the first e-mail programs for machines connected to Arpanet in 1972, choosing the @ symbol from the few available punctuation marks on his Model 33 Teletype and creating the internet's most recognisable icon in the process.

Acronyms

Programmers and technicians use acronyms or abbreviations to reduce lengthy and complicated terms to manageable proportions. Some, when spelled out, are reasonably self-explanatory, such as GUI (graphical user interface). Others, like CORBA (common object request broken architecture), are rather harder to visualise and remember. Not all acronyms are technical. In NEWSGROUPS you may come across figures of speech such as IMHO (in my humble opinion) and IYSWIM (if you see what I mean). The popularity of CHAT, in particular, has stimulated the creation of many less useful examples. BRB, for instance, is short for "be right back", an indication that its author may have found something more useful to do.

ActiveX

A loosely defined set of standards from MICROSOFT for creating software components. Often misleadingly compared with JAVA, the most visible aspects of ActiveX to internet users are controls, small pieces of software that extend the capabilities of web BROWSERS such as Microsoft's INTERNET EXPLORER and NETSCAPE'S NAVIGATOR. These controls may perform many functions, such as displaying animations or allowing access to CHAT rooms, and can be written in many languages, including Java.

A

ActiveX has raised many concerns about security on the web. Unlike most other downloadable chunks of code, ActiveX controls can access nearly all the functions of a WINDOWS-based PC, including those relating to the hardware. This gives them great power and flexibility, but exposes unwary users to potential security hazards. Malicious HACKERS can easily write small programs that will shut down a computer without warning or delete the entire content of its hard drive. More worryingly, several researchers and hackers have demonstrated apparently innocent controls that are harmless on their own but become malicious when installed alongside other ones.

Java fans and many security consultants cite these problems as good reasons to avoid the use of ActiveX. Microsoft, however, says that the use of a DIGITAL SIGNATURE to identify controls from trusted companies will guarantee user security. Whoever is right, it appears that more and more people are shunning ActiveX in favour of Java APPLETS and FLASH applications, which are now much more common on the web.

ADSL

Asymmetric Digital Subscriber Line, one of several BROAD-BAND technologies designed to increase the BANDWIDTH available over standard copper telephone wires (see also DSL). ADSL's design is based on the assumption that most homes and businesses consume more data than they generate. Accordingly, such a connection may theoretically provide an incoming (or downstream) data speed of up to 8MBPS and an outgoing (or upstream) speed of less than 1mbps, although in practice ISPS are likely to provide much slower connections than this (typically 512KBPS) to keep costs down. The actual data transmission speeds possible depend on the quality and integrity of the copper connection and associated equipment, as well as the distance of the user from the exchange.

ADSL is suitable for one-way applications such as web browsing, video on demand and software distribution, but much less so for those with two-way needs such as VIDEO-CONFERENCING. This makes it ideal for home users and small businesses, who are slowly beginning to adopt it as ISPs and telecoms companies broaden the reach of their broadband networks and improve their marketing. Most large ISPs in Europe now sell ADSL connections for both home and business use.

Because ADSL runs on standard copper wires with a direct one-to-one link to the exchange, rather than across shared cable, it will provide much more consistent performance than most of the alternatives. It requires only a special MODEM and, in some cases, a separate device to split the data and voice channels. It is also much more widely available than equivalent services from cable networks, which require expensive investment and disruptive engineering work to extend their wires to people's doorsteps. But many potential ADSL subscribers, especially those in rural areas, have been disappointed to discover that they live or work too far from their nearest exchange to receive it. This is one reason why only 9% of UK internet users subscribed to broadband services in January 2003.

Advertising

The internet has provided yet another medium through which products, services and brands can be promoted through advertising. For most of the web's brief history, advertising has been seen as a much more reliable source of income for WEBSITE and CONTENT owners than subscription revenue, because people can get so much information ONLINE without having to pay for it. The web has unique attractions for potential advertisers too. Web audiences can be tracked and carefully targeted, and it is easy to monitor which sites visitors come from, how long they spend at a site and where they go next. Such information is difficult and expensive to acquire in the real world, which is why many companies with products and services to sell have turned to the web instead of magazines or television.

Such faith in the new medium appeared to be justified until as recently as 2000, when the Internet Advertising Bureau reported that internet advertising revenue reached $8.2 billion, nearly twice that of the previous year. But in 2001 the market declined by nearly 12%, and the outlook seemed bleaker still in

A 2002, when mid-year figures suggested a further decline of more than 20%. Such figures are an inevitable reflection of the collapse of the DOTCOM phenomenon (dotcoms contributed as much as 70% of the advertising spend in 2000) and even the biggest internet companies have suffered. YAHOO, historically one of the web's more reliable performers, saw its advertising revenue drop from $1 billion in 2000 to a mere $538m in 2001. Part of the reason for the decline may be that consumers have become less tolerant of online advertising. A study by Burst Media, an advertising sales network, in 2002 showed that 36% of web surfers would leave a website if it was too cluttered with adverts, and they were even more disparaging about the explosion of POP-UPS, the advertisers' latest weapon.

It is not surprising that in these circumstances advertisers have become a lot more cautious in their online activities. Not only do they now display much greater discrimination about where they advertise, but they have also changed the way in which they do so. One reason for this change is the decline in the usefulness of the BANNER, still the principal form of advertising on websites but now considered the least effective. Whereas pioneering sites such as HOTWIRED (the self-proclaimed inventor of the banner ad in 1994) once claimed CLICK-THROUGH rates of 10% or more, in the United States the figure plunged to 0.3% in 2001. Faced with abysmal returns from this once rich source of revenue, advertisers are turning to more sophisticated RICH MEDIA advertising techniques to boost their sales.

Despite this apparently bleak picture, online advertising seems to be recovering slowly. Many businesses now report more interest from advertisers as the web economy revives, and most analysts remain optimistic. Forrester Research estimates that online advertisers will spend €6.4 billion in 2007 in Europe alone, representing 6.3% of the total advertising spend for all media. Some industry sectors are performing especially well; for example, spending on online travel advertising rose by as much as 39% in 2002 compared with a year earlier. Meanwhile, content owners continue to seek other forms of revenue, many returning to the idea of selling their content to subscribers rather than giving it away for free and relying on advertising to provide their revenue. Smaller advertisers are turning to other, cheaper devices such as affiliate marketing programmes (in which a supplier of goods or services exchanges a LINK to its website for a share of any profits accruing from sales generated as a result) and E-MAIL advertising to sell more goods online. AMAZON's affiliate marketing programme, for example, offers websites that display links to its bookselling pages a share of the profits from any resulting book sales. Smaller businesses have been well served by such networks as the MICROSOFT-owned Banner Network, which offers schemes including free exchange of banners between sites as well as various inexpensive ways of advertising on high-profile sites such as Yahoo.

Agent

A piece of software designed to find and process information automatically, especially across a NETWORK. Grandiose claims are made for the potential of agents, but most of them have yet to be fully substantiated. The most advanced forms watch a user's behaviour and adapt to it, becoming more useful and accurate the more that they are used. Currently, they are used mainly for retrieving regularly visited web pages, scouring NEWSGROUPS for articles of interest and automating other, similarly repetitive tasks. Other varieties seek out news stories and stock quotes.

Agent technology remains a hot topic despite the fact that it has not matured as fast as originally expected. As the SEARCH ENGINES struggle to keep up to speed with the ever expanding web, the vaguest promise of intelligent and individually tailored entities that can deliver precisely targeted information is an enticing one for many investors and developers. A particular area of interest is shopping, where agents can help by searching retail sites for the best-priced items. (See BOT.)

AIML

Artificial Intelligence Mark-up Language. A relative of XML, AIML is being used to create artificial online "intelligences", especially

A   CHATBOTS, which can respond to queries from users. One such creation is ALICE (short for Artificial Linguistic Internet Computer Entity), which can understand and respond to simple questions about food, weather, sex and even knock-knock jokes.

Ain't It Cool News

A film critique WEBSITE run by Texas-based Harry Knowles, now the internet's most prominent film pundit. Ain't It Cool News has acquired a fearsome reputation among the big film studios, thanks to its detailed reporting and analysis of film screenings and insider secrets several months before the films themselves are released (or even finished, in many cases). Knowles's site is regarded as a premier source of industry gossip and rumours, often supplanting Hollywood magazines as the information source of choice for filmgoers and professionals alike. His network of spies inside the big studios has given him many exclusives, although his apparent scoop listing the 2000 Oscar winners in advance proved to be highly inaccurate, much to the delight of leading film executives, who made the most of their first opportunity to ridicule him.

AltaVista

One of the first SEARCH ENGINES for the WORLD WIDE WEB. AltaVista was born at Digital Equipment Corp (DEC) in 1995, the software being developed as a result of an internal obsession with keeping track of old E-MAIL. It was acquired by Compaq as part of its 1998 takeover of Digital, but was sold to CGMI, an investment group, in 1999 in a deal that valued the company at $2.7 billion.

AltaVista caused a stir in Europe in early 2000 when it announced the launch of a free ISP service, complete with free phone calls, the first company to make such an announcement. Whatever its intentions, the service never materialised, severely damaging the company's credibility in the process. Despite its early start in the search engine sector, much of its ground has now been lost to sleeker competitors such as GOOGLE. In early 2003, AltaVista was sold to Overture, another web search company, for $140m, representing a loss of over $2 billion in less than four years for its previous owners.

Amazon

Almost certainly the most visible brand born on the web and one of the most talked-about companies in the brief history of the internet. Amazon was founded by Jeff Bezos in 1994 with the aim of being able to deliver any book in print in the United States, over 1m titles at that time. By June 1999 it had become the first internet company to reach 10m customers (and in fact gained over 10m new customers in 1999 alone, finishing the year with a total of over 16m). At the same time, *Forbes* magazine rated Bezos's personal worth at more than $10 billion and the company, which had never got close to making a profit, was worth twice as much as British Airways.

Bezos's most important contribution to the internet economy has been people; more precisely, shoppers prepared to hand over details of their credit cards to a WEBSITE. No other organisation has done as much to acclimatise people to the idea that buying things on the internet is safe or made shopping ONLINE quite as easy and enjoyable, another important reason for its popularity with its customers. Amazon now sells not just books but also DVDs, CDs, toys, games, electronic goods, health and beauty products and even DIY equipment, all of which make sizeable contributions to its overall revenue. As if all this was not enough, the company has added an auction service and a scheme for third parties to sell their goods on the Amazon site, called Zshops, and has taken over several high-profile special-interest sites, including the highly rated Internet Movie Database. Perhaps more importantly, it has also started to sell its own highly praised software to other web retailers, earning $225m in 2001 from its BUSINESS-TO-BUSINESS ventures and licensing deals alone.

Like most internet companies, Amazon spent most of its early years losing money. But the size of its customer base and the

A health of its revenue stream inspired confidence in the financial community, and in the last quarter of 2001 the company posted its first ever operating profit, albeit a small one. More encouraging results in 2002 have helped renew faith in Amazon's prospects, with growth of 76% in its international markets in the last quarter of 2002. It now has well over 30m customers and annual revenues were nearly $4 billion in 2002. In common with other dotcom businesses, Amazon's stockmarket value dropped by over 80% in one year, with the share price plunging to less than $6 in September 2001 from a high of $221 in 1999. But its stock price remained relatively stable in 2002 and the future looks promising.

Anon.penet.fi

A Finnish computer system used to protect the identities of internet users (see REMAILER).

Anonymiser

A service that allows surfers to visit WEBSITES without revealing information about themselves or their computers. Nearly all websites collect information of some kind about visitors, in particular their IP ADDRESSES, which web SERVERS need to send pages back to the right place. Many sites also use COOKIES to track visitors and link E-MAIL addresses to particular IP addresses, allowing marketers to identify users and add them to mailing lists. By subscribing to a web-based anonymity service, users can hide their IP addresses and prevent websites from installing cookies on their machine, thus providing them with a greater degree of privacy. Many anonymisers also prevent well-known annoyances such as POP-UP windows.

Anonymisers rely on PROXY SERVERS to act as intermediaries between users and the websites they are trying to visit. Instead of sending information directly to the site, the anonymising service redirects all requests for web pages to its own proxy servers, from where the request is subsequently dis-

patched. As a result, website owners see only the IP address of
the service, rather than the user, and can theoretically gather no
information about the person or computer actually looking at
the site. In practice, however, a determined site owner can
exploit advanced features of modern web BROWSERS to effectively bypass these services, usually by using JAVASCRIPT or
special HTML tags to collect IP addresses and silently redirect
traffic away from the intermediary. Several of the most popular
anonymisers are vulnerable to these tactics.

The popularity of anonymisers has risen dramatically in line
with the huge volume of unwanted e-mail received by most internet users and an increasing awareness that their behaviour is
being tracked. They are especially popular with people visiting
sites with questionable content, such as PORNOGRAPHY, who
hope that their tracks will be covered and their identities secure.
Ultimately, however, anyone with a good reason to discover
those identities (law-enforcement agencies, for example) can
simply recover them from the service, so they are not a safe
refuge for people engaging in illegal ONLINE activities.
Anonymisers can also interfere with the normal operation of
many useful websites, which may refuse access to users who
disable cookies or pop-up windows. (See also REMAILER.)

AOL

America On Line, the world's largest provider of internet access
and ONLINE services, with over 35m subscribers and another
2.3m under the COMPUSERVE umbrella. AOL made its mark by
attracting subscribers with interactive services such as CHAT via
the distribution of hundreds of millions of trial disks, comfortably the biggest such marketing programme in history. It then
exchanged access to those subscribers for original CONTENT
from big media names such as Time Warner, CBS and New Line
Cinema, alongside free ADVERTISING with those companies.
The result was a service rich in information and flush with visitors, which, for a while at least, made real money in an otherwise profitless sector.

Long regarding itself as a media concern as well as a provider

A of online services, the company spent most of the late 1990s figuring out ways to bring its content to ever more people in ever more varied ways. Nobody was surprised when AOL bought NETSCAPE in 1998, marking its first real interest in the business sector. The company spent much of 1999 forging deals with suppliers of BROADBAND and satellite communications in a big push to provide subscribers with high-speed access to its enhanced services. It moved into online music distribution, buying two digital music companies, and it made some aggressive moves towards the retail sector.

In January 2000, AOL announced a £150 billion takeover of entertainment giant Time Warner. By the time the merger was completed a year later, the stockmarket was a few months away from collapse and confidence in the new company was receding. AOL Time Warner has struggled to live with its status as the world's biggest media company. Despite a 100m-strong subscriber base and a vast distribution NETWORK, it failed to capitalise on its immense existing content assets from its component businesses, choosing instead to concentrate its efforts on cross-promotional marketing activity, video-on-demand trials and digital music subscriptions.

All this is now seen as evidence that the company's detractors may have been right all along. Few technology companies have attracted as much vitriol as AOL, or AOHELL as it is known in some circles. Often criticised for its poor service to dial-up subscribers, its nannying and censorious behaviour, the ineptitude of its software and a huge SPAM problem, it now also appears to be a company whose management badly misread the market for its services. Following the report that the company had lost a staggering $99 billion in 2002, Steve Case, AOL's chairman and founder, announced his departure from the company early in 2003.

Apache

Software for running web SERVERS. Unlike similar software from giants such as NETSCAPE and MICROSOFT, Apache is free, which has led to its rapid adoption by millions of WEBSITES. A

Netcraft survey in February 2003 showed that 63% of websites polled were running Apache, putting it streets ahead of commercial products such as Microsoft's IIS (27%). **A**

Apache, so named because it was originally based on a "patchy" version of an NCSA web server, runs on many kinds of computers, including Intel-based WINDOWS machines and UNIX-based systems, and is an important part of the OPEN SOURCE movement. Not only is the actual program code freely downloadable, but so is the editable SOURCE CODE, making it possible for users to customise the software.

Applet

A small computer program usually dedicated to a specific task. In the context of the WORLD WIDE WEB, applets are built into web pages to perform functions such as displaying animations or performing calculations. Typically written in JAVA, such programs are designed to run in any BROWSER supporting that language.

It shouldn't be too much of a surprise that the internet has evolved into a force strong enough to reflect the greatest hopes and fears of those who use it. After all, it was designed to withstand nuclear war, not just the puny huffs and puffs of politicians and religious fanatics.
Denise Caruso

Arpanet

A pioneering NETWORK that formed the basis of the internet. Arpanet began life in 1969 as a testbed for new networking technologies funded by the United States Defense Advanced Research Project Agency (DARPA). Its decentralised structure, in which no single NODE has overall control of the network, was conceived amid concerns about the vulnerability of centralised structures to sudden upsets (such as nuclear war). The networks that replaced Arpanet (a new military network, the Defense Data Network, and NSFNet, a network of scientific and academic computers funded by America's National Science Foundation) evolved into the BACKBONE of today's internet. The process continues as this backbone is turned over to a consortium of commercial providers.

ASP

Application Service Provider, a company that gives organisations access to software applications across the internet. Instead of running the software itself, an organisation "rents" it from an ASP, thus freeing itself of the burden of buying and maintaining expensive software, SERVERS and support staff. To date, the most successful offerings have revolved around communications software such as E-MAIL and messaging, and many ASPS also offer payroll, accounting and human-resources applications. Although the ASP model has clear advantages for companies, many are wary of it, worrying about the reliability of the provider, the need for 24-hour availability of the software and the enforceability of complex service-level agreements that are required to ensure protection against failure of the services.

Most analysts have suggested that the size of the market for ASP services will run into billions of dollars in the next few years, with figures as high as $25 billion quoted by some for 2004. IDC, a research company, estimates that the European market alone will be worth $6.5 billion in 2006. Although early interest in the ASP model was limited, it has grabbed the attention of the business community as the world economy has faltered and the need to control costs has grown sharply. Many companies have rebranded themselves as managed service providers (MSPS) rather than ASPS, offering to take over software assets completely in the hope of attracting business in the lucrative outsourcing market. Some estimates predict that over 50% of companies will use the services of an ASP or an MSP within the next three years.

Asynchronous transfer mode

A

A networking technology enabling fast transfer of information. Asynchronous transfer mode (ATM) promises extremely high data transfer rates, perhaps up to 10 gigabytes per second, although current implementations are limited to about 600MBPS, roughly six times the speed of the fastest LOCAL AREA NET-WORKS in popular use.

ATM

Asynchronous transfer mode (see previous entry). This is also the abbreviation for Adobe Type Manager, a font-smoothing program used by Macintosh and WINDOWS machines in conjunction with desktop publishing programs and word processors; and for automated teller machine, a device that dispenses cash. Technology has unfortunately outstripped the alphabet's capacity to abbreviate it (see TLA).

Attachment

A file sent with an E-MAIL message, such as a document or an audio clip. Any disk file can be sent as an attachment, although size is often a limitation for those with slow MODEM connections; sending unannounced huge video segments to friends is generally regarded as bad form.

Files sent as attachments from e-mail programs must be converted into a text-based format using a process known as encoding. The text is then converted back into BINARY FILE format at the receiving end. The most common encoding systems for the PC are UUENCODE and MIME; Macintoshes commonly use binhex. Such conversions occasionally cause problems, as not all e-mail programs understand all formats; this is why e-mail sometimes arrives as pages of seemingly incomprehensible garbage, rather than the expected document or spreadsheet. A bigger contemporary problem is that of VIRUSES such as Melissa and I Love You, many of which now arrive in the form of e-mail attachments.

A   Avatar

A software-generated figure or form taken by a participant in an ONLINE world, gaming environment or CHAT room. Such representations can take many forms, from free-floating heads to cartoon characters. Many avatars have some three-dimensional characteristics, so that fellow participants can move around them. The word comes from the Hindu religion, where it is used to denote a divine incarnation or deity.

B2B

The common abbreviation for BUSINESS-TO-BUSINESS E-COM-MERCE. Some cynically minded individuals have suggested that in the post-DOTCOM climate it should more properly stand for "back to banking", as internet company executives return to more reliable ways of making a living. (See also B2C.)

B2B exchange

A WEBSITE, usually focused on a particular industry or area of interest, where goods and services are exchanged between buyers and sellers. Almost anything can be bought and sold in a variety of ways on such sites, and they have attracted traders in commodities as diverse as almonds and petrochemicals.

Such exchanges attracted much attention and publicity at the height of the DOTCOM boom, but in common with many E-COMMERCE businesses they have largely failed to live up to expectations. The harsh reality of their business model, once pitched by internet gurus as the prevalent way in which goods would be bought and sold ONLINE, has made it impossible for them to function in a flaky economy. To make profits on small percentages of transactions (as little as 0.2% in most cases), sites need to generate huge volumes of business, a problem in the vertical markets in which most exchanges currently operate. Most of the sites doing significant business rely on a small number of customers, with many making as much as 50% of their revenue from just one or two big traders. A 2000 survey by A.T. Kearney, a New York consultancy, showed that less than 15% of them were actually delivering services or complet-ing electronic transactions, and several other studies show that most users of B2B exchanges were unhappy with their per-formance. Some estimates indicate that less than 1% of B2B e-commerce is conducted through industry exchanges, although some companies continue to do well, including DoveBid, which helps people buy and sell equipment from failed START-UPS.

B2C

B Short for business-to-consumer. B2C represents the most visible face of ONLINE commerce. Confidence in the B2C market suffered throughout 2000 and 2001 after the collapse of several high-profile businesses, including boo.com in Europe and eToys in the United States, but ever increasing numbers of web users have ensured that consumers continue to shop enthusiastically online. Nearly 60m Europeans made online purchases between November 2001 and April 2002. Americans spent $13.7 billion during the 2002 Christmas period alone, according to a study by Goldman Sachs, and revenue for 2002 was estimated at $48 billion by Bizrate, an online research company.

One attraction of online retailing is the ease with which you can compare prices. There are now many sites that hunt for the best bargains in almost any kinds of goods, and a trend towards free shipping costs has encouraged people to spend their money online rather than in the high street. Jeff Bezos, AMAZON'S CEO, said that free delivery on orders over $25 was a contributing factor to the company's first ever profit in late 2001. However, the more that online B2C businesses have to compete on price the more difficult it is for them to be profitable. Amazon achieved its market share by selling things so cheaply that it made huge losses. It is impossible to do that forever and survive.

Backbone

A high-capacity line carrying enormous amounts of internet traffic over long distances. Backbones are typically built and funded by large commercial ISPs such as UUNET and BT in the UK and Sprint and MCI in the United States. The present-day internet evolved from government-funded American backbones such as NSFNET, originally built to connect research and education communities.

The internet is so big, so powerful and so pointless that for some people it is a complete substitute for life.
Andrew Brown

Bandwidth

A measure of the range of frequencies occupied by a data signal across a communications channel. The greater the range of frequencies, the more data and thus information can be transmitted in a given time. The term is normally used to refer to the actual amount of information a communications connection can carry; its capacity, in effect.

Generally, the bandwidth required for any given purpose is directly related to the complexity of the task. It takes far more bandwidth to download a full-page colour picture in one second, for example, than a page of plain text, a fact that most regular web users now readily appreciate. In analog systems, such as telephone and television, bandwidth is measured in cycles per second, or hertz (Hz). A typical voice signal occupies about 3 kilohertz (kHz), but a broadcast television signal occupies about 6 megahertz (MHz), or 2,000 times as much. In digital systems, bandwidth is measured in bits per second (BPS) and multiples thereof: kilobits per second (KBPS), megabits per second (MBPS) and gigabits per second (gbps).

There is much confusion about exactly what the bandwidth of networks in widespread use really means in terms of performance. For example, 56K modems can transmit information at only half the 56,000bps that the name promises, and 10mbps Ethernet connections typically achieve only one-third of the advertised speed. Nevertheless, size is everything in the internet world, and both hardware manufacturers and telcos are well aware of the marketing pull of larger numbers. Increased bandwidth is the key to providing enhanced web offerings, such as video, audio and other RICH MEDIA applications, and large-scale software distribution.

The process of building a communications infrastructure that will support affordable high-speed internet access is complex and expensive, and bandwidth providers have been slow to roll out faster alternatives to their existing MODEM-based dial-up offerings. Although many ISPs now provide free (and slow) individual internet access, anyone determined to own one of the fastest T1 or T3 connections can expect to pay handsomely for the privilege. Nevertheless, the widespread availability of new

BROADBAND technologies such as ADSL have made high-speed access much more affordable for home users and businesses. Many advances have been made in wireless communications, too, as telecoms companies introduce new services such as GPRS and the popularity of WI-FI networks grows. Only one thing is certain: however fast your connection, CONTENT providers will find a way to use every last BYTE of it.

Banner

An advertisement on a web page, usually in the form of a GIF IMAGE. Invented by HOTWIRED in 1994, the banner is still the most common form of web ADVERTISING. Most banners contain animations designed to catch a BROWSER's eye and trigger a CLICKTHROUGH to a WEBSITE with the hope of eliciting a sale. Banners are sold on a cost per thousand model (CPM), with advertisers typically paying between $5 and $50 or so for every 1,000 IMPRESSIONS, depending on the profile of the site and the position of the advertisement within it.

The number of website visitors clicking on banners has declined dramatically as their presence has spread to every corner of the web and the curiosity of the audience has waned. Many advertisers have therefore rethought their ONLINE strategy. Nonetheless, banners are still regarded by some as cheap and effective tools, especially in conjunction with a SEARCH ENGINE capable of displaying specific banners triggered by particular KEYWORDS. Many banner advertisements are now being replaced by alternatives based on RICH MEDIA advertising techniques.

BBS

See BULLETIN BOARD.

BCC

Short for blind carbon copy, a copy of an E-MAIL sent to a third
party without the primary recipient's knowledge (see CC).

Bellhead

Describes an engineer, manager or marketer with a phone
company background, especially one that believes in traditionally rigid principles of solving networking problems with dedicated hardware and fixed connections rather than intelligent
software. Bellheads are said to be especially prevalent in companies promoting ATM networks, and they are reviled by IP-
worshipping NETHEADS. The name comes from the
now-defunct Bell telephone company in the United States, the
mother of all phone companies.

Binary file

Technically, a file in which all eight BITS of its component
BYTES are used for data. Unlike ASCII-format text files, which
contain only generic keyboard characters that can be read by
any computer, binary files often contain code specific to the sort
of processor in the machine that created the file. This is why
binary files attached to E-MAIL messages must be converted to
seven-bit ASCII before being sent to a recipient who may be
using a different machine.

Not all binary files contain processor-specific codes. Graphics
files, for example, use all eight bits for data but no machine code.
Other examples of binary files include spreadsheets, programs
such as WINDOWS .exe files and word-processor documents.

Bit

Short for binary digit; in other words, a one or a zero. Bits are
the building blocks of internet data. Every digital transmission

consists of a stream of bits travelling between two points, and most descriptions of BANDWIDTH measure it in bits per second (BPS). Eight bits make up a byte.

B

Blocking software

Programs that prevent access to parts of the internet deemed to be objectionable, sometimes called censorware or filtering software. Blocking software can stop people accessing particular WEBSITES, NEWSGROUPS, mailing lists and CHAT lines, and can even prevent them from typing names, addresses or offensive words. Originally designed to protect children from PORNOGRAPHY and other perceived dangers on the internet, blocking products are now widely used in the corporate world, and most schools and public libraries routinely use them on computers connected to the internet. Most BROWSERS, for example MICROSOFT'S INTERNET EXPLORER, contain facilities for controlling access to websites that have been rated using the PICS scheme.

Blocking software has been heavily criticised for mindlessly discriminating against many harmless sites and interfering unnecessarily with people's ONLINE activities. Some products, for example, have blocked access to any site or newsgroup containing the word "breast" irrespective of its nature, preventing access by anyone seeking advice on breast cancer. A 2002 study by the Electronic Frontier Foundation and the Online Policy Group found that blocking software in US schools could block up to 70% of SEARCH ENGINE results for state-mandated curriculum topics. Outraged by such idiocy, two HACKERS reverse-engineered the CyberPatrol blocking software package in 1999 and distributed a program allowing people to see the list of sites being blocked. Mattel, the program's owners, responded with a lawsuit that forced Matthew Skall and Eddy Jansson to hand over the program and refrain from distributing further copies. But the hacker community continues to take a dim view of such software and many public sites exist that explain how to disable the commonly used programs. Meanwhile, many parents have been dismayed to discover that their children have been able to disable them without any outside help whatsoever. (See also CONTENT FILTER.)

B

Blog

Short for WEBLOG. A blog is an individual's online journal or diary, often with irreverent, whimsical or philosophical over-tones. Someone who maintains a blog is (somewhat inevitably) called a blogger.

Bluetooth

A set of specifications for wireless communications. Bluetooth, named after a king who united Danish provinces in the 10th century, connects electronic devices such as mobile PCs and telephones together across radio waves. Originally started by mobile phone makers Ericsson and Nokia, the Bluetooth con-sortium is now backed by industry giants such as Intel, IBM and Toshiba and over 1,000 other members.

Bluetooth-compliant devices can communicate with each other within a range of 10m or so (or up to 100m if signals are boosted by a powerful transmitter). In the short term, the biggest promise of this technology is that it will free users from the need to carry around cumbersome proprietary cables. Instead, devices need merely be within range of each other's radio signals to communicate. Already, such devices as key-boards incorporate Bluetooth, and the technology has support from MICROSOFT, which now includes Bluetooth capabilities within the WINDOWS XP OPERATING SYSTEM.

Although interest in Bluetooth has been strong, the technol-ogy is struggling to establish itself. It seems unlikely that original estimates of 1.4 billion Bluetooth-enabled devices worldwide by 2004 will be met. Gartner, a research company, estimated that 161m Bluetooth-enabled devices would be sold in 2003, rising to 362m in 2004.

Some of the early concerns about Bluetooth's viability are fading, particularly in the light of the falling cost of the chips that make it work. But concerns remain about interference with other wireless networking technologies, the difficulty of configuration and security. Once seen as a promising way to provide universal data access from single access points (for example, enabling public access to the internet in railway stations or airports), many now see WI-FI as the fastest and most reliable way to connect to the internet across wireless connections. So Bluetooth's principal use may be as a replacement for cables rather than as the pervasive digital glue that will bind together electronics devices of all kinds. Likely areas of growth for Bluetooth are mobile phones, which can be equipped with hands-free Bluetooth headsets, and PDAs, which can use Bluetooth connections with mobile phones to connect to the internet.

Bookmark

A LINK to a WEBSITE address, kept by a BROWSER as part of a list of favourite sites. Nearly all browsers use this term; an exception is MICROSOFT'S INTERNET EXPLORER, which refers to such links as favorites. Bookmarks are notoriously clumsy to manage, as most web users amass a huge list of sites. Modern browsers now include features that remember recent or often visited sites and help users return to them quickly.

Bot

Short for robot. A bot is a small piece of software that automates a task or emulates human behaviour in some way, such as replying to E-MAIL in someone's absence or gathering information from websites. Many varieties exist; most are designed for repetitive tasks but some occasionally stray into more creative fields. CHATBOTS, for example, simulate real humans and can hold conversations (albeit of a limited kind) with WEBSITE visitors or CHAT room users. The most visible results of bot behaviour are seen in SEARCH ENGINES, which use CRAWLER or spider bots to gather their information from the web. Other varieties include shopbots, which might help a user find pricing information, and knowbots, which can seek out specific information on a user's behalf. One recent use for bots is automatic website registrations, often for the purpose of sending SPAM from free e-mail accounts. (See also AGENT.)

Bps

BITS per second, a measure of the speed of a NETWORK connection; in short, its BANDWIDTH. Modern internet connections are typically measured in multiples of at least 1,000, denoted as kilobytes per second (kbps). A standard modem transmits data at roughly 50kbps, depending on the integrity of the telephone line to which it is connected. Faster connections such as cable and DSL may achieve speeds measured in multiple millions of bits (or megabits) per second (mbps) at their upper limits. The fastest connections of all, based on FIBRE OPTIC cables, can now manage data transmission rates of 10 terabits per second, about 180m times faster than a 56kbps MODEM.

Broadband

Strictly, a form of data transmission in which several parallel channels pass across a single cable or wire. A good example of a true broadband medium is cable TV, which pumps huge amounts of data to viewers across very fast landlines. The term is used more generically to describe high-speed circuits and signals, especially those relating to fast-growing internet technologies such as ADSL and cable. Many CONTENT providers and PORTALS are upgrading their systems in preparation for the rapid uptake of broadband by consumers, and are preparing to offer enhanced high-BANDWIDTH services based on audio and video.

Brochureware

A generally pejorative term for a WEBSITE or page that simply

B

replicates a company's paper-based marketing materials. The brochureware approach was widely adopted in the early days of the web before the new medium's potential was fully understood, and it is still an attractive option for smaller businesses unwilling to pay for more complex web presences. Despite the sneers of NEW-MEDIA gurus and professional web designers, brochureware still has some real benefits for companies offering simple products and services, at the very least ensuring that casual browsers stand a chance of finding them, especially in conjunction with a good SEARCH ENGINE. Many low-cost tools for helping them create it are available.

Few influential people involved with the internet claim that it is a good in and of itself. It is a powerful tool for solving social problems, just as it is a tool for making money, finding lost relatives, receiving medical advice, or, come to that, trading instructions for making bombs.
Esther Dyson, *New Perspective Quarterly*, spring 1997

Browser

Software for viewing web pages, and thus the key to the explosion of the internet in the 1990s. Browsers have come a long way since their text-only beginnings at CERN in the early 1990s. Kick-started in 1993 by the NCSA's MOSAIC, the browser business was transformed by NETSCAPE in 1994, with MICROSOFT belatedly joining the party in late 1996. The latest versions of programs such as Microsoft's INTERNET EXPLORER, Netscape's NAVIGATOR and Opera Software's OPERA are more than just HTML viewers: they are sophisticated multimedia tools in their own right. Modern browsers can play high-quality audio and video; manage secure connections to E-COMMERCE sites; send and receive E-MAIL; and run JAVA APPLETS, ACTIVEX controls and plug-ins that extend their capabilities in other ways. And they no longer just run on PCs; mobile phones and PDAS are now routinely equipped with sophisticated browsers, enabling people to access web pages while on the move.

It is their status as doorways to the web which has made browsers the subject of fierce debate in the net COMMUNITY, a source of acrimony among software vendors and, ultimately, the cause of the highest-profile antitrust case in recent American history. Own the browser, the theory goes, and you own the web audience and maybe its wallet too: a theory to which Microsoft has readily subscribed. Netscape's seemingly unassailable market share of over 80% in 1996 had been steadily whittled away by Microsoft to less than 25% at the beginning of 2000, largely because of the latter's inclusion of its browser software with the latest version of the WINDOWS OPERATING SYSTEM, an act that led to a high-profile antitrust suit against the company. By the end of 2002, Microsoft was estimated to have cornered 95% of the market, to the great discomfort of industry analysts and legislators alike.

The so-called browser wars have imposed heavy costs on web users and site builders. Users have been plagued by security flaws in successive versions of Internet Explorer, whose close integration with the Windows operating system has made them vulnerable to many forms of attack from malicious outsiders. As fast as Microsoft patches one hole, another seems to appear, yet another reason why so many people oppose the company's dominance of the browser market. Meanwhile, web developers are shackled by the need to build support for multiple versions of several different browsers into their code. Many now only support people with version 5 browsers or higher, effectively excluding owners of older machines or operating systems.

Surfing on the internet is like sex; everyone boasts about doing more than they actually do. But in the case of the internet, it's a lot more.

Tom Fasulo

Bulletin board

A computer system used for posting electronic messages, storing files and chatting with other users. Many bulletin board systems (BBS) are devoted to particular topics; others serve the interests of a variety of special-interest and discussion groups. Anyone with a computer and a MODEM can start a bulletin board providing

B

they have the right software. This led to the establishment of over 50,000 such systems worldwide by the beginning of the 1990s.

Despite a strong and distinctive culture, the popularity of stand-alone bulletin boards has declined with the growth of the internet, largely because all their functions can be easily duplicated on WEBSITES that are reachable by any internet user instead of only a handful of individuals. However, many bulletin board systems now operate their own websites alongside their original BBS software and remain prosperous.

Burn rate

The rate at which a new company or venture spends its capital while waiting for profitability. Most internet START-UP companies became well acquainted with this term, which was widely used as an indicator of their likely lifespan. Routinely burning money faster than they could earn it, few of them are still around to try to increase it. The DOTCOM with the most highly publicised burn rate, fashion retailer boo.com, spent $135m of investment capital between its inception in 1998 and its closure in 2000, while accumulating millions of dollars of additional debt.

It's easy for the press to say that we spent $135 million on Concordes and champagne, but we only drink vodka.
Ernst Malmsten, co-founder of boo.com

Business-to-business

The exchange of goods, services, information or money between businesses, which in ONLINE jargon becomes B2B. Although media attention on E-COMMERCE has been focused on consumer and retailing ventures, most analysts predict that most money (perhaps more than 90% of all online business) will be spent (and earned) in the business-to-business sector. Research firms have in the past made many wild predictions about the level of B2B e-commerce, but its online importance is undeniable. In 2002 the US Census Bureau reported that B2B e-commerce in 2000 accounted for $777 billion of online sales, compared with $29 billion for sales to consumers. Forrester Research predicted that ONLINE trade in Europe alone would reach €2.2 trillion in 2006, with much of the growth being stimulated by the petrochemicals and logistics industries.

For many companies, it is the savings in time and money that make the B2B sector so appealing. The internet allows firms to buy goods more cheaply, process invoices more efficiently and deal with customers more effectively. A 1999 report by the Giga Information Group estimated that doing business online would save companies around the world an estimated $1.25 trillion by 2002, and other studies showed that average delivery times for goods and services could be reduced by up to 95%. Despite these predictions, many suppliers of B2B technology have found the going hard since the dotcom bubble burst, and some of its biggest players have faded from view. Newish technologies such as WEB SERVICES promise to contribute greatly to the B2B economy.

Byte

Eight bits (see BIT).

Cable modem

A MODEM enabling the connection of a PC to a local cable television line. Cable modems provide fast, always-on connections to the internet in areas where the necessary coaxial cable has been laid. They can theoretically achieve data-transfer speeds of up to 30MBPS, but in practice they are limited by the speed of an ISP's internet GATEWAY and the unwillingness of consumers to pay for more BANDWIDTH than they need. Most European systems provide a data-transfer rate closer to 1.5mbps, still much faster than prevalent modems or ISDN lines, although this is shared between all local users of the cable.

Cache

An area on a computer's hard disk used by a web BROWSER to store recently downloaded pages. When a user returns to a stored page, it is retrieved from the cache rather than the original internet SERVER, loading the page faster and reducing the load on the NETWORK. Some ISPs cache popular sites on their own servers, allowing users to DOWNLOAD a local copy rather than the original from a busy remote site.

CC

A copy of an E-MAIL message sent to one or more recipients other than the main addressee. The other recipients' addresses appear in the cc box at the top of the message so the principal recipient can see who else it was sent to. Most e-mail programs also include a blind carbon copy (BCC) function, which copies the message invisibly; that is, addresses in the BCC box will not be seen by other recipients. The term dates back to a time when the only way of creating a copy of a letter or memo typed on a typewriter was to lay a sheet of carbon paper between two sheets of typing paper, thus creating a carbon impression of the original on the lower sheet.

Censorship

The growth of the internet continues to highlight issues of censorship; that is, the banning of material considered to be against the public interest. PORNOGRAPHY involving children and terrorism have been two particular concerns of the authorities.

It might seem straightforward to prevent a country's citizens from accessing particular kinds of material ONLINE, but there are technical, legal and practical issues that make it hard to do. Part of the problem is the easy global reach of the internet. Because laws on such matters as indecency and obscenity vary widely from country to country, material that is acceptable in Italy may not be in Iran. Even within national boundaries, debate persists over what sorts of CONTENT should be regulated. In the United States one answer was the Communications Decency Act (CDA), signed by Bill Clinton in 1996 but overturned by the courts the following year. Their ruling that regulation of speech on the internet was unconstitutional followed months of challenges from civil liberties groups, ISPs, content providers and internet enthusiasts.

Some countries have denied access to particular sites at ISP level or blocked specific addresses on individual PCs. In 2001, the Chinese government closed thousands of internet cafes in an attempt to stop their visitors accessing pornography and potentially subversive material, and forced thousands more to install monitoring software that would allow it to track the use of public computers for purposes it considered illicit. In 2002, it blocked access to the popular GOOGLE SEARCH ENGINE from all Chinese internet users prior to the Communist Party congress.

Such attempts to prevent citizens accessing undesirable material, such as criticisms of government policy in Singapore or neo-Nazi sites in the United States, usually fail in the long term. Although it is easy to shut down a WEBSITE containing material deemed inappropriate, many authorities quickly discover that the material itself seems to have a life of its own. Often, it is copied quickly from SERVER to server, thus becoming more rather than less widely available.

The last hope for censors is self-regulation by websites and ONLINE SERVICE providers (OSPs). Attempts by OSPs to censor material themselves have led to several embarrassments; AOL, in particular, faced savage criticism when its screening software accidentally shut down a forum for discussing breast cancer because it mentioned breasts. Other content providers have had more success with PICS, a content rating scheme administered by the Internet Content Rating Association (ICRA).

Would-be censors are beginning to discover that blocking access to questionable material is not always in their best interests anyway. By monitoring visitors to particular sites, they can often catch far more transgressors than they can by more conventional means. One recent investigation of visitors to a US site hosting child pornography resulted in thousands of arrests around the world.

It is no exaggeration to conclude that the internet has achieved, and continues to achieve, the most participatory marketplace of mass speech that this country and indeed the world has yet seen ... [It] deserves the broadest possible protection from government-imposed, content-based regulation.
Judge Stewart Dalzell,
during the US Communications Decency Act hearings, 1996

Censorware

See BLOCKING SOFTWARE.

CERN

The European Laboratory for Particle Physics, CERN (formerly the Conseil Européen pour la Recherche Nucléaire, hence the acronym) is famed as the origin of the WORLD WIDE WEB. An initiative to improve collaboration among workers in the physics community, led by Tim Berners-Lee and Robert Cailliau, led directly to the development of HTML, HTTP, the first text-only BROWSER and the first web SERVER. The rest is history.

Certificate

See DIGITAL SIGNATURE.

C

CGI

Common Gateway Interface, a PROTOCOL that helps to extend the capabilities of otherwise dumb web pages. CGI links a web page to a small computer program that performs a specific task, such as processing the contents of a form and sending back a confirmation message. A CGI program, known as a SCRIPT, can be written in several languages, including PERL, C++ and JAVA.

Chat

One of the most popular uses of the internet, particularly among newcomers, and widely regarded as the driving force behind the success of AOL. Once viewed as merely an internet enthusiast's version of CB radio, chat is now at the heart of the ONLINE COMMUNITY and has attracted the attention of most of the big players in the internet world. A good illustration of chat's success is the program ICQ (bought by AOL in 1998), which now has 135m registered users.

Chat on the internet takes many forms, from the free-for-all Internet Relay Chat (IRC) channels to one-to-one programs such as ICQ and AOL's Instant Messenger. Most work around a simple, text-only window where messages to an individual or group are typed and the responses read, but more advanced chat programs also include VIDEOCONFERENCING and voice communication features. Many people use chat as a cheap alternative to long-distance or international phone calls, but there are channels and rooms on many thousands of subjects, and some services allow users to set up private rooms for more intimate conversations. Many companies now use chat technology on their WEBSITES to provide customer-service features, such as live one-to-one technical support for software products, in preference to phone calls.

Chat rooms have become a more visible part of the internet culture as a result of cases in which adults, posing as teenagers, have arranged meetings with children. So many chat rooms aimed at young people are now scrutinised by the authorities, who are not shy of prosecuting those they find are seeking to break the law.

Defenders of the chat culture point to the community-building virtues of such rooms as evidence for their continuation. Meanwhile, the rapid growth of INSTANT MESSAGING software has given the chat phenomenon new credibility with a previously sceptical audience of professionals. This in turn has caused problems: some employees are spending large parts of their day in chat rooms rather than working, and there are surveys that indicate that chat-room encounters could be responsible for up to one-third of divorces in the United States.

My favourite thing about the internet is that you get to go into the private world of real creeps without having to smell them.

Penn Jillette

Chatbot

An artificially intelligent program designed to interact with users of ONLINE services, especially chatroom and customer-service applications. Chatbots are not yet gifted conversationalists, but they are capable of returning simple answers to simple questions and they can be programmed to return information on specific subjects. A golf chatbot, for example, might respond to queries about problems with a golf swing, and a technical support chatbot could provide useful information for people with hardware or software problems. The current capabilities of such programs are limited, but researchers expect that applications like these will become practical in the near future. Meanwhile, accurate predictions about the evolution of truly intelligent computers are still hard to find.

Circuit-switched

Describes a NETWORK in which the two ends of a connection are linked by a fixed circuit. For the duration of this connection the communicating parties have exclusive use of the BAND-WIDTH it provides. Ordinary telephone voice calls are circuit-switched. Contrast with PACKET-SWITCHED.

Click

One of the defining activities of the WORLD WIDE WEB. Mouse clicks take visitors from one web page or site to another by way of the hyperlinks on which the web is based. Much to the delight of advertisers, they also take people from a suitably attractive BANNER to a place where they can be sold things. (See LINK.)

In five years, there won't be any internet companies because they'll all be internet companies. Otherwise they will die.

Andy Grove, 1999

Clicks and mortar

Describes a company with its roots and assets in the "old economy" that also exploits the power of the internet to expand and streamline its business. A good example is Barnes & Noble, a traditional bookseller that was forced to embrace the web following the success of AMAZON.

"Pure-play" internet companies can still outperform their slower moving real-world competitors in some areas, as the success of companies like Amazon proves. But recent history shows how few internet companies have been able to make it on their own. Most large companies now have some kind of web-based presence and are capitalising on their advantages over net purists. The lower cost of customer acquisition, better-established brands and more reliable cash reserves have given real-world companies of all kinds a more solid footing for their

ONLINE ventures. A good example of this is in the grocery sector, where many internet-only companies failed to make a lasting impression. Tesco.com, part of the British supermarket giant, is now one of the biggest online grocery retailers in the world, with a turnover of £356m in 2002.

Clickstream

A record of the CLICKS made as web users travel within and between sites, and thus a record of the pages visited and the order in which they were visited. Web marketers and advertisers use clickstream information to determine the popularity of site sections, time spent on various activities, usability of individual features and the response to BANNER advertisements.

Clickthrough

An advertising term for a single instance of a CLICK on an advertisement. Clickthroughs are regarded as a better way of measuring and paying for audience response than the number of IMPRESSIONS, as they imply real interest on the part of the viewer. However, clickthrough rates have declined dramatically as web audiences tire of BANNERS, and many advertisers have been forced to pay for the number of times a banner is displayed, irrespective of whether or not somebody clicks on it.

Client/server

Describes a computing model in which one program, a client, requests information from another, a SERVER. The client/server model is one of the most important concepts in NETWORK computing, as it provides a good way for organisations to make use of programs and data that are distributed widely across different machines or networks. The WORLD WIDE WEB is based upon a simplified and more elegant version of this model, in which a BROWSER acts as the client requesting information from any one of millions of web servers.

The open society, the unrestricted access to knowledge, the unplanned and uninhibited association of men for its furtherance – these are what may make a vast, complex, ever growing, ever changing, ever more specialised and expert technological world, nevertheless a world of human community.
J. Robert Oppenheimer

Community

A collection of individuals or users of a WEBSITE, MAILING LIST or NEWSGROUP, generally united through a common interest. Community-building is one of the biggest challenges faced by website owners, for whom unclicked BANNERS, empty CHAT rooms and discussion groups, or unclaimed web space presage doom. The rules for encouraging the development and retention of such communities are not clearly defined, and many theories circulate about how best to attempt this. Howard Rheingold's book *Virtual Communities*, available ONLINE, provides one of the best such discussions.

Broadly speaking, there are two types of online communities. Websites such as Geocities and Tripod have built successful businesses by renting web space to anyone who wants it, organising people or businesses into neighbourhoods and creating a sense of place in an otherwise flat and sterile environment. More specifically, stand-alone commercial or special-interest sites use chat technology, moderated E-MAIL discussions, user forums and relationships with other sites to build audiences and encourage participation. Newsgroups, too, constitute communities in their own right, albeit ones whose discussions are unmoderated and whose members are less predictable in their movements and habits. Many of the principles behind successful community-building have their roots in organisations such as the WELL, one of the first online communities.

Compression

A technique for reducing the size of files, commonly used to speed transmission and DOWNLOAD times. Most compression algorithms work by removing or replacing redundant information from text or binary files, such as blank space or often repeated characters. Picture files are especially suitable for compression, as they often contain large blocks of colour that can be represented in much simpler ways. Many picture formats, such as GIF and JPEG, are compressed.

Compuserve

A pioneering ONLINE SERVICE. Compuserve has a special place in the hearts of internet old-timers; for many it was their first experience of E-MAIL and CHAT. Originally conceived as a computer time-sharing service in 1969, the service expanded rapidly into a forum-based information resource of immense proportions. Widely used by computing professionals, Compuserve was the undisputed leader in online services for many years, despite its reliance on old proprietary technology, an arcane command-line interface and a clumsy subscriber ID system. The arrival of a WINDOWS-based interface made navigating the system somewhat easier, but despite a belated transition to ISP status it never achieved the mass appeal it hoped for. One possible reason for this is that H & R Block, Compuserve's owner for many years, was a firm of accountants. The company was sold to AOL in the early 1990s.

The future will become vivid
Spreadsheets will crumble before creativity
Information will marry entertainment
They will have many children
Sony advertisement, Wired magazine

Content

The constituent information of a WEBSITE or other source. Content can take many forms, including text, sound, video, animation and numerical information. As many organisations have found, the process of accumulating content is expensive and time-consuming, irrespective of its subject. Few web users will pay for it as there is a vast amount of information available free on the web, and businesses that depend on the sale of content have been proved unrealistic time and time again. Even the biggest organisations have had their fingers burnt by the content issue. MICROSOFT, for example, was unable to persuade subscribers to its MSN service to pay for the content it offered separately.

Despite the unwillingness of people to part with their money, some websites are returning to the paid-content model as ADVERTISING revenues have become less reliable. Meanwhile, PORNOGRAPHY continues to be the only form of content for which people seem happy to pay. (See also MICROCONTENT.)

Content aggregator

A company that gathers web CONTENT from multiple ONLINE sources which can then be reused or resold. Many WEBSITES use content aggregators as a practical way of drawing the world's attention to their content without the need for expensive marketing or ADVERTISING campaigns. At the other end of the line, web publishers can obtain all of their information from a single source, rather than having to sign deals with many separate content providers. Most aggregators offer a wide range of information for syndication to third-party sites, typically including news, financial data and sports results alongside more esoteric items such as cartoons and video clips.

Content filter

A mechanism or strategy for preventing access to specific kinds of ONLINE information, usually that deemed to be objectionable by the people who enforce it. BLOCKING SOFTWARE is probably the most widely used form of CONTENT filtering, but several other kinds exist. Company FIREWALLS, especially, are often routinely configured to prevent employee access to particular WEBSITES or kinds of material and to filter out incoming E-MAIL that contains objectionable words or LINKS to external websites.

Convergence

The coming together of disparate technologies, such as internet services, television and other forms of entertainment. Nearly everyone knows how to work a television set, but PCs are much harder for them to master. This has been the push behind initiatives aimed at making the television a central source of digital information, whether it be E-MAIL, the web, satellite and cable television, video-on-demand or video games.

However, associated with merging these technologies there are a variety of issues to be considered. For one thing, television-watching is a largely passive activity, whereas playing games demands interaction. Design, in terms of what people see and react to, is crucial, but more crucial these days is access to high-speed cable, satellite or other digital networks necessary to use the internet effectively.

Throughout the world, there has been little enthusiasm for interactive services that link the internet with the TV. This is a blow to those keen on interactive ADVERTISING and advanced services such as video-on-demand. Many analysts now agree that the most likely future for interactive television services involves either betting or voting. The biggest noise in the convergence world is now being made by supporters of high-speed wireless technologies such as UMTS who say that the biggest consumers of combined, interactive media services will be owners of PDAS and other smart devices such as next-generation mobile phones. A 2002 survey by the UMTS Forum estimated that the global market for these services would reach $320 billion by 2010.

Cookie

A text file left by a WEBSITE on a hard disk. Cookies record information about site visitors, especially information that can be used to make life easier for users on subsequent visits. When a visitor returns, the site retrieves the cookie and reads it for PASSWORD or LOGIN information, user-configured preferences such as page layout, or credit-card numbers, for example. Advertisers and WEBMASTERS make extensive use of cookies to track the behaviour of site visitors, noting the sections and pages that they visit, keeping track of dead-ends that force users to go back on themselves and watching their response to BANNER ADVERTISING.

Sites that use cookies generally claim that they are beneficial to users. But the mechanism by which cookies work is subject to criticism because of its invisibility. Unless told to do otherwise, BROWSERS accept cookies and share information without the user's awareness, raising concerns about security and privacy. Many people argue that the storing and transmission of browsing information is unethical, and fear that it may be sold to marketing organisations or retailers.

The question of intellectual property promises to be the Vietnam of the internet.
Mitchell Kapor

Copyleft

A software licensing scheme in which programs can be modified, redistributed or even sold, with the proviso that anyone who does so also passes on the freedom to make further changes. The copyleft idea came from Richard Stallman, founder of the Free Software Foundation (FSF), in the collaborative spirit that created UNIX. It applies particularly to the FSF's GNU software. Unlike COPYRIGHT, copyleft favours the rights of users above those of commercial software makers, and ensures that anyone who wants to make improvements to the code for their own use or that of others can do so freely.

Copying all or parts of a program is as natural to a programmer as breathing, and as productive. It ought to be as free.

Richard M. Stallman

C Copyright

The issue of who owns what on the internet is a complex one. Like obscenity laws, copyright laws differ from country to country, making regulation on the internet difficult. The internet has also thrown up some new and effectively ungovernable ways of distributing copyrighted material. A good example is the MP3 music format, which allows owners of CDs to copy and distribute CD-quality audio files by E-MAIL, on WEBSITES and especially using P2P programs with little chance of being tracked down and prosecuted.

Organisations such as the World Intellectual Property Organisation (WIPO), a UN agency and a forum for discussion and arbitration of copyright issues, have tried to garner support for new global copyright schemes, in particular protecting the content of DATABASES and the copies of material made during transmission over the internet. Other initiatives, such as the Strategic Digital Music Initiative (SDMI), established by the music industry to prevent piracy of its works, have underestimated the resourcefulness of the net COMMUNITY and alternative approaches are being considered.

Finding and prosecuting every copyright infringement on the net is an impossible task. In a world where intangible assets such as copyright have become more and more important to businesses, you can be sure that legislation will become tougher and copyright holders more aggressive in protecting their intellectual property. But to what effect: in the United States, the 1998 Digital Millennium Copyright Act, originally designed to protect works such as DVDs, may have curtailed the use of NAPSTER by music pirates, but other file-sharing networks continue to thrive.

Many argue that the big copyright owners should adapt to the new internet world rather than use the legislative club to fight it. Much better, they say, to develop new and imaginative distribution mechanisms which might persuade people to pay for their intellectual property. By strangling resources such as internet radio and surreptitiously attempting to corrupt file-sharing networks, it is argued, organisations such as the Recording Industry Association of America (RIAA) have made more enemies than friends.

Corportal

Short for corporate PORTAL. Also known as an enterprise portal, a corportal is a WEBSITE designed to improve employee access to important business information and applications. Corportals provide a consistent, centralised interface for accessing everything from internal websites and INTRANETS to DATABASES, calendars, training applications, customer support and E-COMMERCE applications, reducing the time spent swapping between them and even providing a single LOGIN point for all of them. This kind of integration is well-suited to the application of WEB SERVICES, and most portal software vendors are now designing their products around web-service-enabled components.

Many cite the flexibility and timesaving features of portals as a major factor in increasing the efficiency of technology in the workplace; this is being keenly exploited by software vendors. A 2001 survey by Ovum, a research company, estimated the size of the market for portal software at $1 billion, a figure it expects to grow to $7 billion by 2005. In 2002 a survey by Forrester, another research company, suggested that over one-third of a group of companies known as the Global 3,500 planned to buy portal software in 2002.

Cracker

Someone who breaks into someone else's computer system, usually on a NETWORK. Crackers may operate for profit, malice, ideology, braggadocio or plain old altruism; many have cracked systems simply to demonstrate security holes. Not to be confused with HACKER. (See also WAREZ.)

C

Crawler

A program that visits web pages and reads their contents, usually on behalf of a SEARCH ENGINE responding to a request from a WEBSITE owner. Once read, the information is returned to the search engine, indexed and made generally available to the outside world. A crawler cannot penetrate a FIREWALL, which limits its effectiveness.

Cyberspace. A consensual hallucination experienced daily by billions of legitimate operators, in every nation, by children being taught mathematical concepts ... A graphic representation of data abstracted from the banks of every computer in the human system. Unthinkable complexity. Lines of light ranged in the nonspace of the mind, clusters and constellations of data. Like city lights, receding ...

William Gibson, *Neuromancer*

Cyber-

A rather hackneyed prefix denoting a person, object or idea related to technology, especially that of the internet and its culture. The term was introduced in 1948 by Norbert Weiner, a scientist at the Massachusetts Institute of Technology (MIT), who derived the word cybernetics from a Greek word meaning helmsman or governor to denote the new science of control systems. Its reappearance in popular culture can be traced to Doctor Who's cybermen, although it was most famously used in the term cyberspace, coined by William Gibson to describe the geography of the ONLINE world in his novel *Neuromancer*. It is now appropriated for use in many contemporary terms, including cybercafe, cybernaut, cyberpunk, cyberrights, cybersex, cyberstalker and CYBERVENTING.

Cybersquatting

The practice of acquiring a DOMAIN name with the intention of selling it on to a company or individual who wants to use it for their own purposes, especially those who feel their claim is more legitimate. The first-come, first-served nature of the domain name registration process and the lack of authentication by registrars mean that many companies have found the domains they wanted for their web presences have been bought by quick-thinking entrepreneurs, tipped off, in some cases, by employees of ISPs who know a company is in the process of registering a domain name. Some companies have had success in reclaiming domains they see as their rightful property, notably MTV and McDonalds, but many less well-known businesses have not had the same co-operation from the courts and have found it cheaper and easier simply to pay up and move on.

Despite the efforts of organisations such as ICANN and the International Trademark Association, which has campaigned for new international legislation on cybersquatting, the issues surrounding it are unlikely to be resolved soon. Part of the problem is that unlike the real world, where companies with the same name have generally coexisted happily for decades, the web demands unique identifiers for addresses. No reliable worldwide process exists for settling disputes over this kind of intellectual property, despite ICANN's introduction of its much-criticised Uniform Dispute Resolution Policy (UDRP).

In the United States, the Anti-Cybersquatting Consumer Protection Act was introduced in 1999 to help resolve disputes between domain and trademark owners, and is used on a case-by-case basis to determine who has the right to own a name. Under the act, trademark owners, if they are to prevail, must show that their opponent acted in bad faith when registering a disputed name and harmed the trademark owner's commercial interests. Its principal benefit is that unlike other trademark legislation it makes allowances for distinctive trademarks rather than just famous ones, giving smaller companies a better chance of defending their turf.

Cyberventing

Letting off steam about your employer, boss or colleagues in public, usually on a WEBSITE designed for the purpose. Many such sites now exist, for example, www.workingwounded.com, and some companies such as Wal-Mart have sites devoted entirely to their perceived inadequacies as employers or businesses. Although many employees feel better after a good cybervent, some have been tracked down and even fired by their bosses, especially after revealing confidential information.

Cybrarian

A librarian or researcher specialising in the internet, rather than books, as a source of information.

Database

A computerised filing system forming the core of most corporate computer systems. Databases are, on the face of it, simple tools used to store and retrieve information. In reality, they are big and complex programs that are subjected to extreme pressure as the demand for sophisticated analysis of corporate data grows. Until fairly recently, databases handled only numbers and text, but the acceptance of MULTIMEDIA technologies has added a requirement for storage of more complex forms of data such as video and graphics.

Databases are commonly used as the engines driving WEBSITES. Retail sites, for example, use databases to store the details of their customers (not a trivial task in the case of companies such as AMAZON, which have tens of millions of them) and the items they have for sale, and many sites now use database technology to manage the display of editorial CONTENT. Many website databases also contain demographic information about subscribers, and ONLINE retailers and banks use them to store credit-card and other financial information. Unsurprisingly, the presence of such repositories of potentially valuable data has attracted the attention of CRACKERS, and database security has become a major concern for anyone storing information on computers attached to the public internet. The importance of database technology to the internet world is reflected in the massive growth of companies like Oracle.

Day trader

A stockmarket enthusiast who trades from a PC, perhaps as many as 50 times a day. Day traders are viewed with animosity by some investment managers, who have accused them of distorting the stockmarket and causing volatility in share prices. Their very existence is a tribute to the democratising power of the internet is the response. On the net anyone can be a trader, not just the elite. Many of them, however, must now be wishing they had stuck to more traditional investment strategies. A 2001 report by the North American Securities Administrators Association claimed that over 70% of day traders would lose not just money, but everything they own as well. The general risks of day trading, allied with the collapse of global stockmarkets, has made it a less popular activity than it was at the height of the DOTCOM boom, but hundreds of websites offering advice to would-be investors still exist.

D

Demon Internet

The first ISP in the UK to offer full dial-up internet access to consumers. Demon Internet's "tenner-a-month" pricing policy and its full range of internet services established the model for British ISPs, which was only recently superseded by free-access providers such as FREESERVE. Founded in 1992 by Cliff Stanford, Demon started with modest ambitions, aiming for 200 members in its first year and 4,500 by the end of 1995, a figure it exceeded by a factor of 10. By May 1998 the total number of subscribers exceeded 180,000. The company was sold to Scottish Power for £66m later that year. In April 2000 Demon agreed to pay damages to Laurence Godfrey, who took action against the company for refusing to remove allegedly libellous comments about him from NEWSGROUP postings. The case caused some panic in the British ISP community, for which the prospect of being held responsible for the content of over 1m newsgroup messages a day was not a welcome one. Demon is now owned by Thus, a telecoms company, which was demerged from the ScottishPower group in 2002.

Denial of service attack

Describes a particular form of electronic attack against a WEBSITE or other digital service that results in a temporary loss of service and access to resources. Denial of service (DOS) attacks rarely damage data or equipment, but they can be expensive for their targets, especially if the attack is prolonged. In February 2000, some of the world's largest websites, including YAHOO, AMAZON and EBAY, were forced offline for several hours by such attacks. More recently, an unknown assailant attacked the computers at the heart of the internet's DOMAIN NAME SYSTEM, bringing down several core SERVERS and disrupting internet activity all over the world.

Distributed denial of service (DDoS) attacks are almost always made by malicious CRACKERS. They usually involve the sending of vast amounts of data across the internet to a server that is not equipped to deal with it, from either a single computer or, more commonly, a widely distributed group of computers (known as zombies) that have been programmed to attack a particular site at the same time. Some targets have reported that servers were being flooded with as much as 1 gigabyte of data per second. A high-profile attack on Gibson Research Corporation's site in early 2001 was co-ordinated by a 13-year-old boy from 474 separate PCs, and a subsequent invasion involved the transmission of over 2 billion malicious data PACKETS.

Some companies have been accused of crying DoS attack to mask server crashes and other self-generated errors, in the hope of diverting attention away from serious internal problems. Many kinds of DoS attacks are known, including the SYN, Teardrop and Smurf varieties. Most security experts agree that there is no good defence against a determined DDoS attack once it has started, and have called for changes to some elements of the internet BACKBONE system to allow blocking of packets before they reach their target.

We cannot have a stable internet economy while 13-year-old children are free to deny arbitrary internet services with impunity.
Steve Gibson

DES

Data Encryption Standard, a widely used method of data ENCRYPTION judged so difficult to break by the US government that its export to other countries was prohibited. Based on a 1970s IBM algorithm called Lucifer, DES was adopted as an official standard by the US government in 1977. It uses a PRIVATE KEY method, in which one of 72 quadrillion keys is used to encode and decode a message. A sample DES message was cracked in June 1997 by DESCHALL, a project involving thousands of people and computers linked by the internet using a brute force attack to test all the possible keys. (See DISTRIBUTED COMPUTING.)

D

DHTML

Dynamic Hypertext Mark-up Language, a collective term for the combination of advanced HTML features, style sheets and scripting. Used together, these elements allow the contents of a web page to change after the page has loaded, without the need for complex programming or reference back to the web SERVER. Often seen examples include text paragraphs or images changing colour and shape when the mouse is moved over them, although it can be used for more sophisticated animation or drag-and-drop effects. DHTML is built around the W3C's Document Object Model (DOM), in which each element of a web page, such as a heading, paragraph or IMAGE, is viewed as an object that can be controlled using JAVASCRIPT or VBSCRIPT.

Digital divide

A term used to describe the imbalance in access to information technology among diverse social groups. Although this divide is most apparent in developing countries, where only the rich and well-connected have access to even the simplest types of communication such as telephones and fax machines, a 2000 US government study entitled *Falling Through the Net: Towards Digital Inclusion* found that it is still apparent even in more affluent societies. US households with incomes of over $75,000 were ten times more likely to have access to the internet than those at the lowest income levels. The good news is that the divide appears to be shrinking across income and ethnic groups. Black and Hispanic households, for example, were adopting internet technologies at rates of over 30% between August 2000 and September 2001, nearly three times the rate of households in the higher income brackets.

One development that promises to help close these sorts of gaps is the VOICE PORTAL, which may eventually let people without computers or internet access obtain information from the web using nothing more complex than a telephone and their own voice.

D

I'm an enemy of what I call "computer theology". There's a class conflict out there. There's a techno-elite that lives in a different world.
Walter Mossberg

Digital signature

A device that uniquely identifies the sender of an electronic message or document, based on PUBLIC KEY CRYPTOGRAPHY. The purpose of a digital signature is to guarantee that senders of such messages really are who they claim to be, an increasingly important concern for businesses considering E-COMMERCE strategies. Without such signatures it is hard to be sure that an E-MAIL is not forged or that a web-based vendor of goods and services is trustworthy.

Digital signatures are issued by certificate authorities such as VeriSign, an American company specialising in authenticating the digital identity of people and organisations. Typically, a signature will contain the user's name, a serial number, expiry dates and a copy of the certificate holder's public key. It also contains the signature of the issuing authority to verify that the certificate itself is real. Unfortunately, this system is not yet bullet-proof. In early 2001, VeriSign was tricked into issuing two certificates to someone falsely claiming to be a MICROSOFT employee, thus potentially allowing them to issue malicious software or build fake WEBSITES that appeared to have Microsoft's official seal of approval.

D

Disintermediation

The process by which producers and consumers are brought closer together, making middlemen redundant. This ugly word, borrowed from the banking world, is especially relevant to internet technologies which allow their users direct access to information that might otherwise require a mediator. Examples include medical and legal websites, which may bypass the need for real doctors and lawyers or at least change the relationship with them.

Any business model that relies upon disintermediation ignores the fact that most of the successful internet companies work in precisely the opposite way, acting as INFOMEDIARIES rather than disintermediators. AMAZON and EBAY, for example, bring buyers and sellers together; they are middlemen, albeit of a sophisticated kind.

Distributed computing

See GRID COMPUTING.

DNS

See DOMAIN NAME SYSTEM

Docuverse

A description of the HYPERTEXT world envisaged by Ted Nelson (see XANADU).

Domain

One or more computers on the internet that are described by a particular name and IP ADDRESS. For example, computers that are attached to the network at *The Economist* are within the domain economist.com. Domains and their names are organised hierarchically by the DOMAIN NAME SYSTEM. At the top of this hierarchy are the top-level domains (TLDs) seen at the end of an internet address, such as .com, .uk or .net. Below these are the names of specific institutions or parts thereof within that group, such as "economist", and lastly a name referring to a specific machine, such as "www". The whole constitutes an internet address that uses easily memorable, recognisable letters and words; www.economist.com is a good example.

D

The administration of the domain system is a complex business involving a mix of quasi-public organisations, registries for individual TLDs and private companies acting as registrars. Exactly who has the right to assign and manage domain names, and who should profit from that arrangement, is still under discussion. Another problem is that of CYBERSQUATTING: the appropriation of a domain name resembling another company's trademark, usually in the hope of selling it at a profit.

A 1999 survey of 25,500 standard English-language dictionary words found that 93% of them had already been registered as .com domains. The rest followed shortly afterwards.

Domain name system

The means by which DOMAINS are organised on the internet. The domain name system (DNS) is also the means by which a domain name (such as www.economist.com) is translated into the IP ADDRESS (such as 165.117.52.149) used to find and identify an internet location. Lists of domain names and their corresponding addresses are distributed throughout the internet on DNS SERVERS.

In June 2001, there were over 30m unique domain names registered worldwide. At the beginning of the year over 400,000 new registrations were being added each week.

Domain sniper

A person or company that buys expired DOMAIN names, usually in the hope of selling them back to their original owners for a profit. Domain snipers take advantage of the fact that domain names must be renewed periodically by their original registrants, many of whom forget to do so or erroneously assume that they own the name. Once a registration lapses the name becomes available for anyone to buy. In some countries, it is estimated that the number of lapsed registrations now exceeds the number of new ones, making the sniping business potentially lucrative for those prepared to seek them out. Some unscrupulous snipers redirect visitors expecting to see the old WEBSITE to a more embarrassing or offensive one, in the hope of persuading recalcitrant businesses to pay up.

Short of invoking expensive intellectual property rights litigation, there is no clear defence against domain snipers other than making sure that registration fees are paid on time. Some name registrars have a grace period during which the name may not be resold to anyone except its original owner. (See CYBER-SQUATTING.)

Doom

A violent computer game created by id Software. Doom was the first game to exploit the try-before-you-buy software distribution model now accepted as standard practice by thousands of software companies. Instead of buying the whole game unseen, players could download the first third of the game free of charge from websites and BULLETIN BOARDS, providing a teaser which proved irresistible to millions of gamers around the world.

id's creation was largely responsible for the popularity of ONLINE GAMING. Designed originally for solo play, it also included multiplayer facilities for LOCAL AREA NETWORKS. Its successor, Quake, added internet-based play, allowing anyone with a net connection to join games on one of hundreds of Quake servers around the world. Nearly all contemporary games now offer similar facilities.

Dot address

A number such as 194.153.0.126, the numerical equivalent of a particular DOMAIN name. (See IP ADDRESS.)

D

Dot-bomb

A term describing a failed WEBSITE or internet company. Although it is generally used by gloating journalists in its noun form, it can also be used as a verb, as in "I hear that Paul dot-bombed again last week". A related adjectival expression, dot-gone, is favoured by some as the best way of describing those no longer engaged in DOT-COMMERY.

Dotcom

The spoken version of .com, one of seven generic high-level DOMAIN names used originally to sort US addresses into broad categories. A .com address generally denotes a commercial organisation (contrasting with a .org address, for example, which theoretically indicates a non-profit organisation). Such addresses are considered to have a kudos greater than country-specific domains such as .co.uk. There were more than 21m registered .com addresses at the beginning of 2003.

The expression dotcom is also used to describe an internet company, generally one that depends entirely on its ONLINE activities for its revenue. Boasting about a new dotcom job was once considered fashionable and many real-world companies (and even some people in towns) rebranded themselves by adding .com to their names at the height of the frenzy for internet companies, but it has acquired a less desirable stigma as dotcoms have become DOT-BOMBS.

Dot-commery

The engagement in new kinds of internet-based commercial

activity, usually by people leaving jobs in traditional businesses to form their own START-UPS. Dot-commery is a dying art, and most of the traffic is now in the other direction: B2B, otherwise known as "back to banking".

D

Download

To transfer information from a remote computer, such as a website or mail SERVER, to a local computer's hard disk across a NETWORK or MODEM connection. (See also UPLOAD.)

Drive-by hacker

Someone who breaks into computer networks via a wireless link from outside a building, particularly across WI-FI connections. Relying on the fact that most companies using wireless technology rarely secure or encrypt their connections, would-be BANDWIDTH thieves and intruders can simply walk or drive through likely looking parts of town armed with a laptop and a suitable wireless data card, waiting for their equipment to detect a signal from an exposed network. Many such intrusions are moderately harmless and involve nothing more sinister than the borrowing of free, high-speed internet connections by people who need to check their E-MAIL on the move. Unsurprisingly, however, not all drive-by hackers are good citizens, and there are more worrying tales of people stealing or corrupting data. Some estimates in 2002 suggested that as many as 60% of corporate Wi-Fi networks were unsecured from outside attacks of this kind. Drive-by hacking is also known as war-driving (or, if the attacker is on a bicycle, war-pedalling) and has been made much easier by the emergence of WARCHALKING.

Drop-dialling

A way for WEBSITES to collect small payments from customers unwilling or unable to use their credit cards, often used when charging for website CONTENT. Drop-dialling requires visitors to DOWNLOAD a small program from the site in question. When the program is run, it cancels (or "drops") the current connection to the internet and dials a premium-rate number to connect to the site directly. The income derived from the call is entirely dependent on the length of time the user then spends on the site, and is thus an unpredictable way of generating revenue. Unless the content in question displays a high degree of STICKINESS, profits are likely to be small and unrepeated.

One popular application is PORNOGRAPHY, and many adult sites use diallers like these to encourage shy visitors. Many visitors to these sites have had a nasty shock when their phone bill arrives; some unscrupulous site operators have configured their diallers to make expensive international calls, often unbeknown to the user. Users of drop-dialling services may also be vulnerable to attack by VIRUSES and TROJAN HORSE programs concealed in the dialling software.

DSL

Digital Subscriber Line (or sometimes Loop), a BROADBAND technology used to connect computers to the internet. DSL services are designed to improve BANDWIDTH connections over ordinary copper phone lines. There are a number of variants, each with a different initial reflecting differences in the volume and direction of the data being transmitted, so it is sometimes known generically as XDSL. The best known variant is ADSL, now becoming widely available in Europe and the United States. The biggest DSL success story is in South Korea, which had 5.6m subscribers in May 2002 (more than in the United States) thanks to government loans to ISPS enabling them to upgrade their equipment and market the services to subscribers. The UK has been the slowest of the major developed economies to adopt DSL technologies because of a late start by the incumbent telecoms company and absurdly high pricing strategies.

Dungeon

See MUD.

D

Dwelltime

The time a WEBSITE visitor can be persuaded to spend hanging around looking at advertisements, a quantity closely related to the site's STICKINESS. Although many studies have been made of the average visitor's dwelltime, few have managed to suggest practical ways of increasing it. The problem has got worse as the amount of free information on the web has grown; the less useful or relevant that information is, the faster dwelltime moves towards zero. The problem is especially severe for PORTAL sites, which have a conflict between keeping people on the site long enough to see the ADVERTISING and being useful enough to serve as a jumping-off point for exploring the rest of the web.

802.11

See page 242.

E-

Short for electronic. Almost as tired as CYBER-, the e- prefix is
now used extensively to describe new, digital forms of old practices: E-MAIL, E-COMMERCE, e-tailing.

eBay

An ONLINE AUCTION company.

E-book

A generic term for electronic books, in essence devices designed
to replace printed pages with electronic equivalents. Early e-
books were hardware devices with flat-screen LCD displays
dedicated to a single task: displaying the text of books, magazines or other documents that could be downloaded from internet sites. Unwilling to carry yet another piece of equipment
around with them, consumers were slow to catch on to the idea,
and the market for such devices remains small. But advances in
screen technology have brought the e-book concept to more
mainstream computers, and reader software is now available
(notably from MICROSOFT and Adobe) that lets people display
downloadable books on any kind of computer screen, complete
with the formatting and graphics that they expect from paper-
based books. This has been especially well-received by users of
small portable computers and PDAs, particularly those based on
the Pocket PC format running a version of WINDOWS.

E-books proponents argue that the ability to reuse electronic
books again and again will in time spell the end of the paper-
based book as we know it. Critics cite their comparatively poor
readability, the weight of the portable devices on which most of

them are read, their limited battery life and their incompatibility with bathtubs as reasons to avoid them. Nevertheless, some researchers are trying to find ways to build book-like devices that can display electronic book documents. Joseph Jacobson, an assistant professor at Massachusetts Institute of Technology (MIT), is working on a project that uses "digital ink" to display text and pictures on turnable pages. Whether or not the deeply entrenched symbolic power of books in our culture can be replicated by a few ounces of silicon and plastic remains to be seen. Most people agree that the bookless library is about as likely to happen as the paperless office: that is to say, not at all.

E-business

Another term for E-COMMERCE.

E-cash

Electronic money. E-cash can be stored and spent in a number of ways which generally involve storing digital tokens representing dollars, pounds or any other currency in some sort of electronic medium, such as a smart card or an electronic wallet on a computer's hard disk. Anyone wanting to spend money transfers these tokens to the recipient's electronic piggy bank, either by transmitting them across an internet connection or by handing over the smart card.

E-cash's principal advantages are the speed and security of the transactions it allows. There are hundreds of e-cash systems in commercial development, and companies such as Mondex have conducted consumer trials in the UK, the United States and Europe. Each uses its own complex blend of ENCRYPTION technologies, including DIGITAL SIGNATURES and systems such as SSL, which make it hard for unauthorised people to intercept payments or break into electronic storage mechanisms.

One form of e-cash that seems likely to succeed is the electronic purse, a smart card armed with a chip that can DOWN-LOAD cash from suitably equipped ATMs. Users of these cards will be able to make small purchases from participating retailers and have the cost deducted straight from the chip on the card rather than via a complex banking transaction. Banks and credit-card companies such as Visa and Mastercard are pursuing this idea with vigour, although their efforts are currently being hampered by the difficulty of enforcing suitable standards on a global basis.

E-commerce

Broadly, the buying and selling of goods and services on the internet. With the possible exception of PORNOGRAPHY, no other area of the internet has attracted more attention than retail e-commerce. The rise of companies such as AMAZON and EBAY has alerted the public to the possibilities of electronic shopping. The real money, though, is likely to be made in the BUSINESS-TO-BUSINESS sector, where companies can save money and streamline processes by automating procurement, negotiating deals electronically, reducing transaction costs and managing supply chains. (See also B2C.)

A friend called me up the other day and talked about investing in a dotcom that sells lobsters. Internet lobsters.
Where will this end? The next day he sent me a huge package of lobsters on ice. How low can you stoop?
Donald Trump

EDI

Electronic Data Interchange, a standard way of exchanging data between companies that predates the internet. It is especially suitable for sharing information such as prices or parts numbers. EDI has been used widely in the corporate world for over a decade, and now is being integrated into some internet technologies (see EXTRANET).

EFF

Electronic Frontier Foundation, a non-profit organisation that campaigns for ONLINE civil liberties. The EFF, founded in 1990 by John Perry Barlow and Mitch Kapor, is a loud voice against CENSORSHIP and an influential supporter of free speech and privacy.

E

Egosurfing

The practice of searching for mentions of yourself or your company on the web or in other internet resources such as NEWSGROUPS. Although egosurfing can safely be regarded as a resolutely self-indulgent activity for those with too much time on their hands, it has at least one beneficial use for businesses: it can reveal the number of sites that mention or point to their own, thus giving a measure (albeit a fairly imprecise one) of its popularity or general interest.

E-mail

Short for electronic mail, an electronic message sent from one computer to another.

Emoticon

A short string of ASCII characters used to add an expression of emotion to an E-MAIL or other ONLINE message. Most emoticons are designed to represent a simplified facial expression such as a smile (hence the alternative name "smiley") or a frown. So :-) is used to signify amusement either at someone else's wit or, at least as often, the author's own. Invented by Scott Fahlman and others at Carnegie Mellon University in 1982, the smiley has mutated into dozens of forms signifying everything from anger to flirtation. Although popular among users of CHAT rooms and INSTANT MESSAGING software, emoticons are still regarded somewhat snootily by the net's self-appointed intelligentsia, for whom they symbolise the death of irony and clarity of expression. :-(

Encoder

A program that converts data from one form to another, often with the aim of reducing its size and shortening DOWNLOAD times. In digital audio technology the best-known example is an MP3 encoder, which converts a sound recording (often in the WINDOWS WAV format) into a much smaller, but still near-CD quality, MP3 file. Encoders are also used to convert and optimise digital video files. Fierce competition exists between MICRO-SOFT, which wants everyone to encode their digital music and video into its own WMA and WMV audio and video formats, and other digital CONTENT providers, who prefer to rely on industry standards.

Encryption

The conversion of a message or data file into a form that cannot be understood by unauthorised readers. Encryption is the technology that makes E-COMMERCE possible because it underlies the security systems used to protect electronic financial transactions. Many forms of encryption exist, ranging from simple ciphers such as ROT13 to intricate mathematical algorithms.

Whatever their level of complexity, all encryption techniques require at least one KEY, which describes how a message is encoded and how it can be decoded. Single-key systems, usually called secret key or PRIVATE KEY encryption, are used by algorithms such as DES. The problem with single-key systems is that if the private key held by the sender and recipient of a message falls into the wrong hands, it can quickly be used to decipher any message. It also requires a separate key for every transaction or business partner, so anyone trying to build an e-commerce-based business must generate millions of different private keys and then find ways of sending them securely over the internet: an impractical task.

So far, the best solution to this problem is PUBLIC KEY EN-CRYPTION, which relies on a two-key system. To send a private message, the recipient's public key, which can be listed in the equivalent of a phone directory or on a WEBSITE, is used to encrypt it. Once so encrypted, only the private key held by the recipient will reveal the contents of the message. A DIGITAL SIGNATURE works the other way round, being encrypted with the sender's private key and decrypted with their public key.

Keys are complex entities, and their usefulness is directly proportional to their size. The bigger the key, the more secure ("stronger") is the encryption. Key size is measured in BITS. Adding one bit to the length of the key doubles the computing power taken to crack it, so a 56-bit key is theoretically twice as secure as a 55-bit key. Keys measured in tens of bits are regarded as easily crackable with today's powerful computers, with some schemes being broken in days or even hours; those over 1,000 bits long are effectively unbreakable, even by the fastest commercially available computers. Many attempts to break strong encryption schemes now rely on GRID COMPUTING techniques, in which many computers can work on the problem simultaneously.

Strong encryption technologies (the PGP program is a good example) are already widely available on the internet, often at little or no cost, and many people routinely use them to protect the contents of their E-MAIL communications. For years, governments have been doing their best to restrict such use of encryption software, arguing that it will place terrorists, drug smugglers and paedophiles beyond the reach of the law. One result of the 2001 terrorist attacks on New York and Washington was to put legislation against encryption back on most governments' agendas after a period in which controls were being gradually relaxed. In the United States, a new Domestic Security Enhancement Act was in draft form at the beginning of 2003; it includes a provision to regulate domestic use of encryption software. In the UK, the much-criticised REGULATION OF INVESTIGATORY POWERS ACT already gives authorities the power to monitor electronic communications and demand the handing over of encryption keys. Opponents of such regulation include campaigners who support individuals' rights to say what they like discreetly, and e-commerce suppliers, who worry that their business will be seriously undermined without the ability to secure financial transactions.

> *Encryption ... is a powerful defensive weapon for free people.*
> *It offers a technical guarantee of privacy, regardless of who is running the government. It's hard to think of a more powerful, less dangerous tool for liberty.*
> Esther Dyson

E-tailer

An electronic retailer, usually one selling something on a WEBSITE. Many e-tailers suffered in early 2001 as a result of the DOTCOM collapse, and even those with significant sales volumes and strong branding have not been shielded from market forces. eToys, one of the web's best-known retailers, collapsed at the beginning of 2001. Its demise was followed by that of hundreds of smaller players who were unable to generate sufficient sales to cover their running costs. Most of the successful remaining e-tailers have big brands behind them: either ONLINE brands such as AMAZON and eBay, or CLICKS-AND-MORTAR brands such as Toys "R" Us.

The collapse of the dotcom market convinced many sceptics that online shopping was doomed to fizzle out, but there are few signs that consumers are suffering from the same lack of confidence. A 2002 survey by Nielsen NetRatings, an internet research firm, showed that online shopping is growing 15 times faster than general retail sales in the UK, and three times faster than the equivalent growth in the United States. Some 60% of the UK's online population visited an e-tailer over the Christmas 2002 period, spending over £1 billion in November 2002 alone.

Evernet

A term used to describe the convergence of the internet, BROADBAND and wireless technologies in a way that enables users to remain continuously connected to the web from almost any device. Viewed by some as the next logical progression of internet technologies, the Evernet promises to connect not just PCS, PDAS and phones to the web but household appliances, cars and office equipment too. This vision of uninterrupted connectivity currently has little technical underpinning, although many new technologies such as BLUETOOTH are already making some of its ideas possible. The real barrier to its emergence is a lack of the BANDWIDTH required to connect hundreds of millions of people and devices simultaneously. Widespread adoption of always-on connections such as ADSL and, in particular, the wireless GPRS and UMTS 3G standards, may hasten the Evernet's arrival, assuming that the companies providing the relevant services do not run out of money or steam first.

E-wallet

Simply an electronic version of a wallet, used to store money, personal information and other data for use in ONLINE transactions. Such a wallet typically lives in a secure area on a user's hard disk and is used to identify individuals and handle financial transactions on retail or business WEBSITES. One of the great advantages of e-wallets over other payment schemes is that users need to enter information about themselves and their money into it only once; when they visit a website equipped with the appropriate software, their details can then be transferred when a request for payment is made. Various attempts have been made to establish e-wallets by software companies and banks anxious to help customers protect their funds, but a lack of standards and enduring concerns about security and privacy have prevented their use from becoming widespread. (See also E-CASH.)

Extranet

A NETWORK built on standard internet technology, typically used by an organisation to share information with customers, suppliers and other business partners. An extranet is generally an extension of a company's INTRANET, modified to allow access by specified external users.

Although they are based on standard internet technology, extranets are much harder to build than this simple description suggests. One problem is security, an important issue when considering what sort of data to make available, so FIREWALLS, DIGITAL SIGNATURES and message-level ENCRYPTION are commonly used. A potentially bigger problem is that of standardising data formats and business processes across organisations. Industry standards such as EDI and, increasingly, XML and WEB SERVICES are important parts of the solution to this problem.

E

404 Not Found

See page 241.

FAQ

Frequently Asked Questions. Most NEWSGROUPS contain a self-explanatory list of questions and answers designed to guide newcomers, explain the purpose of the group and give guidelines for posting messages. For reasons of NETIQUETTE (and self-preservation), it is a good idea to read the FAQ before posting questions such as: "What's this newsgroup all about then?" Repeating an oft-asked question without consulting the FAQ is likely to attract at least one FLAME. FAQS are a regular feature on the customer-service pages of commercial WEBSITES, theoretically helping site visitors to find answers to questions about a company or a product.

Some discussion forums and ONLINE COMMUNITIES now include a neat reversal of the FAQ idea. Called FQA (Frequently Questioned Answers), it gives people an opportunity to debate or dismiss so-called facts presented by others. For infrequently asked questions visit www.economist.com/diversions.

Fibre optic

A fine glass fibre that transmits light, sometimes known as optical fibre or just fibre. Fibre optic cables transmit data faster than copper wires and are less susceptible to electromagnetic interference. Most long-distance telephone and internet traffic travels across fibre, which now connects nearly all telephone exchanges and forms most internet BACKBONES. The first transatlantic fibre optic cable, laid in 1988, can carry nearly 38,000 simultaneous telephone conversations. Some of the latest fibre optic systems can transmit data at a staggering 10 terabits per second, nearly 180m times faster than a 56K MODEM.

Much has been made of the potential benefits of "bringing fibre to the kerb" by replacing the existing copper wires on which telephone systems are currently based and linking the fast fibre connection to the home using standard coaxial cable. But fibre optic technology is costly to install, and the widespread availability of local fibre is still a long way off. It is expensive to manufacture and needs more physical protection than existing wires. Meanwhile, technologies such as ADSL are demonstrating that copper still has plenty of life left in it.

F

File server

A computer responsible for the central storage and management of data files that can be accessed by other computers on the same NETWORK. File servers are typically equipped with large, fast hard disks for rapid transfer of information, lots of memory and often more than one processor. (See SERVER.)

Filter

A program (or part of one) that examines a message for specified criteria and then processes it accordingly. A good example is represented by the rules in many E-MAIL packages that allow a user to determine what happens to each incoming message. For example, e-mail from anybody at economist.com can be placed automatically in a folder called "Economist", or all messages without subjects can be deleted without being read. Filtering is also used extensively by BLOCKING SOFTWARE.

Firewall

A system composed of hardware or software, or both, that enforces access control between two networks, usually between a private LOCAL AREA NETWORK and the public internet. Most firewalls are installed to prevent unauthorised access to networks by potentially malicious outsiders, although they are often used in corporate environments to control the use of internet resources by employees. Home users are increasingly vulnerable to attack by CRACKERS armed with PORT SCANNERS, especially those with always-on connections via cable or ADSL, and personal firewalls are now available that are designed to protect individual PCs. The latest versions of popular OPERATING SYSTEMS now include firewalls as standard.

Firewalls are flexible tools that can be configured to provide security at many levels. Some allow only E-MAIL traffic, for example, and others block only incoming traffic from specific sites or services. They may also provide logging and auditing functions, allowing administrators to see how much and what sort of traffic passed across the NETWORK, how many illegal access attempts were made and even where those attempts came from. This is a potentially useful way of tracking down intruders. Personal firewalls may also stop outgoing traffic from a PC, preventing MALWARE such as TROJAN HORSES and VIRUSES from "phoning home" or redistributing itself.

Although often seen as the ultimate in network security, no firewall can prevent an employee walking out of the building with a bag full of corporate data stored on disk or tape; equally, a firewall may not be able to protect a network that allows dial-up access to a MODEM pool or a maintenance port on a photocopier. Increasingly, firewalls are being seen as tools that reinforce a comprehensive overall approach to security rather than the last line of a network's defence. A new generation of distributed firewalls attempts to provide security for every point on the network, rather than a single barrier that can easily be stepped around.

Flame

An abusive communication from a fellow internet user, usually in a NEWSGROUP but sometimes by E-MAIL or in a CHAT forum. Many things can trigger a flame. Common causes are failure to observe NETIQUETTE, ignorance of a FAQ and simple stupidity, or intemperance on either side. Flames often induce considerable shock in first-time recipients, who may be surprised by the vehemence and forthrightness of the attack. Braver individuals may respond in kind, which may ultimately result in escalation to a full-scale flame war. Such frank exchanges of views are generally discouraged by the local COMMUNITY, but they can be tremendous fun for a LURKER.

Flash

A popular software package used by web developers to create glitzy effects and animations on web pages. Many people use Flash technology to create slick, animated interfaces for their sites, largely because of the speed at which its graphical effects download even across comparatively slow connections. Flash-enabled sites often include high-quality music and interactive features as well as just pretty graphics.

Frame relay

A high-speed PACKET-SWITCHED network PROTOCOL, often used in local and wide area networks. Unlike other packet-switched connections, which use data segments of fixed size, frame relay connections put data into variable-sized units (called frames) before transmission. Delivery of these frames can be prioritised, so that companies can choose levels of service quality in which some frames are deemed more important than others. Frame relay connections take advantage of unused BANDWIDTH to optimise data transmission, via a special circuit called a permanent virtual circuit (PVC). PVCs provide many of the benefits of an always-on LEASED LINE without the associated high cost, but they are not ideally suited to voice and video transmission.

Free-mail

Any form of free E-MAIL service, especially one that is web-based. Free-mail services have been extremely successful as they enable anyone with access to a BROWSER to have their own e-mail account. Often used by students and travellers, free-mail is also popular with people who need to keep business and personal e-mail accounts separate. The biggest free-mail service by far is MICROSOFT'S Hotmail, which now claims over 110m users. Some estimates show that the total number of free-mail accounts worldwide now exceeds 600m.

Despite their low-rent image, free-mail accounts are broadly equal in capability to traditional POP-based accounts, with the added advantage that they make it possible to pick up e-mail from almost any machine in the world with an internet connection. Most provide the ability to FILTER incoming mail; send, receive and VIRUS-check ATTACHMENTS; maintain an ONLINE address book; copy messages to multiple recipients; and even retrieve mail from POP accounts.

There are, inevitably, some problems with free-mail. Performance is generally slower than POP, as SERVERS are often heavily loaded and it takes longer for messages to DOWN-LOAD. More worrying for unwary users is security, especially on shared machines, as incoming mail is stored in the browser's CACHE and can often be accessed by anyone with a little browser knowledge. The biggest problem for most users is the vast amount of SPAM that free-mail accounts generate. Well over 1 billion messages a day are sent from Hotmail accounts alone, many of which are unsolicited by the people who receive them. Anyone can set up an anonymous free-mail account simply by providing unverified personal information, and many people do so for spamming purposes alone. In conjunction with an ANONYMISER service, free-mail accounts are effectively untraceable unless you resort to expensive court proceedings against the service provider.

Freeserve

A UK-based ISP, and the first to provide free internet access to its subscribers. Freeserve was founded in late 1998 by Dixons, a high-street retailing group. Within six months of launch it was the biggest ISP in the UK, easily overtaking stalwarts of many years' standing such as DEMON and AOL, and it now has over 2.5m subscribers. Unlike most ISPs, which charged a flat fee or an hourly rate for internet access, Freeserve's original business model was based on making money from a share of the telephone calls to the service itself and to its premium-rate technical support line.

Freeserve's success triggered a revolution in the ISP business in the UK, with many existing companies abolishing their monthly fees and many others starting new free services. Freeserve's initial public share offering, in July 1999, was massively oversubscribed. But many of the free ISPs that were set up have closed down. Freeserve itself was bought by its French rival Wanadoo, part of France Telecom, in December 2000, and now looks a lot more like a traditional ISP. It is one of the biggest suppliers of ADSL in the UK, claiming nearly 50,000 subscribers at the end of 2002.

Free Software Foundation

An organisation dedicated to eliminating restrictions on copying, redistribution and modification of computer software. Founded by Richard Stallman in 1983, the Free Software Foundation (FSF) develops and distributes GNU, a UNIX-like OPERATING SYSTEM that can be freely modified by users within the provisions of the COPYLEFT system. (See also LINUX.)

FTP

File Transfer Protocol, a standard way for computers on the internet to exchange files. Like HTTP, FTP programs use the TCP/IP protocols on which the internet is based to manage the transmission of BINARY FILES from one place to another. Many HTML authors use FTP to transfer web page files to their web SERVER, and it is commonly used to DOWNLOAD programs and other binary files from host computers on the internet. Most browsers are capable of downloading files using FTP.

Gateway

A device connecting different networks, especially those using different standards or PROTOCOLS. Gateways are an essential part of the internet, as they allow systems that know nothing about each other to exchange information. A good example is an E-MAIL gateway which connects two different proprietary e-mail systems, allowing the users of each to communicate as if they were on the same NETWORK. Gateways typically reside on a dedicated SERVER, which may also host a FIREWALL and PROXY SERVER.

Geek

Traditionally, someone whose fascination for technology over-whelms all other pursuits, with all the negative stereotypes this implies: in short, a NERD. For most of the history of personal computers the term was derogatory, but geekdom, especially of the internet variety, has now become stylish. Nearly all the people who have built high-profile internet businesses are geeks of one kind or another; evidence, perhaps, that the geek shall indeed inherit the earth.

There are three roads to ruin: women, gambling and technicians. The most pleasant is with women, the quickest is with gambling, but the surest is with technicians.

George Pompidou

Get Big Fast

An E-COMMERCE mantra first attributed to Jeff Bezos, CEO of AMAZON.com, and the title of a book of the same name. Bezos is said to have distributed T-shirts with this slogan at the first company picnic in 1996, and his idea that the scale of his business would be a critical part of its success has been adopted by many other internet START-UPS. Some have suggested that a version more appropriate in today's climate might be "Get Bought Fast".

GIF

Graphics Interchange Format. GIF files are INTERLACED graphics files widely used on the web, especially for simple computer-generated pictures and animations but also for digital photographs. Most BANNERS are in GIF form. In 1994 COMPU-SERVE, the owner of the GIF specification, decided to make software developers pay for the privilege of including GIF support in their programs, which dismayed many who had considered GIF a free and open standard. More recently Unisys, owner of the COMPRESSION patents on which GIF is based, has tried to extract payment from small software developers and anyone using "unauthorised" GIF files on their sites, an even less popular move that resulted in the Burn All GIFs campaign in 1999. Nevertheless, GIF is likely to remain an industry standard despite the technical superiority of alternatives such as PNG and JPEG because it is the only common graphics format that supports animation.

Gnutella

A system for exchanging files between internet users. Although it can be used to exchange any sort of electronic information stored in files, its most popular use is for sending and receiving music files in the MP3 format. Gnutella's popularity has grown since NAPSTER, once the internet's most popular source of MP3 files, was forced to close after becoming embroiled in legal action by music COPYRIGHT holders.

One crucial difference between and Gnutella and Napster has kept it up and running. Instead of a centralised directory of files available for DOWNLOAD, Gnutella operates on a P2P basis in which users can directly access the files held by other users on the Gnutella network. Because Gnutella has no central point of administration it is effectively immune to the legal weaponry of the music industry, and it has become correspondingly popular with those who believe that music should be freely available. Its name derives partly from a popular hazelnut spread and partly from the GNU project run by the

FREE SOFTWARE FOUNDATION, to whose OPEN SOURCE standards the program conforms. Many of the popular file-sharing programs such as BearShare, Morpheus and LimeWire are based on the Gnutella standards.

Google

A SEARCH ENGINE founded in 1998 by Larry Page and Sergey Brin, two students at STANFORD UNIVERSITY. Google was a comparatively late entrant to an already crowded market, but it has rapidly grown to become the largest and most visited search engine on the web. Its success is largely due to some clever search algorithms and a unique page-ranking system that ranks sites on their popularity with other site owners as well as simple KEYWORDS, by way of an equation that it claims uses 500m variables. At the beginning of 2003 Google had indexed more than 3 billion URLs, making it the largest publicly accessible repository of web information, and was responding to 150m search requests every day.

Much of Google's popularity stems from its sparse, uncluttered design and its consistent ability to deliver more relevant results than its competitors. Although it originally concentrated on indexing the web alone, it now includes features for searching 425m images, over 700m USENET posts dating back over 20 years and tens of millions of non-HTML documents such as PDF files and telephone numbers for every city in America. Such is its presence that in a 2003 survey by brandchannel.com, an Interbrand company, it was rated as the world's top brand ahead of much longer established companies including Coca-Cola and Apple. Some of its fans have expressed concerns about the rapid expansion of the company into areas that they say dilute the purity of its search function, such as a news service and various shopping features.

Gopher

A PROTOCOL used to find information on the internet. Gopher is said to be named after the mascot of the University of Minnesota, where it was originally developed. For many years Gopher provided the easiest way to find information on the internet, but its popularity has declined with the advent of web technology. Nonetheless, many of the original archives survive, especially in universities, and can be accessed with most web BROWSERS. Gopher is still used extensively by specialist researchers looking for information not accessible to the main SEARCH ENGINES.

G

GPRS

General Packet Radio Service, the first of a series of improvements to the wireless GSM standard, enabling data to be transmitted to a mobile phone or PDA at higher speeds than the original specification allowed. With suitable equipment, subscribers to GPRS can check E-MAIL on the move, browse the web and even indulge in INSTANT MESSAGING. But despite early promises of its performance, GPRS data services have proved to be less spectacular than the ISPs who sell them had hoped. User uptake has been slow because of late availability of the costly new handsets and the expensive pay-per-MEGABYTE costs of using them. A further barrier is speed: most commercial offerings in Europe deliver data speeds of about 40KBPS, almost ten times less than the theoretical maximum. Many users appear to be waiting for the arrival of faster 3G services.

Grid computing

The application of the resources of many networked computers to a particular task. Hailed by some as "the internet's next big thing", grid computing is particularly well-suited to the cracking of scientific or technical problems requiring massive amounts of computing power. By farming out parts of a problem to hundreds or even thousands of computers, researchers can take advantage of unused processing power on idle machines and thus quickly complete tasks which might take months or years on a single, dedicated machine.

The first well-known application of grid computing was SETI@HOME, which enlisted the help of internet users in analysing radio telescope data as part of the search for extra-terrestrial life. The popularity of the SETI project has prompted many other organisations to follow suit, and programs now exist in which grids are deployed to help design new drugs, diagnose illnesses, crack ENCRYPTION algorithms, model the consequences of environmental disasters and even simulate the universe's Big Bang. Some companies, notably IBM, now sell commercial software with built-in grid computing capabilities.

Groupware

Software that helps people work together more productively and share knowledge more efficiently. The groupware concept was popularised in the early 1990s by Notes, a product developed by Lotus Development (creator of the famous 1-2-3 spreadsheet). It has since been embraced by nearly every vendor of software that allows more than one user, including MICROSOFT, NETSCAPE, Novell and a host of smaller companies.

Some groupware products have a broad generic scope that helps with simple office automation tasks and the sharing of resources. Others have much more specialised roles in markets such as computer-aided design (CAD), where it is important for people to be able to collaborate on drawings and diagrams. Even word processors and BROWSERS are now packed with groupware features, the former for aiding multiple contributions to documents and the latter for building sophisticated mailing lists and discussion groups. One of the most important applications is scheduling, an area where once-simple personal information management software has mutated into big, complex programs for planning meetings, building resources and managing multiple diaries.

Generally, these applications rely on expensive proprietary technology, and are thus threatened by the more open and flexible possibilities offered by internet standards. INTRANETS, in particular, are much cheaper than large-scale Notes installations and generally more flexible. From there, it is a short step to an EXTRANET capable of embracing customers, suppliers and business partners. With this in mind, companies such as Lotus have been forced to lower their costs and add TCP/IP-based features to their existing products.

Groupware is viewed with some suspicion by companies committed to old-style hierarchical management teams. Like a NEWSGROUP, it often fosters an electronic soapbox mentality, encouraging employees to express views they might keep to themselves in more traditional face-to-face environments. Reaching any sort of consensus using groupware tools can be a challenge, and many systems are thus used primarily as decision-support tools for senior management rather than free-for-all company-wide discussion groups.

GSM

Global System for Mobile communications, a standard for digital mobile telephones widely used in Europe. GSM and its variants are rapidly being adopted elsewhere in the world, especially in Asia and Australasia. GSM allows phones to send and receive data at up to 9,600BPS in conjunction with a personal computer or PDA. It is not generally suitable for surfing WEBSITES designed to be accessed by PCs, but it is adequate for E-MAIL and text-only websites that have been designed with low-BANDWIDTH connections in mind. New, faster versions of the GSM standard are now available, although most wireless operators have delayed the launch of their fastest 3G services. An intermediate solution to the wireless bandwidth problem, GPRS (sometimes referred to as 2.5G) is now widely available from most European mobile telephone operators, although many of these still have trouble explaining exactly why their subscribers need it. The biggest use for data exchange via GSM is still text messaging (SMS).

Hacker

Broadly, someone who enjoys exploring, using and extending technology, particularly but not exclusively computer technology. This is to simplify the issue, however, and debate persists over what a hacker is and who qualifies for membership of the essentially meritocratic hacker community. Some people consider that to be a true hacker a person must be an enthusiastic programmer, preferably for the UNIX OPERATING SYSTEM. Others maintain that an expert or enthusiast of any kind qualifies. Perhaps the most useful definition is simply someone who enjoys intellectual challenges and creative problem-solving, especially within the context of technology. One generally recognised truth is that people who call themselves hackers are probably not: the honour is conferred by their peers rather than by the individuals themselves.

The word is often used to describe someone who is actually a CRACKER, which enrages the hacker community. As Eric Raymond says in his enlightening essay "How To Become A Hacker", "hackers build things, crackers break them". And build things they do: UNIX, USENET, the WORLD WIDE WEB and the internet itself are all the work of hackers.

I want to get to know the hacker community better.
These people are America's future.
Jeffrey Hunker, US National Security Council

HDML

Handheld Devices Mark-up Language (see WML).

Hit

A single request for a file as logged by a web SERVER. When a BROWSER requests an HTML page, the server must deliver not just the HTML code but any associated objects such as IMAGE files. Each one of these counts as a hit, so a single web page with nine images – common enough, given the number of graphical elements used for design and NAVIGATION purposes in a typical web page – will generate ten hits. Hits are therefore a good indicator of the amount of work a server is doing but an unreliable measure of how many pages are actually being viewed. In the early days of the web disingenuous marketers used hits as a measure of a site's popularity. People (especially advertisers) have seen through this ruse and IMPRESSIONS are now the measure of choice.

Home page

On a WEBSITE, the page that acts as a front door to everything else. Home pages typically provide a comprehensive index of the site's content and the NAVIGATION tools needed to move around it. Usually, the website's main address is also the home page address.

For web surfers, the home page is the first page that appears when they start their BROWSER, often a PORTAL or other site preset by their ISP or browser manufacturer. Pressing the "Home" button in the browser returns a user to this page. Any other site can be specified as the default browser home page; a SEARCH ENGINE, for example, or a different portal.

When I took office, only high energy physicists had ever heard of what is now called the World Wide Web ... Now even my cat has its own page.
Bill Clinton, 1996

Honeypot

A computer or internet SERVER set up to lure unsuspecting CRACKERS or SCRIPT KIDDIES. Honeypots serve several purposes, especially as tools for trapping and identifying would-be intruders into corporate networks. Honeypots typically mimic real computer systems or networks but contain no useful data or information; instead they may be populated with good-looking but falsified data, or merely be given a name that makes them attractive to passing criminals. Careful monitoring of these systems often yields useful information about how intruders choose targets, how good their cracking skills are and what steps they take to cover their tracks. Many companies use honeypots to discover potential weaknesses in their real systems and to help design more secure alternatives. There have been some notable honeypot successes; in 2000, for example, a group of Pakistani hackers was identified when it tried to use a US computer system to attack websites in India.

Increasingly wise to the ways of their enemy, sophisticated intruders are getting better at spotting traps and may completely destroy systems that they suspect are fakes. Meanwhile, some security experts have criticised the honeypot approach for distracting people from the real business of protecting their own networks, pointing out that most serious attacks come from inside organisations rather than from the internet. A new form of honeypot is evolving around WI-FI technology, designed to identify DRIVE-BY HACKERS.

Host

Broadly, any computer acting as a repository for information, data or services that can be accessed by another computer across a NETWORK. On the internet the meaning is more specific, encompassing any computer that has its own IP ADDRESS and full two-way access to other NODES on the network.

Hotwired

A WEBSITE originally established by *Wired* magazine, now owned and run by LYCOS. Hotwired is best known for its invention of the BANNER advertisement.

HTCPCP

Hypertext Coffee Pot Control Protocol (see RFC).

HTML

Hypertext Mark-up Language, used to create documents and LINKS on the WORLD WIDE WEB. HTML is a simple, text-based set of instructions, known as TAGS, which describe how the elements of a web page should be laid out and how they connect to other documents or programs. Much of the web's success can be attributed to the accessibility and simplicity of this language, which anyone with a text editor and a simple reference guide can write. Despite (or perhaps because of) this simplicity, writing reams of HTML code is dull work, and many programs now exist to automate the process.

Unlike real programming languages such as C++ or JAVA, which need to be compiled for a specific OPERATING SYSTEM, HTML is – in theory, at least – interpreted by all browsers in the same way, regardless of their manufacturer or the type of computer they run on. HTML standards (including the latest, version 4) are administered by the W3C, which works hard to ensure that they are widely adopted. But the BROWSER manufacturers have not been co-operative in enforcing these standards. Both MICROSOFT and NETSCAPE have hijacked the HTML specification and made their own incompatible additions to it, with the result that code written for INTERNET EXPLORER may look completely different (or not work at all) in NAVIGATOR, and vice versa. This represents a problem for site developers, who must consider writing at least two versions of their pages to ensure that everyone can read them properly.

H

HTTP

Hypertext Transfer Protocol, the PROTOCOL used to transfer web pages between a web SERVER and a BROWSER. HTTP was created at CERN by Tim Berners-Lee and his team as part of the development of the WORLD WIDE WEB.

Hyperlink

See LINK.

Hypertext

Text that can be read in a non-linear fashion by following a series of LINKS between related sections of material. Typical applications for hypertext include encyclopedias or dictionaries, where interesting or useful explanations of highlighted words in the text can be reached by clicking on them with a mouse. Many computer help systems use hypertext to guide users and illustrate common procedures; and hypertext is slowly creeping into our culture in the form of novels and video installations.

By far the biggest hypertext application is the WORLD WIDE WEB, which uses its HTML and HTTP technologies to link together billions of individual pages. (Strictly speaking, the web is a hypermedia system, as it incorporates graphics, video and audio into the text framework.) The web makes something of a mockery of the many lofty hypertext theories that have been propounded over the years, most of which want to impose a predetermined structure and format on hypertext documents. Despite the lack of consistent guiding principles among its builders, the wonderful thing about the web is that it works.

The term hypertext was coined by Ted Nelson in the 1960s to describe his XANADU system. But hypertext-like systems had been described before, most presciently in 1945 by Vannevar Bush, whose theoretical microfilm-based "memex" device included features for linking together information recorded on microfilm. In 2000, BT, a British telecoms giant, claimed that it owned the intellectual rights to the hypertext link idea, based on a patent originally filed in 1976. It subsequently invited ISPS and other telecoms companies to license hypertext technology, an invitation that was treated with derision by the internet community and its legal representatives. In 2002, an American federal judge rejected BT's claims for royalty payments from Prodigy Communications, a large American ISP.

ICANN

The Internet Corporation for Assigned Names and Numbers, a private non-profit organisation responsible for managing the systems and PROTOCOLS that keep the internet running. In particular, ICANN is responsible for allocating IP ADDRESSES, managing the DOMAIN NAME SYSTEM and taking over other tasks currently under US government contract to other agencies, such as the Internet Assigned Names Authority (IANA). ICANN was formed in 1998 to help bring an independent, international focus to the management of the internet.

Many believe that ICANN has failed to meet its obligations. It has been widely criticised for its choice of board members and its failure to bring clarity to the processes by which domains are administered. But it is most unpopular for its failure to consult the TLD operators and registries that it claims to represent, some of whom claim that it has excessive power to make decisions about the TLDs that they believe to be their own property. Some of these operators have threatened to abandon ICANN and consider proposals for a scheme that would attempt to take over some of its powers.

ICQ

Messaging software that lets people communicate electronically in real time; in effect, a CHAT program. ICQ (a contraction of I Seek You) has attracted millions of users, who can not only chat but also send files and URLS, play games and even communicate by video, either individually or as part of a group. This rapidly growing COMMUNITY, which now has over 135m users, inevitably attracted the attention of AOL, to which the program's developer Mirabilis was sold in 1998.

ICRA

The Internet Content Ratings Association, an organisation providing guidelines on the rating and filtering of potentially harmful web content. Originally formed as the Recreational Software Advisory Council (RSAC), which was designed to rate computer games according to their level of violence and use of obscene or offensive language, the ICRA now helps WEBSITE owners and creators of other sorts of material to rate their CONTENT on all sorts of criteria. Unlike many organisations distributing BLOCKING SOFTWARE and arguing for the removal of offensive content from the web, the ICRA does not itself rate anything. Instead it promotes the PICS standard, which lets content owners rate their own material and parents or other concerned web visitors choose which kinds of content can be displayed in their BROWSER.

I

IETF

The Internet Engineering Task Force, a self-organised group which shepherds the development of new technical standards for the internet. Its brief includes identifying technical problems, proposing and specifying the development of solutions to these problems and providing a forum for the exchange of information within the internet COMMUNITY. Despite the fact that the IETF is not a traditional standards organisation – its ad hoc structure and open-to-all policy would make the leaders of most analogous organisations shudder – it produces many specifications that become internet standards. Its main unit of currency is the RFC (Request For Comments), a document that details a new technological solution to a particular problem. Comments from relevant experts then guide the development of that technology. One of the IETF's stipulations for any proposal is that the standard in question must actually exist, preferably in prototype. This is one of the reasons for the internet's rapid technical progress.

We reject kings, presidents and voting.
We believe in rough consensus and running code.
Seen on an IETF T-shirt

IM

See INSTANT MESSAGING.

Image

A picture stored in electronic form. Images that appear on web pages are generally stored in one of the few formats that can be understood by a web BROWSER: GIF, JPEG or PNG. All of these formats use COMPRESSION techniques to reduce the size of the image files and thus speed up DOWNLOAD times.

I

Image map

A clickable IMAGE used to help users navigate around and between WEBSITES. An image map is divided into several different hotspot areas, each of which is linked to another destination. A CLICK with the mouse on one of these hotspots will take the user to the URL associated with it.

IMAP

Internet Message Access Protocol, a standard way of retrieving E-MAIL from a mail SERVER. The main advantage of IMAP over older protocols such as POP3 is that users can manipulate remote mailboxes as if they were on a local machine. This makes it much easier for recipients to specify how they receive their e-mail. They can, for example, view just the subject and sender of an e-mail before deciding whether to download it, or specify that only messages meeting certain criteria should be viewed.

I-mode

The name for the world's largest wireless information service, operated by Japanese telecoms operator DoCoMo. I-mode has become the model to which European mobile operators aspire, thanks to its huge and active subscriber base, over 20m in March 2001. More than 40,000 independent websites provide services for i-mode subscribers, who are billed on the amount of data they transmit rather than the amount of time they are ONLINE.

Impression

A single instance of the display of a specific web page or, more commonly, a BANNER advertisement. Impressions are measured by the number of requests from BROWSERS for particular banners, as counted by specialised ad counters. Advertisers pay for a number of impressions, rather than a number of HITS.

Infomediary

An electronic intermediary that helps buyers and sellers do business on the internet, usually by providing unique or exclusive information and services. There are many examples of infomediaries, the best-known being consumer-driven WEBSITES such as lastminute.com and EBAY. Both of these bring buyers and sellers together in ways not practical before the advent of public electronic networks by consolidating geographically isolated customers and suppliers. But the real future for infomediaries is in BUSINESS-TO-BUSINESS transactions, where the ability to provide up-to-the-minute pricing information, supply goods at rock-bottom prices or merely host a conveniently neutral dealing platform may give internet-based businesses a huge advantage over their real-world equivalents. For an interesting contrast, and an example of the difficulty of making predictions on internet trends, see also DISINTERMEDIATION.

Infonesia

The inability to remember where you came across a particular piece of information. This irritating ailment is becoming much more prevalent as the number of digital information sources in people's lives increases, and most infonesiacs are long-term users of E-MAIL, NEWSGROUPS and MAILING LISTS. A related condition, internesia, is common among avid web surfers and CYBRARIANS.

> Where is the wisdom we have lost in knowledge? Where is the
> knowledge we have lost with information?
> T.S. Eliot

I

Information appliance

A device that connects to a digital network or broadcast service for the purpose of gathering or distributing information. After the telephone, the internet-connected PC is still the most common and useful information appliance. But many new devices to help people connect to information resources have come on the market or are being developed that are less bulky and less expensive and offer other advantages. One example is the personal digital assistant (PDA), which is capable of making wireless connections to the internet and may be equipped with powerful processors that are capable of running popular business software.

Instant messaging

A form of messaging technology that allows internet users to communicate in real time, rather than using asynchronous tools such as E-MAIL or BULLETIN BOARDS. The technology behind instant messaging (IM) has been available to users of university networks and internet CHAT rooms for many years. But the advent of stand-alone programs such as ICQ, MICROSOFT'S MSN Messenger and AOL's AIM has allowed anyone with an internet connection to chat to friends, strangers and business acquaintances all over the world.

At its simplest, IM software lets people communicate quickly, privately and often anonymously by typing ordinary text messages into a small window on the screen. IM has become one of the internet's most widely used and important tools, and it is considered an essential part of the strategy of all the big PORTAL companies. As well as providing simple chat facilities, most IM clients now include features that allow files to be sent between users and even enable voice conversations and VIDEOCONFERENCING applications.

The immediacy and simplicity of IM has attracted businesses keen to find ways of communicating quickly and privately with colleagues and clients, but there are some problems to solve before it becomes a completely secure medium for these sorts of communications. Lawyers, doctors, financiers and even the US navy have adopted IM on a wide scale as an important adjunct to existing e-mail services, but they are aware that it is subject to the same security issues as any other form of digital exchange. With this in mind, several companies now sell products based on advanced ENCRYPTION algorithms that protect instant messaging exchanges from eavesdroppers, authenticate the identity of the people involved in discussions and record an irrefutable audit trail of conversations. Such developments are becoming popular with some financial institutions, which use them to manage communication among brokers, traders and clients.

Over 41m Americans used IM software from home in May 2002 (over 40% of the active internet population), and nearly 13m business people sent messages from work. IDC, a research company, predicted that businesses would spend $133m on instant messaging products in 2002, and over $1 billion by 2005. Even allowing for duplications and users of more than one product, these are numbers big enough to attract the attention of not just software companies but industry regulators too. One problem with IM software is the incompatibility between products from different companies. AOL has fiercely resisted all attempts to allow its software to communicate with that from other vendors such as YAHOO and Microsoft, a stand that aggrieved its competitors and, in relation to its merger with Time

Warner, led to some stern words from the US Federal Communications Commission (FCC) regarding unfair competition. After some unseemly tit-for-tat "chat wars" between AOL and its opponents, in which AOL repeatedly rewrote its software to block incoming messages from other sources, the opposition took a different tack. Microsoft, Yahoo, AT&T and several smaller companies joined forces in 2000 to form a standards-based body called IMUnified, an alliance notable for the absence of AOL. IMUnified's work has yet to bear fruit.

Meanwhile, most companies developing IM programs are seeking ways to integrate them successfully with the SMS services available on mobile phones, thus guaranteeing an exponential increase in the number of annoying beeping sounds now heard in most public places.

Internet2

An experimental high-speed NETWORK. Formed in 1996 by a consortium of American universities, Internet2 was designed as a testbed for new networking technologies and applications, especially those needing very high speeds. Despite its name, it is not a replacement for the existing internet; rather, its operators hope that research and developments stemming from Internet2 will find their way on to the mainstream internet as higher BANDWIDTH and better technology becomes available. Current areas of research on Internet2 include delivery of educational and health services, digital video, IP v6 and MULTICASTING. Over 180 universities, many of which are connected to other high-speed networks such as VBNS, are now members of Internet2.

Internet Explorer

Software for browsing the WORLD WIDE WEB developed by MICROSOFT (see BROWSER).

Internet Open Trading Protocol

A PROTOCOL designed to standardise electronic payment transactions on the internet. As anyone who has bought things from more than one WEBSITE will testify, most internet retailers use their own complex and incompatible systems for financial transactions, agreeing only on the ENCRYPTION standards. The Internet Open Trading Protocol (IOTP) tries to recreate some of the accepted practices that govern real-world buying and selling, complete with subtleties such as the way a transaction is conducted, the presentation of offers and the delivery and receipt of goods.

Theoretically, IOTP should make life much easier for consumers, who will be able to use a consistent interface for buying and ordering goods and services, as well as for merchants and banks, who will have more consistent ways of collecting and processing payments. In practice, it is likely to be a long time before it is widely used. Bodies implementing new internet standards do not always share users' views about consistency and ease of use, and many good ideas like this have yet to be usefully implemented anywhere. A further problem is that successful retailers have become fiercely protective of their own patented shopping and trading mechanisms and may not embrace attempts to make them all behave in the same way.

Internet Society

An international non-profit organisation which guides the development of the internet. Formed in 1992, the Internet Society is the organisational home of the bodies that govern technical internet standards, including the Internet Engineering Task Force (IETF) and the Internet Architecture Board (IAB).

Internet telephony

Techniques for transmitting voice and fax over the internet. There are two ways of making telephone calls across the internet.

The first, which relies on the use of a PC, has the attraction of being essentially free, regardless of distance. The only charge is for the local call between the PC and an ISP, the same as any other dial-up internet connection used for browsing the web or sending E-MAIL. A combination of hardware and software compress and convert the sound of a voice (or a fax machine) into a BINARY FILE, which is then broken up into PACKETS just as any other message would be. The PC at the recipient's end of the call then converts the packets back into an audible voice signal.

The technology behind this sort of communication has advanced significantly and a version of it is now included in the most popular INSTANT MESSAGING programs. Armed only with a microphone, users of these programs can talk to each other freely without the need to buy expensive bespoke hardware or software. But there are problems with this sort of communication. In particular, the quality of service (QOS) is far from perfect because of the inherent difficulties in managing time lags across the internet and reassembling packets in the right order.

The second way of using the internet to make phone calls is to use a normal telephone, but instead of the call being routed all the way on public telephone networks, it is converted into IP packets and then routed via the internet. At the other end, the digitised voice is converted back again by a local SERVER. Although this kind of call suffers from the same packet reassembly problems, it gets over the compatibility issue: sender and receiver need only standard telephone equipment. It has many benefits for businesses, which can use the same network to transmit voice and data rather than rely on two separate sets of cables. Concerns about quality of service remain, however, and many important requirements of a hybrid service such as accounting, billing and roaming support for mobile devices have yet to be fully worked out.

Internet time

Time taken to get things done in the fast-moving internet environment. Not a clearly-defined fraction of standard linear timescales, but nonetheless a measure of the fact that things happen faster on the internet than in the real world. This transformative effect is especially apparent in the software and hardware industries, where an already rapid rate of change has been greatly accelerated by extreme competition and massive demand for new products and services.

The term is also used to describe a new, standardised global time measurement system proposed by Swatch, a Swiss watch manufacturer, which divides the day into 1,000 units called beats. Interest in this idea has so far been limited.

I | Internic

Until recently, the American organisation responsible for registering and maintaining top-level DOMAIN names, in conjunction with Network Solutions. Since 1998 the registration process has been open to competition, with ICANN assuming responsibility for accreditation and the appointment of new registrars.

Interstitial page

A page inserted into the structure of a WEBSITE that displays an advertisement or other form of promotion. When visitors CLICK on a LINK, the interstitial page pops up for a few seconds before taking them to the page they intended to view. Some sites force users to endure interstitial pages before the HOME PAGE loads, either for creative effect or to maximise exposure to an advertisement which can be sold for much more money than a typical BANNER. Poor site design has occasionally resulted in interstitial pages leading directly on to other interstitial pages, locking site visitors into a perpetual loop of advertisements.

Intranet

A NETWORK based on the same technical standards as the internet but designed for use within a single organisation. Intranets are replacing proprietary networks in companies because they are generally simpler and cheaper to administer. Indeed, it is possible to build an intranet without paying for any software at all by running free E-MAIL, BROWSERS and web SERVERS on top of the TCP/IP software supplied with all major OPERATING SYSTEMS. In practice, most organisations use commercial software from networking companies such as Novell and IBM to build and administer their networks.

Intranets are extremely flexible and are used to create everything from simple employee directories (much cheaper than printing 1,000 copies) to complex DATABASE and GROUPWARE applications. The open technology on which they are based makes intranets much easier to customise than proprietary products like Lotus Notes. Unfortunately, it also makes them more open to attack from the outside, so intranets must be carefully protected by a FIREWALL and a solid security policy. This is particularly important once the logical leap to an EXTRANET is made. Despite their general usefulness, a report by the Office of National Statistics showed that just 10% of UK companies were using intranets at the end of 2001.

IP

Internet Protocol (see TCP/IP).

IP address

The address of a particular computer on the internet, used to identify it uniquely for communications purposes. Every computer that sends or receives information on the internet must have an IP address, expressed as a 32-BIT number, which is attached to every message that is sent. Thus the recipient of any message has a return address to which it can reply if necessary. This is especially important on the web, where a SERVER must know exactly where to send back a requested page.

According to the current version of the IP PROTOCOL, version 4, the number itself is arranged in four groups of up to three numbers and has two parts: one identifies the network on which a machine resides and the other is for the machine itself. Each group is represented by a number between 0 and 255, giving numbers like 170.224.17.153. These numbers are translated into the alphabetic names associated with them (in the above example, www.economist.com) by a NAME SERVER.

Although a huge quantity of individual addresses are supported by this system, many numbers are reserved for special purposes and are not available for use by companies or individuals. The incredible growth of the internet has rapidly depleted the available numbers, especially those designated for use with small networks (known as Class C addresses). Enter IP version 6, already implemented in some OPERATING SYSTEMS, which will use 128-bit numbers. This new system, sometimes known as IPng (for "new generation"), theoretically enables 340,282,366,920,938,463,463,374,607,431,768,211,456 possible addresses; that is, 665,570,793,348,866,943,898,599 for each square metre of the Earth. This should be enough for even the most information-hungry economy.

IPO

Initial Public Offering, a term for the first sale of publicly tradeable shares by a company that has previously been privately owned, otherwise known as going public. IPOs are a crucial stage in a company's evolution, as they generate substantial income from the sale of the initial batch of shares and, more importantly, establish the company's credentials with the trading community. Internet companies have become famous for the success of their IPOs, which generated fortunes for the owners of Cisco, EBAY, NETSCAPE, YAHOO and hundreds of others in the early days of the web. In 2000 the IPO for AT&T's wireless division raised over $10 billion on the first day's trading, a US record for any company. But in early 2000 the markets demonstrated their unpredictability, as high-tech stocks took a dive not long after successful IPOs of such companies as Lastminute.com in the UK, which led to ALTAVISTA and others delaying their IPOs. The continuing downturn in high-tech stocks between 2000 and 2002 severely reduced the number of successful IPOs, and start-ups now find it much harder to attract staff on the basis that they might get rich when the company goes public.

IRC

Internet Relay Chat, a popular way of communicating on the internet. Using special CHAT software, users connect to one of many chat SERVERS around the world. Each server contains a number of chat areas, called channels, which are in theory devoted to a particular subject: #cricket, for example, should be about cricket. Once connected to a channel, anything you type is instantly readable by anyone else on the channel.

IRC attracts an enormous number of enthusiasts and, unsurprisingly, more than its fair share of eccentrics. Many an IRC NEWBIE finds its arcane commands and lively participants a little harsh when compared with the cosiness of web-based providers' chat rooms. Nonetheless, IRC has been used to transmit news from some otherwise inaccessible places: inside the Russian parliament building while it was being shelled in 1993, for example.

IRL

In Real Life, commonly used in CHAT rooms and NEWS-GROUPS. A typical comment is "So what do you look like IRL?", often accompanied by a SMILEY.

ISDN

Integrated Services Digital Network. Long touted as the next generation of high-BANDWIDTH digital communications services, ISDN is still the most widely available alternative to the plain old telephone system (POTS) as a means of connecting to the internet.

As its name suggests, an ISDN line integrates data and voice calls, so that it is possible to make phone calls while connected to the internet or other services.

Phone companies typically charge considerably more for ISDN than POTS, despite the fact that it is often cheaper for them to support. It also requires a special piece of equipment, called a terminal adapter, to connect a PC to ISDN, adding more cost to the package. These factors, and some poor marketing, have held back ISDN's progress in the UK, although it is popular in the United States and elsewhere in Europe. New technologies such as ADSL are rapidly superseding ISDN.

I

ISP

Internet Service Provider, a company that provides direct connections to the internet. ISPs form the GATEWAY between the public telephone network and the internet itself, and make it possible for anyone with a computer and a MODEM to gain access to a full set of internet services. All ISPs supply subscribers with an E-MAIL address. Most provide web-hosting facilities, allowing anyone with a text-editing program and a smattering of HTML knowledge to build their own WEBSITE.

Few kinds of companies have been forced to evolve as fast as ISPs. Since their advent in the early 1990s they have had to cope with massive increases in the numbers of internet users, PORNOGRAPHY and libel issues and drastic changes in technology, not to mention commercial challenges. Many have not survived, and in its characteristically democratic way the internet has made life hard for ISPs. Additional subscribers are hard to find – or attract from competitors – and so finding new sources of revenue has become important. This is one reason why ISPs such as FREESERVE have sold out.

In this kind of market, differentiating yourself from a competitor is difficult, and it is getting harder. BANDWIDTH and consistency of service, the two biggest issues for subscribers, have levelled out across ISPs, and customer demands have become much more sophisticated. No longer satisfied with pay-by-the-minute dial-up access, many subscribers now demand flat-rate, unmetered access to internet services as a minimum, which ISPs must find a way to subsidise, usually through PORTALS and ADVERTISING. Meanwhile, the rush for always-on services such as ADSL is forcing ISPs to strike deals with telecoms wholesalers and invest in expensive new technology in order to hold on to their customers. A report by IDC, a research company, estimated that user spending on BROADBAND services will grow by nearly 13 times between 2001 and 2006, with a corresponding decline in the number of dial-up connections.

Janet

ACRONYM for Joint Academic Network, a high-speed UK BACK-
BONE connecting several hundred academic and educational in-
stitutions. Janet and its fibre-based BROADBAND cousin
SuperJanet are part of the global internet.

---

*The most important thing in the programming language is the name. A
language will not succeed without a good name. I have recently invented
a very good name and now I am looking for a suitable language.*
Donald Knuth

Java

A programming language created by SUN MICROSYSTEMS
which began life as a way to connect intelligent devices in the
home. It has since evolved into a sprawling set of NETWORK
software technologies that allow information to be transmitted
and shared by a wide variety of devices. Java has generated enthusiasm bordering on religious mania in the software development community, and it is now routinely used by hundreds of
thousands of programmers in preference to older, well-established languages. All sorts of programs are now written in Java,
including many games and financial applications.

From a programmer's viewpoint, Java is easier, faster to use
and more elegant than languages such as C++. It can still be used
for large-scale projects, and several commercial software
vendors have released Java-only versions of their business and
graphics software applications. But Java's greatest promise is that
software programs written in it will run on any computer, regardless of the OPERATING SYSTEM or processor it uses. Such
PORTABILITY is achieved by way of a VIRTUAL MACHINE (VM),
a piece of software specific to a particular operating system,
which interprets the bytecode in a Java program and translates it
for use in the local environment. This "write once, run anywhere"
property is immensely attractive to software developers, who
have previously been burdened with the necessity of writing separate versions of their programs for each PLATFORM or operating

system: one for WINDOWS, one for Macintoshes, and so on.

A second benefit of Java is security. VMS insulate Java programs from the HOST machine's hardware and software, and thus limit their ability to damage the system. This is often cited as one of Java's main advantages over ACTIVEX technology.

These two attributes have done much to popularise Java in the developer community. But its third characteristic, modularity, is arguably the most important. Many people associate Java only with APPLETS and the WORLD WIDE WEB, but its reach is far broader. Java is a fully OBJECT-ORIENTED language, well-suited to the creation of components, each with their own specific functions, which can communicate locally or across networks, on SERVERS and in clients.

Such far-reaching usefulness sounds too good to be true, and in some ways it is. The missionary zeal with which Java's evangelists promote it conceals some awkward truths that have prevented Java from becoming quite the ubiquitous language that its creators hoped for. In particular, the "write once, run anywhere" promise has turned out to be misleading and irrelevant, as developers have discovered the need to use specific features of operating systems to make their products really useful. This in turn has compromised Java's much-vaunted security model.

Java is at the centre of bitter disputes between Sun and Microsoft, which has produced a range of supposedly Java-compliant products that, Microsoft claims, improve on Sun's lowest-common-denominator originals. Java's popularity forced Microsoft to include support for it in Windows operating systems and browser products, but it chose to write its own VM rather than include its competitor's code and stated that it would include Java only until 2004. After Sun accused Microsoft of leaving important features out of some Java products, an American judge ordered Microsoft to include Sun's version of Java in its operating systems.

Despite its failure to live up to its initial promise, Java is still a powerful force on the internet. In particular, it represents an opportunity for Sun to capture a sizeable proportion of the lucrative emerging WEB SERVICES market. Once again, though, Microsoft may prove to be its most dangerous enemy. Its .NET strategy, in particular, is designed to compete directly with many of the services that Java offers to developers of next-generation web-service applications, and some fear that Microsoft is again introducing compatibility problems for users of non-Microsoft products.

Javascript

A programming language designed to enhance the capabilities of web pages. The brainchild of NETSCAPE, Javascript is a relative of C++ but is designed for completely different tasks and is much easier to learn. It should not be confused with JAVA. Its main purpose is to help a web BROWSER do things that are beyond the scope of pure HTML, such as popping up special windows in response to mouse CLICKS or displaying messages in its status bar.

Many Javascript applications on the web are decidedly trivial, but it has some powerful features and forms a central part of DHTML. It is used to create many of the "live" effects seen on web pages. Other common uses include checking web forms for completeness before returning them to the SERVER and changing the colour of text blocks when the mouse pointer passes over them. Its most visible and annoying use is in displaying POP-UP advertising.

Jello

A term used by web designers to describe the placement of CONTENT in the exact centre of a web page, no matter what the size or resolution of the screen on which it is displayed. Jello pages sometimes spill off the edges of the screen, so designers also use "ice" pages (in which content has a fixed width and is aligned to the left of the screen) or "liquid" pages (which reflow to fit snugly into a display of any size).

Jini

A way to connect hardware devices on a NETWORK intelligently, irrespective of their make or type. When a device is added to a Jini-based network, it posts a list of its resources and capabilities to a central DATABASE used by every other device on the network. When something else comes along that wants to use those services, the instructions for how to do so are already contained in the database. Thus a Jini-enabled printer can be used by all the PCs, wireless PDAS and even televisions on a particular network, without the need for each to have special driver software or even the same OPERATING SYSTEM.

Jini is the invention of SUN MICROSYSTEMS and is based on its JAVA technology. Jini's various champions have described a gigantic future global computer network, in which everything understands everything else and technology is freed from the tyranny of large, monopolistic suppliers of operating systems. But this Utopia has so far failed to materialise. Massive indifference from hardware manufacturers, in particular, has scuppered many of Sun's plans, and the technology underlying Jini is now being deployed in other more immediately relevant areas such as WEB SERVICES.

JPEG

A type of compressed IMAGE file, based on a specification by the Joint Picture Experts Group. JPEG-encoded images (often known simply as JPGs) are often used on WEBSITES because of the comparatively small size of their files. (See also MPEG.)

Junk e-mail

See SPAM.

Just-in-time compiler

A program that turns JAVA bytecode into processor-specific executable software. Just-in-time (JIT) compilers can help overcome the sluggish performance of a web BROWSER'S VIRTUAL MACHINE, which runs bytecode one instruction at a time. If the code in which a Java APPLET is written is translated into native code that the computer understands, the underlying program can often be run much faster. JIT compilers are supplied with virtual machines from many companies, including IBM, MICROSOFT, NETSCAPE and SUN.

K

Abbreviation for kilo-, used to denote a multiplier of a thousand. So a 28.8K modem receives data at 28,800 bits per second, and the Motorola 68000 chip found in older Apple computers is sometimes referred to as the 68K.

Kbps

Short for thousand of bits (or kilobits) per second, typically used as a measure of the speed of a MODEM connection to the internet (see BPS).

Key

A string of data used to decode an encrypted message. The length of the key, usually quoted in BITS, determines how secure the message is. (See ENCRYPTION.)

Keyword

An index entry in a DATABASE that identifies a document or record. Keyword searches form the basis of the operation of SEARCH ENGINES such as ALTAVISTA, which search web pages for unique words and index them accordingly. The simplicity of this approach belies the difficulty of obtaining useful results from databases of several million documents, and most search engines use additional criteria to determine the relevance of a particular keyword's occurrence.

Some search engines have attracted controversy by selling keywords to advertisers and ranking searches for these words preferentially. Many others associate keywords with particular advertisements, so that a search for "computer" will display a computer vendor's BANNER at the top of the search results page. PORNOGRAPHY sites have taken particular advantage of this feature, to the displeasure of many web users confronted with graphic advertisements following innocent searches, especially for words describing parts of the body.

Key escrow

A scheme whereby anyone using PUBLIC KEY CRYPTOGRAPHY must deposit a copy of their key with a designated agency or TRUSTED THIRD PARTY. When security agencies wish to eavesdrop on encrypted conversations or read encrypted files, a warrant of some sort would allow them to retrieve the key from its escrow. Unsurprisingly, there has been worldwide opposition to key escrow schemes by privacy campaigners. (See ENCRYPTION.)

> *Gentleman do not read each others' mail.*
> Henry Stimson, US secretary of state, on ordering the closure of the "Black Chamber" cipher bureau in 1929

K

Killer app

A piece of software that creates the market for a promising technology. The best-known example of a killer app is the spreadsheet, first in the shape of VisiCalc and then Lotus 1-2-3. The latter drove the early market for IBM PCs by offering number-crunching facilities for which every business could see an immediate use. Most successful computer technologies have a killer app behind them, often a generic one. The most obvious example from the 1990s is E-MAIL, undoubtedly the application that has attracted millions of businesses and consumers to the wider internet.

LAN

See LOCAL AREA NETWORK

Latency

Broadly, a term used to describe a delay in transmitting data between two computers. Latency is the time taken to transfer a PACKET of information from one point to another, and is often cited as one of the reasons for the sluggish performance of internet connections.

Many factors influence the latency of a NETWORK connection, including the nature of the medium (cable, fibre and so on), the number of ROUTERS, the efficiency of a MODEM or network card and, ultimately, the speed of light. Although the delays introduced by each of these are measured in milliseconds, they add up to a significant total when applied to every packet of data sent across the network. This is one of the reasons that modes of communication which rely on sending a large number of messages back and forth, such as VIDEOCONFERENCING and ONLINE GAMING, are susceptible to latency problems.

LDAP

Lightweight Directory Access Protocol, a PROTOCOL which helps find people, computers and other resources on a NETWORK. Designed to work with existing address-book standards and improve compatibility between widely differing systems, the LDAP standard was adopted by the IETF in 1997 and now forms the basis of many white-page directories on the web. It has also been incorporated directly into some software programs and OPERATING SYSTEMS, making it possible to find E-MAIL addresses without visiting a directory site.

Leased line

A communications line that is rented for private use. Leased lines, sometimes known as dedicated lines, have a number of benefits for companies sending or receiving large amounts of data. The biggest is that the fixed BANDWIDTH of the line (which can vary from POTS speed to high-speed fibre or satellite rates, depending on how much you are prepared to pay) is not shared with anyone else, thus guaranteeing a particular level of service. This contrasts with FRAME RELAY connections, which share lines with other users.

Link

A connection between two HYPERTEXT objects, used to help people navigate on the WORLD WIDE WEB. Generally, a link takes the form of a highlighted word, phrase or graphic IMAGE on a web page. Clicking on a link then displays the object to which the link points, known as the target, which can be a different web page, a marked location further down the same web page or even a program on an FTP site. For all their simplicity, hypertext links are the key to the web's power. As well as forming its skeleton, they are an increasingly useful measure of the relevance of WEBSITES. Some SEARCH ENGINES, notably GOOGLE, rate the importance of pages on the basis of the number of links to them from elsewhere. BT, a British telecoms company, attempted to hijack the ownership of the hypertext link idea in 2000, claiming that it held a patent which predated the invention of the web.

Linkrot

A gradual process whereby LINKS from web pages to other pages or sites become unusable, usually resulting in a 404 NOT FOUND message. Linkrot is generally caused by sites reorganising their structure and moving or deleting pages in the process, or by the closure of a site. Despite the availability of many site management tools that track and maintain links, some surveys show that almost one in four web pages contains bad links.

Linux

A powerful, freely available computer OPERATING SYSTEM. Linux was created by Linus Torvalds, a Finnish student, as a result of his frustration with commercial operating systems such as MICROSOFT's WINDOWS and Apple's MacOS. Originally based on a slimmed-down version of the UNIX operating system, called Minix, Torvalds's creation has become an impressive and highly capable operating system in its own right.

Although Linux was originally the work of Torvalds, the system has evolved from the efforts of hundreds of programmers working collaboratively and philanthropically in the OPEN SOURCE spirit. The heart of the system is still written and maintained by Torvalds and a handful of "generals", who regularly add new features and tweak old ones. Additions to the system, such as drivers for printers and scanners, are written and tested by members of the far-flung Linux community, working and communicating through a number of dedicated NEWSGROUPS. Through this real-world testing and development, Linux has achieved a degree of stability and usefulness that matches or even exceeds that of commercial operating systems.

Many ISPS now use Linux as the basis for their services in preference to Windows or Unix, and it has gained a solid reputation in some vertical markets such as advanced graphics and IMAGE processing. It is also the operating system of choice for many web SERVERS because of its robustness and its ability to handle hundreds or thousands of simultaneous users, and over 1m WEBSITES now run on it. Many people see Linux as a real alternative to Windows in the business community, as the tools for configuring and administering it become more sophisticated and business applications become more widely available, especially DATABASES. Most of the big server hardware companies now sell machines running Linux alongside their Windows-based products.

Most estimates suggest that Linux has a long way to go to catch up with Microsoft's products, which dominate the market for personal computers. But a 2002 survey by IDC, a research company, showed that although Microsoft commands nearly 50% of the market for new operating systems in the business world, Linux is holding its own at 25%. It predicts that the market for Linux-based servers will grow by nearly 25% between 2001 and 2006. Proof that large companies are taking it seriously comes from a 2002 survey by Goldman Sachs, an investment bank, which showed that 39% of IT managers in 100 US multinational companies had deployed Linux in some capacity. However, critics of Linux still cite its independence as a major problem for corporate users needing guaranteed technical support and managed upgrades for business-critical systems. Many versions lack a graphical user interface (GUI) and are considered hard to install and configure. But fully supported commercial versions with GUI front-ends are available from companies such as Red Hat Software, and because the Linux SOURCE CODE is freely available, organisations with sufficient resources can build custom versions to meet their specific business needs.

LINX

Shorthand for the London Internet Exchange, a neutral interconnection point for many British ISPs and the largest IXP (point of network interconnection) in Europe, acting as a central hub where data can be moved quickly between carriers and BACKBONES. LINX, which is housed in London's Telehouse, is designed to speed traffic between ISPs by providing a direct link between them at a single central point. The flaw in this apparently good idea became abundantly clear in 1997, when a power surge at Telehouse caused much of the UK's internet to disappear for 10 minutes. Several other IXPs have since appeared, including MANAP in Manchester and SCOTIX in Scotland, with the aim of spreading the risk of future NETWORK failures.

List server

A program that manages the distribution of electronic newsletters and other messages to a MAILING LIST's subscribers. List servers respond to E-MAIL requests, automatically adding or removing subscribers to a list and arranging for all future messages to be sent to them. Nearly all aspects of list server administration can be handled by e-mail, making them easy to operate remotely. Two popular list servers are LISTSERV and MAJORDOMO.

Listserv

A popular LIST SERVER (see also MAJORDOMO).

Local area network

L

A NETWORK that links nearby computers to one another. A local area network (LAN) is usually used to connect computers in the same room or on the same floor of a building, and often forms part of a much bigger corporate network. Most LANS are based on one or more FILE SERVERS, which hold centralised applications and files that can be accessed from the network's constituent workstations. Most LANS use either the Ethernet or Token Ring methods of managing information flow across the network, alongside network OPERATING SYSTEMS such as Netware or WINDOWS, which manage users and network resources. Increasingly, LANS use standard internet PROTOCOLS such as TCP/IP for transmitting data rather than proprietary ones, and thus form the underlying skeleton for an INTRANET.

Local loop

The link between a customer's telephone socket and the nearest telephone switch. Each loop is dedicated to a single customer. Most existing links were designed for voice transmission using analog devices, rather than modern digital equipment, and still consist of a pair of copper wires. Local loops are the most unpredictable parts of the telephone system, as the wires may be old and damaged. This is one potential barrier to the widescale implementation of new digital technologies such as ADSL, which are partially dependent on the quality of the local loop cables.

Login

A user validation process imposed by many computer systems before they can be used. A successful login generally depends on a user entering a valid name and a PASSWORD before access to the computer's resources is granted, although some OPERATING SYSTEMS demand extra steps. Some versions of WINDOWS, for example, require users to press the Control, Alt and Delete keys simultaneously as protection against TROJAN HORSE programs designed to break system security. It may also be referred to as logon.

Lurker

Someone who hovers in the background in CHAT rooms and NEWSGROUPS without contributing to the discussion; effectively, an electronic voyeur. Lurking is generally regarded as a harmless pastime, especially among NEWBIES and the terminally shy. The process of breaking silence and contributing to a discussion for the first time is called delurking.

Lycos

One of the first SEARCH ENGINES. Launched in 1995 with technology developed at Carnegie Mellon University, Lycos was named after the wolf spider family, the Lycosidae. In 1996 Lycos's IPO made it the youngest company to go public in the history of the NASDAQ stock exchange. The company has diversified widely since its inception, acquiring several web communities such as Tripod and Angelfire, as well as E-MAIL company MailCity, the Hotbot search engine and the HOTWIRED network. In May 2000 the company announced a $12 billion merger deal with Terra Networks, a spin-off of Telefonica, a Spanish telecoms giant.

Mailing list

An E-MAIL distribution list, used to circulate requested information or group discussions. Mailing lists rival NEWSGROUPS in their diversity, and are used for everything from the simple dissemination of product information to heated discussions of the finer points of non-ferrous metal welding.

Anyone with access to an internet SERVER can set up a mailing list (hence the vast number of lists in circulation) using server software such as LISTSERV or MAJORDOMO.

Mail rage

The digital equivalent of road rage. Mail rage (or E-MAIL rage) describes the sense of anger that may be felt by recipients of inflammatory or annoying e-mail messages, prompting them to send abusive or ill-considered replies. E-mail programs are easy to use, and their immediacy has prompted some individuals to respond aggressively to perceived provocation or irritation without pause for thought. Most mail-rage incidents involve nothing more serious than an undignified and usually private exchange of views, although careers have been damaged by intemperate reactions to unwelcome messages. Some companies now routinely advise their employees on appropriate techniques for controlling mail rage while at their desks.

Majordomo

Software used to manage a MAILING LIST. Unlike LISTSERV systems, which all interconnect with each other and provide access to a global list of lists, Majordomo hosts are independent, stand-alone entities.

Malware

Any kind of malicious software, distributed across networks, that is intended to cause damage to computers, files or internet connections. VIRUSES, TROJAN HORSES and WORMS distributed via E-MAIL may all be regarded as malware. Many malware programs exploit security flaws in the WINDOWS OPERATING SYSTEM and its associated programs to do their damage. The phenomenon has even spread to the latest generation of "smart" mobile phones, some of which run a version of Windows.

Mbps

Short for millions of BITS (or megabits) per second, typically used as a measure of the speed of a fast internet connection (see BPS).

Mbone

Multicast Backbone, a high-speed internet BACKBONE designed for sending large files such as video segments to multiple users. Unlike normal internet transmissions, which rely on the one-to-one capabilities of the IP PROTOCOL, Mbone transmissions allow material such as live concert footage or radio broadcasts to be sent to thousands of people simultaneously. Instead of sending a copy of the file to everybody, the multicast protocol sends out a single file which copies itself only when necessary. So if 50 people at economist.com request a copy of a 20-MEGABYTE news broadcast from an American server, just one copy of the file is sent and duplicated once it arrives at the economist.com NETWORK.

M

M-commerce

Mobile commerce, which is widely predicted to be the next wave of E-COMMERCE. Sometimes known as m-business, it encapsulates any kind of information transfer or transaction that can be initiated from a mobile phone or other portable

INFORMATION APPLIANCE device. Commonly cited examples include booking of services such as flights or other tickets, personal banking and share trades. Some schemes have concentrated on smaller transactions, such as the buying of pizzas or newspapers. Currently, the biggest market for m-commerce services is in Europe, where mobile-phone penetration is extremely high and still growing faster than anywhere else.

A 2000 report by the Boston Consulting Group estimated that global m-commerce revenue could reach $100 billion by 2003, although most such estimates have since been substantially revised. Dissatisfaction with speed, the awkwardness of typing on mobile devices and security concerns have conspired to slow the uptake of m-commerce services, and many consumers have already abandoned their use. But Frost & Sullivan, a consulting and research firm, estimated that the value of mobile transactions would still reach $25 billion in 2006, about 15% of total e-commerce consumer spending.

Meatspace

The physical world, as described by participants in ONLINE conversations. Contrast with CYBERSPACE.

Megabyte

A unit of data storage, equivalent to about 1m BYTES. Generally, a megabyte is considered to be equivalent to 2 to the 20th power bytes, or 1,048,576. Some authorities, however, claim that for purposes of data storage and transmission a megabyte is exactly 1m bytes. A HACKER would argue that only the first definition is correct, as bytes should logically be measured in powers of 2.

I guess this must be my 15 megabytes of fame.
Anonymous web developer, on making USA Today's Hot List of sites

Melissa

See VIRUS.

Meme

An idea, skill or habit passed from person to person. The term was coined in 1976 by Richard Dawkins, a British biologist, in his book *The Selfish Gene*. Dawkins speculated that memes are to cultural information what genes are to genetic information and might thus play a crucial role in the evolution of the human brain and language. The internet is seen by some as a new mechanism for the rapid dispersal of memes.

Some jerk infected the internet with an outright lie.
It shows how easy it is to do and how credulous people are.
Kurt Vonnegut,
in response to a widely circulated speech supposedly given by him

M

Microcontent

Small chunks of CONTENT that are easily and quickly digestible, particularly those that express single ideas or address specific subjects. Originally conceived by Jakob Nielsen to describe head-lines and page titles on web pages, the microcontent concept has broadened to include any kind of information in short form, such as a weather forecast, a stock price, a WEBLOG entry or a cinema timetable. Arguing that most of the information people actually need from online sources is in microcontent form, some people have suggested that a specific piece of software called a micro-content client is needed as a replacement for web BROWSERS. Such clients might run on PDAs and mobile phones as well as on larger computers, allowing the user to gather, organise, create and cross-reference snippets of information quickly and flexibly. Several attempts to create such clients are in progress, most of them relying on XML-based data which can be easily found, iden-tified and formatted according to the needs of each user.

Micropayment

A small amount of money used to buy goods or services over the internet. Micropayment systems are designed to allow CONTENT to be purchased in small quantities – one magazine article, say, or a single track from a CD – without the need to supply credit-card details for every transaction. Instead, an E-WALLET on the buyer's PC transfers the requisite sum of money to the vendor in token form, and the vendor later reclaims the actual cash from a third-party bank.

This form of E-CASH is secure and convenient, but micropayments have not yet become popular with sellers of information. There is, as yet, no KILLER APP or trend-setting model, and many developers of micropayment technology are moving into other areas of E-COMMERCE. One problem with micropayments is keeping the cost of performing the transaction lower than the cost of the goods being exchanged. A bigger stumbling block is the subscription-based model that has become widely adopted among WEBSITES for text-based services, especially in the United States. The money obtained from credit-card-based transactions and ADVERTISING sales is a more reliable source of revenue than an unpredictable stream of buyers each paying a few cents for content. In Europe, where credit cards are not as strongly entrenched, micropayments may have a rosier future.

Microsite

A small WEBSITE that is an offshoot of a larger overall web presence. Some companies create microsites to help market new products or promote different parts of the organisation. They can retain the same look and feel of the main site, live on the same physical web SERVER and even share some of the same code, but they generally have a different URL. Microsites are sometimes referred to as sitelets.

Microsoft

A software company. Despite a feeling that it is impossible for any one organisation to own the internet, none is likely to come closer than Microsoft. Much has been made of Bill Gates's apparent failure to appreciate the importance of the internet in 1995, when Microsoft seemed irreversibly committed to its proprietary Microsoft Network (MSN). But its subsequent turnaround surprised even those accustomed to Gates's willingness and ability to change the direction of his business.

Within months of the launch of the first version of NETSCAPE'S NAVIGATOR, Microsoft had bought a BROWSER from a rival company, ditched its original plans for MSN and embarked on a massive phase of growth by acquisition and development that shows no sign of stopping. In less than five years, the firm that made a fortune from its MS-DOS and WINDOWS products took control of the browser market from Netscape, the company that invented it; even the most conservative studies show that INTERNET EXPLORER now has well over 90% of the market. It has acquired or invested in a bewildering array of internet and communications companies, to the extent that it has at least a foot, and often several limbs, in every door. In the process, it has attracted the ire of the US Department of Justice and more or less every company with which it does business, even those with which it does not directly compete, such as PC manufacturers.

Microsoft's dour and unflattering antitrust battle in the US courts highlighted the extent to which it has dominated its business partners and competitors with the ubiquitous Windows. But Judge Thomas Penfield Jackson's decisions in 2000 that the company had broken US antitrust law and that it should be broken up into competing divisions were subsequently overturned on appeal. Microsoft eventually settled the case brought by the government, much to the annoyance of the many companies and states that had brought their own antitrust cases against the software giant. They argue that none of the original aims of the litigation – to prevent Microsoft tinkering with Windows to the detraction of its competitors, and to force it to produce stripped-down versions of its operating system that

M

allow other companies to install their own programs in place of Microsoft's own – has been met, and that it remains free to dominate and manipulate markets as it has done for decades. But some concessions have been made, especially towards PC manufacturers, all of which Microsoft must now treat on equal terms. They can also choose to pre-install non-Microsoft browsers and other programs on their machines prior to sale, thus giving consumers the choice that Microsoft's detractors claimed it had denied them.

Microsoft is unlikely to become a less fierce competitor as a result of the rulings against it. It is still facing dozens of antitrust and class-action suits, and its practices are being investigated by the European Union. But it is showing signs that it is taking a less predatory role in the computing ecosystem, promising to forge closer links with governments and competitors and to spend $5 billion on research. Meanwhile, Microsoft persists in its efforts to stay at the centre of the internet economy, continuing to develop a dizzying array of internet-enabled products and services that remain popular with the people who use them. MSN, the company's portal, was the web's second most visited site in February 2003, with over 45m unique visitors, just 5m fewer than AOL.

MIME

Multipurpose Internet Mail Extensions. MIME extends the text-only capabilities of the original internet E-MAIL PROTOCOL SMTP, allowing people to exchange different kinds of information such as sound, video and still images. Many e-mail clients can encode and decode a file ATTACHMENT in the MIME format, and most BROWSERS can display MIME-encoded files; but users still fall foul of these encoding schemes. A file sent in MIME format can only be read by software that also speaks MIME, which is a problem for owners of programs that only understand other algorithms such as UUENCODE. Such incompatibilities are often the cause of those long, mystifying e-mails full of garbage.

MIP

Mobile Internet Protocol. Designed for mobile devices such as phones and PDAS on GPRS and other mobile networks, MIP allows people using mobile internet connections to stay connected while on the move. Unlike fixed-line connections such as MODEM dial-ups and DSL, mobile devices have no fixed position on the network and thus need a way of telling it where they are at any given time. MIP manages the transitions between different areas of the mobile network without the need for a user to continually reconnect. The latest version, MIPV6, is a subset of the IPV6 PROTOCOL (see IP).

Mirror site

An exact copy of a WEBSITE or FTP server. Many sites that offer files for downloading operate mirror sites at other locations, to reduce traffic on local SERVERS and speed DOWNLOAD times for people a long way from the original source of the files. Many US websites, for example, offer mirror sites in several European countries. Small organisations, which may have limited internet connectivity or slow hardware, often set up mirrors on larger or faster sites.

Modem

ACRONYM for modulator-demodulator, a device that translates a stream of digital data created by a computer into the curious squeaking and hissing sounds that can be transmitted across phone lines. Most subscribers to internet services use modems to connect to their ISPS across the public telephone network, and nearly all PCS are now equipped with modems as standard. Ordinary modem-based connections have maximum speeds of 56KBPS, once considered almost embarrassingly fast but now hobbled by the increasing complexity of modern WEBSITES. Faster connections, such as ADSL and cable, use special "modems" – not, technically, quite the same thing –

that can handle transmission at megabit speeds and higher.

A chip of silicon a quarter of an inch square now has the capacity of the original 1949 ENIAC computer, which occupied a full city block.

Moore's Law

A principle established in 1975 by Gordon Moore, co-founder of Intel, describing the rapid growth in the power of computer microprocessors. Officially, Moore's Law states that the circuit density or capacity of semiconductor chips doubles every 18 months, or quadruples every three years. (Moore's original 1965 article in *Electronics*, an American magazine, observed that the complexity of such chips roughly doubled every year, but he revised his predictions a decade later.) So far, it has proved to be not just an accurate measure of the development of computer chips but also a barometer for an entire industry.

Moore himself predicts that his law will run out of steam in 2012, when 1 billion transistors will be squeezed on to a processor and the limits of current chip fabrication technology are finally reached. Variants of it have been applied to everything from software to the web, both of which have grown even faster than the processors they rely on. The web grew from 10,000 sites at the beginning of 1995 to somewhere in excess of 35m by early 2003.

By the power vested in me by nobody in particular, alpha/beta version 0.5 of NCSA's Motif-based networked information systems and World Wide Web browser, X Mosaic, is hereby released.
Usenet post by Marc Andreessen, announcing the arrival of the first graphical browser

Mosaic

The first BROWSER that displayed more than plain text, developed at the NCSA by Marc Andreessen and others in 1993.

Mosaic's appearance is widely credited with stimulating the tremendous interest in the WORLD WIDE WEB, until then a text-based academic curiosity. Andreessen and his team later used Mosaic as the template for the first NETSCAPE browser.

Mouse potato

Someone who spends too much time in front of their computer, especially those with a compulsion for ONLINE activities. Often used pejoratively, as in "I've been trying to lure Steve out to dinner for weeks now, but he's such a mouse potato these days".

Mousetrapping

One of several techniques used to force a visitor to stay on a WEBSITE. The mildest form of mousetrapping involves the disabling of a BROWSER's Back button, thus preventing its user from skipping back to the last page visited. More extreme techniques, commonly used by gambling and PORNOGRAPHY sites, involve flooding the visitor's screen with an endless series of new windows and POP-UPS every time they attempt to leave the site or shut down the browser, sometimes necessitating the restarting of the computer. In 2002, a mousetrapper in the United States was fined nearly $2m after duping thousands of users into visiting fake sites with a TYPOSQUATTING scheme.

Mozilla

Originally the codename for NETSCAPE's first BROWSER, Mozilla was the name given to the company's dinosaur-like mascot. Most recently and importantly, it has been use to describe the family of web browsers based on the OPEN SOURCE NAVIGATOR code. The Mozilla project is run as an independent group within Netscape, which moderates the development of improvements to the original browser code. Mozilla suffered some major setbacks in 1999 when many of the project's leading lights resigned, citing dissatisfaction with progress and company culture following the AOL takeover in 1998. But the project continues, and many web users still tout Mozilla and other browsers based on the Mozilla code as an essential weapon in the battle to save the world from INTERNET EXPLORER's hegemony. The latest version of Netscape's browser is based on open source code from the Mozilla labs.

MP3

A format for recording near CD-quality music. Short for MPEG 1 Layer 3, an MP3 file is a music track that has been encoded and compressed for electronic distribution or storage. MP3's great trick is to squeeze musical recording into less than 10% of the space it would occupy if recorded in a standard format such as WINDOWS wav. Thus a four-minute song, which as a wav file might occupy 50 MEGABYTES of disk space, uses only 4 megabytes in its MP3 form. This highly efficient COMPRESSION has made MP3 the format of choice for music pirates, who can record and distribute entire CDs across the internet quickly and efficiently. Many NEWSGROUPS and WEBSITES are devoted to the dissemination of illegally recorded music, and the phenomenon has spawned a new generation of inexpensive hardware devices capable of storing and playing dozens of MP3 tracks.

MP3 files are especially popular with students, most of whom have free high-speed access to the internet, but it is increasingly popular with the general public too. Forrester, a research company, estimated that 35m Europeans have downloaded music from the internet, about one-third of the ONLINE population. Estimates of the cost of MP3 piracy vary, but in a 2000 study in the United States by SoundScan, a music-industry data gatherer, showed a drop of 4% in music sales within five miles of university campuses, in stores that historically account for 50% of all offline music sales. The Recording Industry Association of America (RIAA) claimed that online music piracy resulted in a 10% drop in music sales in 2001, a result of 23% of music consumers downloading files rather than paying for CDs.

The big labels reacted to the threat by refusing to allow artists to distribute their music electronically and cracking down on allegedly illicit MP3 distribution services such as the ingenious NAPSTER. A consortium of companies from the music and computer industries formed the Secure Digital Music Initiative (SDMI) in late 1998, with the aim of creating software and hardware-based ENCRYPTION technologies that would make the illicit copying and distribution of music impossible. But their efforts to put this genie back in its bottle are being undermined by the sheer weight of support for MP3 and a new generation of music companies running MP3-based distribution services from their websites.

Although the record companies have had one highly visible success in closing down the Napster music exchange network, the number of people using comparable systems such as GNUTELLA is growing rapidly. At the same time, CRACKERS have made a mockery of the SDMI technology, throwing the music industry's attempts to create new online music standards into confusion and forcing SDMI into hiatus. Many experts, including a group of MICROSOFT researchers, believe that MP3 file sharing will always be impossible to prevent, citing the growth of consumer access to BROADBAND connections and the corresponding increase in the number of available sources for music as insurmountable barriers for the music industry.

You can make more money in this new era of "free" digital music. But only if you break free of label mind control.
Jaron Lanier

MPEG

Motion Picture Experts Group. MPEG systems encode and compress digital sound and video files to a format that can easily be stored on CDs or transmitted across networks. Several varieties of MPEG encoding exist, each tailored to a specific task. Some, such as MPEG 2, are especially useful for video applications, and MPEG 1 Layer 3 (MP3) is an elegant and efficient way of storing music.

MSN

Short for the Microsoft Network, an umbrella term for MICRO-SOFT's dial-up internet access and ONLINE CONTENT business. Inspired by the success of AOL in the early 1990s – modest at that time – MSN started life as a proprietary NETWORK designed to attract people interested in electronic services and original content.

Originally accessible only to WINDOWS 95 users who dialled a local number for access to MSN's SERVERS, the service was slow to attract content providers, with the result that subscribers stayed away in their droves. Nonetheless, Microsoft persisted with its proprietary approach until well into 1996, when it became clear that the WORLD WIDE WEB was where people wanted to be. Several changes of strategy quickly followed, in which Microsoft began to offer internet access as part of a series of differently priced and confusingly wrapped packages. MSN's latest and stablest incarnation is now based principally on its free-to-all PORTAL, a huge site localised for many countries. MSN is now one of the biggest such sites in the world, owing to the fact that most Microsoft browsers are pre-configured to use MSN as their home page. Many millions of Windows users, in particular, are herded towards MSN by default the first time they access the web.

MSP

Managed Service Provider (see ASP).

MUD

Short for multi-user dungeon (or sometimes dimension). A MUD is in essence a large, structured real-time CHAT room, in which participants, usually referred to as players, take part in role-playing games. Typically, a player will adopt a character taken from a sword-and-sorcery list of knights, dwarves, princesses and dragons. Once logged on to the system, players navigate through locations that might include rooms, forests or tunnels; negotiate a variety of traps and puzzles; grapple with the intricacies of the local bartering systems; and, generally, spend a long time doing nothing much.

MUDS were for many years the leading cause of computer addiction among students, for whom such fantasy worlds represented an attractive alternative to lectures. These days, simpler chat rooms and INSTANT MESSAGING probably account for more wasted hours on campus, but research into MUDS and their OBJECT-ORIENTED cousins, called MOOS, continues as the interest in ONLINE VIRTUAL worlds grows. The flexibility offered by MOO languages has encouraged many people to immerse themselves more fully in these environments, perhaps by adopting a different gender, a different personality or even a different species. Such behaviour has inevitably attracted the attention of social scientists and behavioural psychologists, several of whom have written scholarly books attempting to explain it. More useful works have examined the possible extension of MUD and MOO technology into education, teleworking and even medicine.

Multicasting

The transmission of messages from a single sender to many recipients. Multicasting may be as simple as sending a daily newsletter from a WEBSITE to several hundred subscribers, or as complex as updating the software on thousands of machines on a global corporate NETWORK. A specific kind of multicasting is used on the MBONE, a high-speed portion of the internet designed for the delivery of large video and audio files such as live concerts.

Multimedia

The combination of different types of media, such as text, audio, video and animations, into some sort of informational whole that can be displayed on a computer. The role of multimedia in computing has undergone many transformations since its early days. Once a clumsy novelty used merely to entertain, it benefited greatly from more powerful hardware and more imaginative software design tools. Its use in CD-ROM-based educational software, particularly encyclopedias, helped to illustrate its potential. The much-vaunted CD-ROM market proved to be an expensive illusion for many firms involved in producing educational CDs in the late 1990s, but multimedia's promise is stronger than ever because of the internet and its ability to deliver original CONTENT to a widely distributed audience. As more BANDWIDTH has become available to consumers, multimedia usage on websites has grown (although many argue that the taste of its designers has, if anything, decreased) and it is now an important part of RICH MEDIA ADVERTISING.

M

Multiplexing

The combining of several signals in the same communications channel, usually with the aim of increasing the amount of data that can be transmitted. Several types of multiplexing exist, each designed for a particular signal and cable type. Analog signals, for example, are combined using frequency-division multiplexing (FDM), in which the BANDWIDTH is divided into parallel channels of different frequencies. Digital signals can be transmitted using time-division multiplexing (TDM), in which the signals are carried using alternating time slots. On FIBRE OPTIC networks, multiple signals are transmitted as light split into different wavelengths, a process known as wavelength-division multiplexing (WDM). This technique is being widely investigated to improve the speed of internet BACKBONES.

Nagware

Software that literally nags its user into doing something, such as buying a product or registering for a WEBSITE. Nagware typically manifests itself as one or more POP-UPS when a visitor attempts to leave a website without parting with money or leaving personal information, especially sites offering shareware programs.

Name server

A computer on the internet that tracks the relationship between IP ADDRESSES and DOMAIN NAMES. Name servers are responsible for translating alphanumeric E-MAIL and web addresses into the 32-BIT numbers computers use to find each other on the internet, thus making sure that messages arrive at the right place.

Napster

An internet-based system for distributing music in the digital MP3 format, now defunct. Napster was the first large-scale tool for helping owners of digitally encoded music to share their collections with other users of the NETWORK, simply by publishing a list of the files on their computer and allowing anyone else using the software to DOWNLOAD the music to their own PC. The simplicity of the software and the openness of the network attracted millions of users, not all of whom had a deeply entrenched respect for COPYRIGHT law; the music industry responded accordingly, eventually forcing the network to close in early 2002. Napster's troubles began in April 2000, when Metallica, a rock band, collected the names of 300,000 users it claimed were illegally distributing its copyright music and forced Napster to remove them from the system. Napster subsequently proved an easy target for the music industry's lawyers, who forced the shutting down of the company's SERVERS and thus put an end to the company that popularised the idea of internet file sharing.

Napster seemed on the brink of rescue when it was bought by Bertelsmann, a German media company, in late 2000, with the hope of developing a secure music distribution network that served the music industry rather than fought against it. But the depth of feeling against the company led to rejection by the major music labels, which turned down all offers of cash generated by a proposed Napster subscription scheme. The music industry is still struggling to agree on standards and technologies for protecting the copyright of its music, most of which have proved to be impossible to protect from CRACKERS and pirates and have been resolutely ignored by the music-buying public. Meanwhile, Napster's better-designed and technically unassailable file-sharing descendants go from strength to strength, with hundreds of millions of users creating a much bigger problem for the music industry than the network that inspired them ever did.

Perhaps out of spite at its continuing inability to control digital piracy, the music industry sued Bertelsmann for damages of $17 billion in February 2003, arguing that its efforts to prolong Napster's life resulted in an extra year's loss of revenue. Such arguments are unpopular with defenders of Napster-like systems, who say that these revenue losses are imaginary, based on a spurious assumption that people would buy the music if they could not get it for free.

Napster's assets and intellectual property were sold to Roxio, a software company, in November 2002. Its new owner planned to relaunch the site at least in name in mid-2003, although it seems unlikely to appear in its original guise.

It is sickening to know that our art is being traded like a commodity rather than the art that it is.
Lars Ulrich, spokesman for Metallica

NASDAQ

Short for National Association of Securities Dealers Automated Quotation system. Most of the high-tech companies in the United States trade on NASDAQ, which has consequently become one of the most powerful engines driving the Silicon Valley economy.

Navigation

The process of finding your way around a WEBSITE. The provision of adequate navigation tools is one of the biggest challenges facing website developers, who must consider not just how to guide visitors from the HOME PAGE of their site but also how to indicate their exact location within it. Well-designed sites provide a visual equivalent of the "You are here" arrows seen on maps, often a necessity if the visitor has arrived at a deeply buried page from a SEARCH ENGINE or directory.

Navigator

A BROWSER produced by NETSCAPE. Once the market leader, Navigator's innovation and technical excellence made it the browser of choice for millions of neophyte internet users. These characteristics have not been enough to maintain its dominance, and its market share has been gradually whittled away to below 10% by INTERNET EXPLORER since MICROSOFT began giving it away with the WINDOWS OPERATING SYSTEM.

The software has been in the hands of AOL since 1999, and its fortunes have not improved in that time. Delays in bringing new versions to market and a reputation for instability have crippled the browser that helped define the landscape of the web, and AOL's much-vaunted marketing prowess has done nothing to help revive it. Nor has its cause been helped by the fact that AOL continues to supply Internet Explorer, rather than its own Navigator, as part of its consumer package. Version 7 of the software, based on OPEN SOURCE code developed as part of the MOZILLA project, was released in 2002.

NC

See NETWORK COMPUTER.

NCSA

The National Centre For Supercomputing Applications. Based at the University of Illinois, the NCSA is a research organisation specialising in high-performance computer applications in many fields. It is best known for its work in developing MOSAIC, the first graphical web BROWSER.

Nerd

A generally pejorative term for someone of above-average intelligence but who has poorly developed social skills and is sartorially challenged. Nerds are often portrayed as being shy, badly dressed and incapable of forming normal relationships, especially with members of the opposite sex. Real or not, this image has shifted somewhat as the realisation has grown that nerds are among the most powerful people in our society. An oft-cited example of this is Bill Gates, for whom nerdism has not proved a significant disability. Several explanations for the word's origin have been proposed, the most interesting being that it is the name of a character in Dr Seuss's 1950 book *If I Ran The Zoo*.

> *And then, just to show them, I'll sail to Ka-Troo*
> *And bring back an It-Kutch, a Preep and a Proo*
> *A Nerkle, a Nerd, and a Seersucker, too!*
> From *If I Ran The Zoo*, Dr Seuss, 1950

.NET

The name used by MICROSOFT to describe its latest strategy for integrating mainstream computing with the web. Aware that the lifespan of WINDOWS is limited, the company is developing a new range of technologies based on WEB SERVICES, which it hopes will become the standards for a new generation of business applications that can talk to each other regardless of their origin or the underlying systems software. In this new world, the OPERATING SYSTEM in use on a user's computer is irrelevant; as long as it is equipped with a suitably up-to-date BROWSER and the standard web services PROTOCOLS, any device (including a PDA or a mobile phone, for example) can use software of many kinds that is written to .NET standards.

Unsurprisingly, not everyone believes that .NET is the answer to the peculiar set of problems being created by the internet. SUN MICROSYSTEMS's JAVA technology, in particular J2EE (Java 2, Enterprise Edition), is still being pushed as a better way of creating web services, for example. Although the two technologies are theoretically based on the same underlying standards and should therefore be interoperable, Sun has somewhat predictably accused Microsoft of creating yet more proprietary software as part of an attempt to lock people into one way of doing things. Microsoft for its part says more or less the same thing about J2EE.

Although much of the hard work involved in creating .NET revolves around existing technologies such as XML, it nonetheless represents a major overhaul in terms of sheer engineering, and Microsoft expects the emergence of the complete specification to take some years. Windows XP, the latest version of its operating system, includes a subset of .NET features. Ironically, some of the ideas it encapsulates are closer in spirit to those proposed for the NETWORK COMPUTER by Larry Ellison, Oracle's chief executive, in the mid-1990s than they are to the Windows model so successfully marketed by Bill Gates.

Nethead

An engineer or individual who believes in the superiority of intelligent, IP-based digital NETWORKS over their circuit-switched antecedents. Netheads typically favour the use of flexible software to control the way in which data flows across networks, rather than the fixed wires preferred by people with old-telephone-company mentalities. Contrast with BELLHEAD.

Netiquette

The conventions of politeness on USENET. Many relate to the
niceties of posting messages in NEWSGROUPS; for example,
advertising beef products in alt.food.vegan is a clear breach of
netiquette. Individual newsgroups often have their own
conventions, which are usually explained in the group's FAQ.
The penalties for not observing netiquette are generally minor,
although repeat offenders may find that life ONLINE suddenly
becomes extremely uncomfortable. Lucky ones may get away
with a FLAME; less fortunate individuals have found their
credit-card details posted to Usenet, or worse.

Netscape

A company that played a major role in creating worldwide enthusiasm for the internet. It started life in 1994 with a single
product and a handful of programmers. By the time the
company went public just 16 months later it was worth
$2 billion. That single product, the NAVIGATOR BROWSER, de-
serves much of the credit for generating the early interest in
the WORLD WIDE WEB. Founded by Marc Andreessen, a
whizz-kid programmer responsible for MOSAIC, and Jim Clark,
the brains behind Silicon Graphics, Netscape quickly became
an important symbol and inspiration for the burgeoning internet industry.

First indications that it might struggle to keep its head above
water came with MICROSOFT's aggressive entry into the
browser market in 1995. Netscape, which had a single source of
revenue, was forced to charge for corporate versions of Navigator. But Microsoft could afford to give its software away, first
on its WEBSITE and then, much more damagingly, as part of the
WINDOWS OPERATING SYSTEM. What started as a 90% market
share had been slowly but steadily whittled away to less than
10% by the end of 2002.

Netscape was sold to AOL in 1999, prompting widespread
concern about the company's future. Its new owner has been
criticised for its failure to reinforce the Netscape brand, and it

has further marginalised the company and its software by supporting and developing other competing products.

Network

A collection of people or things, linked together to share information or resources. The internet can be viewed as one vast network of computers, although it is probably more useful to see it as merely a huge number of smaller networks connected in an arbitrary and self-organising manner.

Network computer

A low-cost INFORMATION APPLIANCE based on a minimalist design and a centralised networking philosophy. The brainchild of Oracle's Larry Ellison, the network computer (NC), an example of a THIN CLIENT, promised to change the MICROSOFT-driven computing model radically by removing the bells and whistles, such as hard disks and CD-ROM drives, from a desktop computer and managing its resources centrally. NCs can run small, fast, BROWSER-driven applications based on JAVA or another suitable system and thus do not need big, complex OPERATING SYSTEMS like WINDOWS. Every time users need a new version of a software program they DOWNLOAD a copy from a SERVER rather than install it locally from disk or CD-ROM, massively reducing distribution costs. Best of all, network computers should theoretically be a fraction of the cost of a fully-specified PC.

The concept sounds attractive, but sales have been in hundreds of thousands rather than the millions Wintel-busters (those who would like to see Microsoft's and Intel's hold on the industry reduced) would have liked. NCs have proved costlier than anticipated, selling at not much less than an all-singing, all-dancing, NETWORK-enabled PC. But the biggest hurdle for NCs has been the enduring appeal and usefulness of PCs, which despite their undoubted problems are not nearly as unpopular with the general public as they are with SUN MICROSYSTEMS and Oracle.

Despite these drawbacks, the NC model seems sure to become part of the landscape as information appliances of all kinds expand their capabilities and more devices become network-aware. A critical part of this process will be the long-promised hike in BANDWIDTH, especially in the home.

Network externalities

An economic term describing the effect that new members of a NETWORK have on the existing ones. A network containing one fax machine is useless, but as the number of machines added to it increases, the more valuable each becomes. Thus the decision by a newcomer to subscribe to the fax network increases the value of all the other machines. This effect has been the driving force behind the internet, which has become more and more useful as the number of people connecting to it has grown. It has also introduced another, equally interesting, phenomenon: the increasing value of knowledge. In the same way that the usefulness of a language depends on the number of people who speak it, so the usefulness of some kinds of information increases with their dissemination. This is one reason for the rapid rate of development of internet technologies.

All the most promising technologies making their debut now are chiefly due to communication between computers – that is, to connections rather than to computations. And since communication is the basis of culture, fiddling at this level is indeed momentous.

Kevin Kelly

New media

Forms of mass communications driven by the internet and related technologies. New media differ from so-called old media, such as newspapers and television, primarily in that they are targetable and interactive. People and businesses are no longer restricted to mere consumer status but can be producers too, as the rapidly expanding web testifies.

Newbie

A newcomer to the internet, or, more specifically, to USENET and its NEWSGROUPS. Newbies are widely reviled for their lack of NETIQUETTE and are discouraged from participating in some newsgroups. The term is sometimes used a put-down for otherwise experienced Usenetters who upset the locals.

Newsgroup

A discussion group on the USENET. Unlike CHAT rooms, newsgroups are not live; instead, questions and comments are posted to one of many Usenet servers and later redistributed around the rest of the NETWORK. Most ISPs provide a newsgroup feed, which pipes the contents of most of the 40,000 or so newsgroups to anyone who wants to take part in the discussions on offer. Each of these groups is devoted to a specific and often highly unconventional set of interests, and anyone who has wondered about the ins and outs of beekeeping or the relationship between bondage and particle physics will find groups that answer their questions. This openness, and the fact that most newsgroups are unmoderated and unregulated, almost demands a robust attitude on behalf of the inhabitants, and the unwary can get some nasty surprises if they fail to observe NETIQUETTE. Newsgroups have also attracted attention as a primary source of PORNOGRAPHY, and there is much debate about whether or not ISPs should carry such groups. (See CENSORSHIP.)

NNTP

Network News Transport Protocol, the PROTOCOL used to manage traffic on USENET NEWSGROUPS. Most ISPs run an NNTP SERVER, which communicates with others like it to gather and filter the global collection of newsgroups. NNTP is the replacement for the UNIX UUCP (Unix-to-Unix Copy Protocol) found on older networks.

Node

A HOST computer on a NETWORK. A node may be as simple as a stand-alone PC connected to the internet across a dial-up connection or as complex as a SERVER delivering information to hundreds of machines.

1.0

See page 240.

Object-oriented

Describes a popular approach to programming, in which computer programs are built from software objects that do particular jobs. Objects often have functions that resemble those in the real world. A shopping-basket object on a WEBSITE, for example, could keep track of how many items it carries and maintain a running total of their value. This approach has many benefits for programmers, in particular the ability to reuse sections of code to perform multiple tasks and allow different programs to co-operate with each other efficiently.

Online

Connected to the internet or another electronic service such as a BULLETIN BOARD. Its opposite, offline, denotes the lack of such a connection.

Online auction

The latest and, to date, one of the most profitable forms of consumer-driven E-COMMERCE. There are two broad categories of ONLINE auctions.

- The merchant auction, which involves a manufacturer or retailer offering goods for sale, often using an intermediate auction specialist, such as QXL.com in the UK. These auctions are popular because they provide an easy way for buyer and seller to agree a price, especially for old stock or goods approaching the end of their shelf life, and because almost anything can be sold in this way: holidays, computers, cars or cameras.

◪ The personal auction, which provides a way for individuals to trade items with each other.

Online auctions have proved a big success with internet users, largely because they do not rely on the fixed pricing favoured by most online retailers. Most sites run in much the same way as their real-world counterparts. Sellers post a description of their item for sale, set a closing date and an optional reserve price, and wait for customers to bid. Personal auctioneers make money by charging sellers an initial insertion fee and then taking a commission on the sale.

The biggest name in the personal auction field is eBay, founded in 1995 by Pierre Omidyar, following an observation by his wife, a collector of confectionery dispensers, that people with interests in specialist items should be able to trade them online. This has turned out to be one of the internet's most persuasive ideas, as reflected in the large number of companies that have followed in eBay's path. But none has yet matched the enthusiasm of eBay's visitors, who line up online daily to trade millions of items for millions of dollars. Omidyar's COMMUNITY-building prowess has resulted in that most elusive of qualities in an internet company: profitability. This has been achieved as a result of a business model requiring no storing of goods, no carriage costs and, indeed, no interaction at all with the items for sale. The company simply charges the seller a flat fee and a percentage of the sale price.

People can now indulge their passion for auctions everywhere from AMAZON to YAHOO. eBay in particular has done a good job of introducing systems for protecting its buyers, who have continued to trade items of every conceivable type online and helped to maintain eBay's profitability at a time when most other internet companies have been paralysed or extinguished altogether by the downturn in high-tech stocks. In 2002, the company's net revenue exceeded $1.2 billion dollars and it reported 62m registered users; its stock price has remained consistently high as a result.

Despite its continued success, eBay has not felt itself able to provide a service to every customer. One man's attempt to sell his soul online was quickly squashed by the company's lawyers, who claimed that there was either nothing to sell or that it fell under the site's ban on the auctioning of human body parts or remains. More recently, the company has banned the sale of advertising space on a man's body, Nazi memorabilia and remnants of the Columbia space shuttle.

Online gaming

The playing of computer games across a NETWORK connection, usually in competition with other players. Many games, especially those of the shoot-'em-up genre such as DOOM, are now designed to be played by lots of people simultaneously, either on the internet or across a LOCAL AREA NETWORK. Players connect to a central computer, which controls the gaming environment and manages the interaction among the participants. Some kinds of online games, such as MUDS, are simple text-based programs demanding little by way of raw processing power but rather more by way of logic. More contemporary games typically involve complex 3D graphics, dramatic sound effects and a lot of physical interaction between players and their environment.

Online games can support hundreds or sometimes thousands of simultaneous players. Because of their complexity and high degree of realism, they have provided inspiration for researchers into new forms of VIRTUAL reality and even teleworking. Instead of dingy mazes full of axes and chainsaws, people are building online offices full of filing cabinets and fax machines. Such is progress.

Online service

A company offering electronic access to a variety of services besides those available from ISPS. These often include exclusive CONTENT and special offers, proprietary CHAT rooms and other COMMUNITY facilities. Because these services typically use their own closed networks and communications services rather than public WEBSITES, their facilities are available only to subscribers. One such example is AOL.

Provided the development co-ordinator has a medium at least as good as the internet, and knows how to lead without coercion, many heads are inevitably better than one.
Eric Raymond

Open source

A concept describing the development and distribution of software. The open source movement revolves around the idea that software evolves faster and becomes more stable as more people work on it. This idea has long been in practice in the UNIX world, where code-sharing and co-development projects are common, but it is anathema to software companies, which like to develop their products in relative secrecy. One driving force behind the open source concept is the Open Source Initiative (OSI), a non-profit organisation. Software developers that wish to use the Open Source trademark must distribute their software and its SOURCE CODE for free. Much of the movement's inspiration comes from Richard Stallman, the man behind the FREE SOFTWARE FOUNDATION and creator of the legendary EMACS text editor, and Eric Raymond, whose paper *The Cathedral and the Bazaar* first brought the open source idea to the attention of commercial software vendors.

For proof that open source development works look no further than LINUX, an OPERATING SYSTEM written by Linus Torvalds and subsequently tested and tweaked by tens of thousands of users united by the enabling technology of the internet. The intense scrutiny to which Linux has been subjected by its hundreds of thousands of users has created a stable, bug-free system that now represents a substantial threat to costly commercial products such as WINDOWS. This is an extraordinary achievement for a piece of software that is free to anyone.

The first commercial software house to follow the lead of Torvalds, Stallman and other luminaries was NETSCAPE, which in 1998 released the source code to its NAVIGATOR BROWSER into the public domain as the first stage of the MOZILLA project. The latest version of Navigator is based on open source code. Other companies are beginning to follow Netscape's example, but the open source movement has opponents, notably MICROSOFT, which inevitably views it as a threat to its business. One likely result of the open source initiative is a drop in software prices as companies struggle to maintain market share in the face of competition from low- or no-cost alternatives.

Opera

A BROWSER made by a Norwegian software house and much admired for its small size and impressive speed, rare commodities in the modern software world.

Operating system

The operating system is the most important part of any computer or NETWORK. Its main role is as an interpreter between the hardware itself – the processor, hard disks, video system, network cards, and so on – and the applications that are running on the computer which need access to those resources, such as E-MAIL programs, spreadsheets and DATABASES. Thus the operating system (often abbreviated to OS) must be able to speak the complex language of the chips that make up the computer, while also presenting a friendly face that human operators can understand.

This simple explanation belies the complexities of modern operating systems such as WINDOWS, MacOS and LINUX, which now have an extraordinary level of technical sophistication. As well as its responsibilities for managing the hardware and its peripherals (printers, CD-ROM drives, and so on), the OS must look after files, prevent programs from crashing each other, control network traffic and enforce security. This last item is a particularly important consideration in networked environments, where computers are susceptible to attack by CRACKERS, VIRUSES and other malicious entities. Unsurprisingly, operating systems are prime targets for certain crackers, who delight in exposing flaws in the code, especially of Microsoft's Windows. Some operating systems have also acquired a significant political importance (see MICROSOFT).

P2P

Short for peer-to-peer, a way of connecting computers so that each is as important as every other on the NETWORK and can connect to others at will. P2P abandons the notion of clients or SERVERS on a network, instead allowing information to be stored in a decentralised manner. One such use is for anonymously distributing intellectual property such as music and video without the need to create centralised resources that could be shut down by the property's litigious owners. Many programs and systems such as GNUTELLA now use P2P technology for just this purpose, although its proponents claim much greater things for it than merely replacing NAPSTER. P2P has been hailed as an important development by technology gurus from many different spheres of activity, as it frees companies and individuals from the need to create data repositories on expensive servers that are vulnerable to loss or attack. Instead, information can reside on thousands of machines simultaneously, making access simpler and back-ups unnecessary.

Despite the excitement surrounding P2P, few people have been able to suggest a credible business model for it, and concerns exist over the security of the P2P model in sensitive commercial environments. Cynics have suggested that this is yet more technology in search of a problem, and their case is strengthened by the fact that several years after its emergence, few P2P applications exist in the business world. But a 2001 survey by Frost & Sullivan, a consulting and research firm, suggested that over 6m people might be using P2P business applications by 2007, creating a market worth $4.5 billion.

P2P also stands for person-to-person and is usually used in the context of payments, such as small transactions between individuals' bank accounts, often conducted via a web-based service such as Paypal but also via mobile phones and other portable devices. P2P payments have become popular as an alternative to credit-card-based systems, allowing people to pay for goods and services ONLINE without incurring additional charges. To date, this technology has been used to pay for everything from pizzas to Porsches.

Packet

A unit of data used to send information across the internet. Most types of NETWORK communications use the Transport Control Protocol (TCP) layer of the TCP/IP PROTOCOL to split messages into a number of discrete packets before transmitting them. Each packet contains the address of its destination and a number denoting its place in the sequence. Some packets also include information about what sort of data they are carrying, which allows the network to prioritise them; for example, sending time-critical video data ahead of text.

Packets have some significant advantages compared with continuous streams of BITS. Packets from the same original message can travel by different routes across the network, each taking the path that is least crowded at the time of transmission. Once they have all arrived at their destination they are re-assembled into the correct order. Networks that use packets can also transmit parts of several different messages at the same time. The disadvantage of packet-based networks is that the process of splitting up and reassembling messages imposes a time delay and a processing overhead. The degree to which this matters varies according to the type of packet. ATM networks, which use a small packet size, have more work to do and thus impose a greater overhead.

P

Packet-switched

Describes a NETWORK that sends data one PACKET at a time, rather than as a continuous stream. Unlike CIRCUIT-SWITCHED networks, which depend on exclusive use of a connection, packet-switched networks can share out the available BANDWIDTH to several communications simultaneously.

Pagejacking

The theft of information from a WEBSITE, usually with the intention of boosting traffic to a competing site. By incorporating stolen information into their own sites and submitting their new pages to SEARCH ENGINES, pagejackers can fool prospective visitors to their victims' sites into clicking on a LINK to their own sites, or, more often, redirect them to a third-party site, which pays the pagejacker for new visitors. Many companies offering search-engine optimisation services use pagejacking techniques to drive traffic to their clients' sites, receiving a small payment for each new visitor. Victims of pagejacking are often unaware that their material has been copied and stolen. Some big companies like Disney and Discovery Channel have been pagejacked, and the technique is widely used by PORNOGRAPHY sites to steal traffic from other, higher-profile competitors.

PANS

A multipurpose ACRONYM, originally designed to operate in parallel with POTS but now assuming a life of its own. Purists argue that PANS stands for Public Access Network Services, part of a vision of a society in which everyone has access to information sources, regardless of social circumstances, as a basic democratic right. Less worthy sources claim it as the short form of Pretty Amazing Network Services, a general description of new high-speed communications networks such as ADSL. Everyone else thinks that it stands for Pretty Awesome New Stuff, an umbrella term covering more or less every post-POTS technological development.

Password

A sequence of characters required to LOG IN or otherwise gain access to a computer system. Despite widespread publicity about the importance of choosing a secure password, many systems and networks are cracked by deducing the passwords to people's computers. Current theory suggests that passwords should consist of both letters and numbers, as these are much harder to guess than even random combinations of one or the other. Birthdays, telephone numbers, or names of spouses or pets are obvious targets, as are obscene words, cartoon characters, religious expressions and actors' names. Some security experts even advise against choosing any word that is in any dictionary, as programs exist that can try every word from all the most popular lexicons.

Treat your password like your toothbrush. Don't let anybody else use it, and get a new one every six months.
Clifford Stoll

PDA

Personal Digital Assistant, an electronic device that helps people manage information. PDAS take many forms, but all include an LCD screen for displaying telephone numbers, diary dates and E-MAIL. Some, such as Psion's popular machines, have their own built-in keyboard. Others, including 3Com's Palm range, rely on a simple form of handwriting recognition for data input. A customised version of MICROSOFT'S WINDOWS OPERATING SYSTEM has for some years powered machines made by several vendors under the PocketPC brand.

Increasingly, PDAS are being used as fully fledged INFORMATION APPLIANCES, and are equipped with e-mail software and web BROWSERS as standard. Such devices now routinely include software for playing music files in MP3 format, and can even store and play video clips. A new generation of PDAS is emerging that can connect to the internet and corporate networks via wireless technologies such as WI-FI and GPRS.

According to Dataquest, a research company, over 13m PDAS were sold worldwide in 2001. But sales declined by 9% in 2002, and only 30% of PDAS are currently bought by business users, who cite the high cost and complex deployment of wireless versions as a good reason to stick to more mature technologies.

PDF

Portable Document Format, an invention of Adobe Systems designed for distributing documents electronically. PDF files can contain original fonts, graphics and other design elements that faithfully record the layout of the original. They can even contain audio and video sequences. PDF is especially suitable for distributing documents by E-MAIL, as it requires the creation of one extremely cheap electronic file rather than the expensive printing of hundreds of paper versions. The PDF specification is open, and many programs can now create and view such files.

Perl

A flexible programming language widely used in internet environments, especially WEBSITES. Written by Larry Wall, Perl is popular with programmers because it is fast, comparatively easy to learn and, as a bonus, free. Perl programmes will run on any PLATFORM without modifications, so the same code can be used on a WINDOWS box, a UNIX SERVER or a Macintosh. Many CGI SCRIPTS are written in Perl.

How many of you have broken no laws this month? That's the kind of society I want to build. I want a guarantee with physics and mathematics, not with laws, that we can give ourselves real privacy of personal communications.
John Gilmore

PGP

Pretty Good Privacy, an encryption program that the US government tried to ban. Developed by Phil Zimmerman in the early 1990s, PGP has become a byword for E-MAIL security. It has also been the source of some controversy, following its international distribution in defiance of an American ban on the export of strong encryption software and its unauthorised use of the RSA algorithm. Zimmerman sold PGP to Network Associates, a software company, in 1997. Its new owners exported the source code to the Netherlands in book form, rather than as actual code, to circumvent US laws governing the export of so-called munitions, and an international version is currently on sale. PGP is thus one of few programs whose international versions are as secure as their US equivalents. (See ENCRYPTION.)

PICS

Platform for Internet Content Selection, a way of rating the content of WEBSITES. PICS was designed to give parents, schools and companies control over things that their charges view on the internet. Although conceived primarily to prevent access to PORNOGRAPHY and hate speech, PICS can be used to rate lots of other things, such as books or films. Although the primary responsibility for rating sites rests with their owners, third parties can rate them too, so an anti-racism organisation could maintain and rate a list of sites containing racist material. The PICS software on a home computer could then be configured to check that list before allowing access to any of the sites.

The problem facing PICS is that despite its elegant design and relative ease of implementation, almost nobody uses it. Site owners have not shown the hoped-for public-spiritedness, and the web is just too big for third parties to rate it reliably. PICS will probably not go away, but its proponents may have to look for more dependable means of governing access to undesirable material.

P

Ping

A small program used to check for the presence and response time of a remote computer. Most OPERATING SYSTEMS are supplied with a ping program for testing internet connections. The term is also used in reference to people, as in "I haven't heard from Angus for a while. I'll ping him this evening".

Ping storm

A flood of large PACKETS sent to a computer by a PING program, either to test the machine's ability to manage large volumes of traffic or, occasionally, deliberately to cause it to malfunction. The malicious use of ping in this way, sometimes referred to as the Ping of Death, has shut down several large networks. (See DENIAL OF SERVICE.)

PKI

See PUBLIC KEY INFRASTRUCTURE.

Platform

Broadly, the combination of an OPERATING SYSTEM and a processor to form a system on which application programs can run. Nowadays, the term is often used to refer just to the operating system, an assumption having been made that the processor in question is made by Intel. Historically, different versions of the same computer program have often been written to run on different platforms, creating big headaches for software developers in the process. Early versions of NETSCAPE NAVIGATOR, for example, ran on around 20 different platforms, although that number has shrunk as the program's popularity has declined. The JAVA language promised to bring platform independence to the software world but has met with limited success to date.

PNG

Portable Network Graphics, a kind of graphics file designed for creating pictures for web pages. Despite a good COMPRESSION scheme and considerable technical superiority, PNG has so far failed to capture the imagination of web designers, who generally rely on GIF and JPEG files for illustrating their works. One of PNG's weaknesses is that it does not directly support animations, one of GIF's strongest features, making it unsuitable for eye-catching contemporary BANNER ADVERTISING.

POP

Point of Presence, an access point on the internet. Each ISP has at least one POP, to which users dial in when they want to establish an internet connection. Some big ISPs, such as COMPUSERVE, have hundreds of POPS in dozens of countries, ensuring that subscribers can always make a local call to check their E-MAIL. Not to be confused with POP3.

POP3

The latest version of the Post Office Protocol, a standard for retrieving E-MAIL. POP3 is a CLIENT/SERVER PROTOCOL in which the client, an e-mail program, periodically checks a server for new mail. Most mail programs now support POP3, and several web-based e-mail services such as Hotmail can collect messages from POP3 mailboxes. (See also IMAP.)

Pop-up

A small window that appears in front of a web page when it loads or closes, usually in the hope of selling something to the page's viewer. Pop-ups and their relatives are still popular ways of forcing WEBSITE visitors to look at ADVERTISING or subscribe to services they do not want, despite the fact that almost all web surfers find them highly intrusive. Online marketers say that this is exactly the point. A variant of the pop-up known as the pop-under lessens the irritation somewhat by appearing behind the page being viewed, and is thus only seen when a web BROWSER window is closed.

Some advertising agencies have reported that well over one-third of their revenue still comes from pop-ups, which they say are twice as effective as the less annoying BANNER ads that can be more easily ignored. Effective or not, they are still unpopular: 78% of respondents to a January 2003 survey by GartnerG2, a research company, described pop-ups as "very annoying". According to Nielsen NetRatings, over 5 billion pop-up ads were served in the second quarter of 2002, prompting hundreds of thousands of users to download software generically known as pop-up killers, which is widely available and often free. Some ISPS now distribute pop-up killers to their subscribers in an attempt to appease them, and perhaps even prevent them from defecting to other BANDWIDTH suppliers; and some browsers, such as OPERA and MOZILLA, allow users to block pop-ups. In 2002, AOL announced that it was removing pop-up advertising from its sites altogether, replacing them with more lucrative and effective alternatives based on RICH MEDIA formats.

Pornography

One of the internet's biggest businesses. As the world's media never tire of pointing out, pornography is widely available on the net, both in commercialised subscription form and for free. Regulating it has turned out to be a much trickier business than finding it, as every government that has tried to do so has found. Blanket CENSORSHIP, in particular, has proved to be impossible. This is excellent news for the pornography industry, which has taken to the web with relish. Some estimates show that there may be as many as 400,000 WEBSITES selling or displaying pornography in some form. But a lack of rigorous research data makes such figures hard to verify, which is why estimates of the real value of pornography sales vary widely, particularly in an industry where the size of everything is routinely exaggerated. Amounts of between $2 billion and $10 billion are often bandied about, but a 2000 study by eMarketer, an ONLINE marketing firm, reported that online US sales of pornography were only $230m in 2001, representing an ever smaller percentage of total online spend as gaming becomes more popular.

Despite the difficulties in policing online pornography, criminal investigators continue to take it seriously. Child pornography in particular is a significant problem, although the web turns out to be an excellent way of tracking down subscribers to illegal online CONTENT; a worldwide operation in 2002 revealed the names of over 7,000 British visitors to an illegal American site.

Portability

A characteristic of a program which can run on any PLATFORM without modification. It may sound simple to achieve, but it is extremely hard to engineer because of enormous differences between OPERATING SYSTEMS and processors and a general unwillingness by their developers to co-operate. JAVA, SUN MICROSYSTEMS's programming language, promised to deliver this Holy Grail of computing and, maybe, break MICROSOFT's stranglehold on the PC industry in the process. But despite much public wishful thinking on Sun's behalf, only the simplest Java programs have turned out to be truly portable.

Portal

An electronic gateway to the WORLD WIDE WEB. The portal is really an extension of the SEARCH ENGINE idea, but instead of providing lists of sites matching someone's search criteria it relies on a selection process to choose starter sites that new users might be interested in visiting. The biggest portals are run by some of the net's most visible brands, including AOL, YAHOO and MSN. A measure of the importance of portals is that these three companies' sites were the most visited anywhere on the web in February 2003, according to statistics from Nielsen NetRatings.

P

Portals are the latest stage in the endless quest for ways of attracting web surfers and (much harder) making them come back again. Their owners claim to achieve this STICKINESS by providing a range of information services and entertainment so essential that visitors are irresistibly drawn to return. These might include a directory of other sites, a search facility, a weather service, CHAT rooms, free E-MAIL and a selection of sports, cinema and other entertainment sites. To maximise their exposure, ISPS and BROWSER manufacturers invariably preconfigure their software to load their portal sites automatically when they run, thus more or less guaranteeing that a known number of people will visit the site at least once, which is important in attracting advertisers.

Quick-thinking entrepreneurs have moved on to the next big thing in portal concepts, the VORTAL. Other forms of portal are steadily emerging, including the mortal, a site dedicated to mobile computing resources, and even the snortal, a site updating the scratch-and-sniff card concept for the digital age.

Port scan

A digital probe sent by a CRACKER attempting to break into someone else's computer. Port scans look for open conduits into a computer via its internet connection, attempting to discover whether or not an exploitable weakness exists or whether a TROJAN HORSE program is installed. Port-scanning software is widely available on the internet, most of it used by SCRIPT KIDDIES to disrupt hapless users' activities. The best form of defence against port scanners is a FIREWALL. Many new software-only firewalls are now available to protect individual users as well as company NETWORKS.

POTS

Plain Old Telephone Service – in short, what you get when you pick up a telephone (see PANS).

The telephone has too many shortcomings to be seriously considered as a means of communication.
Western Union internal memo, 1876

PPP

Point-to-Point Protocol, a way for two computers connected by a serial interface to communicate with each other. The most common use of PPP is to connect a computer to an ISP across a MODEM and telephone line.

Private key

A type of KEY used to decode encrypted messages, known only to the sender and recipient of a message. Some ENCRYPTION algorithms such as DES rely on a single private key, using the same string of characters to encode and decode a message. This technique has some disadvantages, the main one being the difficulty of exchanging the key between the sender and recipient and figuring out how it should itself be encrypted. If the key is inadvertently intercepted or revealed by either party, the message can instantly be decrypted. Another problem is that every message must have its own unique key, selected from (in the case of DES) one of tens of quadrillions of alternatives. Contrast with PUBLIC KEY CRYPTOGRAPHY, in which only two keys are ever needed (one public, one private) no matter how many messages are generated.

Protocol

A set of rules that determines how two computers should communicate with each other. Many different protocols are used on the internet because the rules for each form of communication it allows vary considerably. E-MAIL, for example, requires a particular set of commands to be understood by both sender and receiver; these commands are described by the POP3 and SMTP protocols, among others. Similarly, the TCP protocol describes how senders and receivers should manage the transmission of PACKETS across a NETWORK. Other common internet protocols are HTTP, IP and FTP.

P

Proxy server

A computer that controls traffic between a LOCAL AREA NETWORK and the wider internet. Many companies use proxy servers to regulate access to internet services such as the web, FTP and TELNET. When a computer on the LAN makes a request for an internet service the request passes through the proxy server, which then decides how to deal with it. If the request is for a prohibited service, the proxy server returns an error. If the service is allowed, it is either passed on to the internet server as usual or in the case of web requests to a local CACHE, from where previously downloaded pages can be more quickly accessed. Proxy servers give companies a fine degree of control over their internet access policies. They can track every request from the NETWORK, for example, including IP addresses and even keystrokes. They are often used to prevent files from travelling in or out of a corporate network, and most ANONYMISER services rely on the use of proxy servers. (See also FIREWALL.)

Public key cryptography

A cryptographic system in which messages are encrypted with a KEY split into two parts. One of these parts is publicly available and the other is private. A message sent with one kind of key can only be decrypted by the other. Public key cryptography uses complex mathematical algorithms based on large prime numbers, and in its most advanced forms is regarded as more or less unbreakable even with the most powerful computers. (See ENCRYPTION.)

P

Public key infrastructure

A complex way of administering large public key ENCRYPTION schemes. The use of encryption to conceal or authenticate the contents of messages between two people is simple enough, but it becomes significantly harder as the number of regular communicants grows. A global company doing business electronically, such as a bank, must find a way not just to publish the public keys of everybody on the network (including employees, suppliers and customers), but also to evaluate the extent to which everyone should trust each other. Anne may trust Bill, for example, who in turn trusts Carla; but Carla may not trust either Anne or Bill, and so requires each of them to prove that their credentials are still valid every time they communicate.

As the number of people in this web grows, the problem of

managing the relationships becomes severe. Public key infrastructure (PKI) schemes handle this with hierarchical certification programs, which associate public keys with individuals or organisations, and validation schemes, which verify that a certificate is still valid. There are many other problems for PKI designers to solve: one is irrefutability, or the ability to say with certainty that an individual definitely signed a document or wrote a message (see DIGITAL SIGNATURE). Such issues have many legal and social aspects as well as technical ones, further increasing the difficulty of implementing PKI on a wide scale.

Pure-play

An internet company that has no corresponding version of itself in the real world; in other words, a site whose business depends entirely on revenue from its ONLINE operations. Some pure-play companies, such as AMAZON and EBAY, have demonstrated that they can stay afloat without the need for support from a bricks-and-mortar operation. But many others have discovered that purity is a virtue they may most of the original pure-players have long since ceased to exist.

P

Push media

CONTENT that is delivered automatically, rather than waiting for someone to come and get it. Push solves a problem common to many internet users who know exactly what information they want but still have to go and get it every time they need it. By subscribing to a push-based service, the information can be delivered straight to their computer as it becomes available. Push is an attractive technology for advertisers, who can be sure that viewers of their material have requested that they be sent information regularly. Text-based E-MAIL is the simplest form of push, and there are variants based on the delivery of entire web pages, complete with LINKS, graphics and tables. More complex push applications, which offer all sorts of real-time information delivered via custom software, have not made a lasting impression.

QoS

Quality of Service, a term used to describe the reliability (or otherwise) of a NETWORK, based on an underlying assumption that it can always be improved. QOS is difficult to guarantee on PACKET-SWITCHED networks as the volume of traffic and behaviour of packets is hard to predict, but some kinds of network connection have special facilities that make it easier. Companies using ATM, for example, can choose a level of service that suits their specific requirements. A special PROTOCOL, RSVP (Reservation Protocol), can be used to reserve channels on some networks for use by time-sensitive, high-BANDWIDTH applications such as video.

Query

Any request for information from a DATABASE, used by everything from SEARCH ENGINES to web-based railway timetables. A special language, SQL (Structured Query Language), is often used to construct queries.

Quicktime

Apple's software MULTIMEDIA technology. Quicktime is used to add audio and video to WEBSITES and other multimedia applications, and is an alternative to STREAMING MEDIA products from Real Networks and MICROSOFT. Despite the fact that versions are available for both Macintosh and WINDOWS PLATFORMS, Quicktime is nowhere near as popular as its competitors and is unlikely to be a major player in the Windows market.

RealAudio

A program for listening to music and other sound across the internet. RealAudio is the invention of Real Networks, a company founded by Rob Glaser, a former MICROSOFT executive, in 1994. Its great achievement was to allow people to listen to music samples as they were transferred across low-BANDWIDTH connections, rather than having to DOWNLOAD an entire file and listen to it afterwards. RealAudio has since evolved into bigger, better STREAMING MEDIA technologies, including video delivery.

RealNames

A now-defunct commercial system designed to take the pain out of remembering and using URLS. Instead of expecting users to remember complex strings of dashes and slashes, the Real-Names system assigned real, simple words to complex web addresses, so that they could be accessed through a direct navigation system rather than a hit-and-miss process based on SEARCH ENGINES.

Despite the apparent usefulness of such a scheme, Real-Names failed to capture the imagination of WEBSITE owners. Part of the reason for their indifference was that the scheme made no attempt to determine which company had the right to use particular KEYWORDS, effectively assigning them to the highest bidder. A second problem was the technology's imperfect integration with BROWSERS and search engines to make it work properly. Many users complained that an attempt to search for a generic category, such as "London plumbers", might well redirect them to a website based in London, Ontario, instead of giving them a list of sites to choose from. The company's early deals with the major search engines faltered, forcing several confusing changes of strategy. RealNames eventually sold a significant part of the business to MICROSOFT, which integrated support for its technology into its INTERNET EXPLORER browser but refused to renew its contract in May 2002, forcing the company to close shortly afterwards.

Regulation of Investigatory Powers Act

Legislation adopted by the UK government in 2000 that increases its powers of surveillance of electronic communications. The act has been subjected to intense scrutiny by privacy and cyber-rights campaigners, who object to the fact that under the new bill the government can anonymously tap all electronic communications, thus, they say, infringing the Human Rights and Data Protection acts. Such infringements have yet to be proved or even tried in the UK courts, but many organisations representing a wide range of commercial and consumer interests have mounted official objections to the act's provisions.

Despite widespread opposition to the original bill, it received the royal assent in July 2000, giving the government many new ways to investigate users of the internet and other technologies. In particular, it allows government agencies to monitor all data traffic, allowing them to see which websites individuals have visited and who they have communicated with. It can also force individuals to reveal the contents of encrypted messages and transactions, which critics say unfairly places the burden of proof of innocence on to people under surveillance. ISPS may be forced to install costly "black box" monitoring equipment at the command of the home secretary, and may be legally required to store data on customer behaviour for six years, an obligation which AOL claimed would require 360,000 CDs each year in the UK and cost £34m.

A report commissioned in 2000 by the British Chambers of Commerce estimated that the loss of confidence in E-COMMERCE resulting from the act could cost businesses £46 billion in its first five years of operation, although this figure now looks somewhat inflated in view of recent e-commerce trends.

If we had a reliable way to label our toys good and bad, it would be easy to regulate technology wisely. But we can rarely see far enough ahead to know which road leads to damnation.

Freeman Dyson

Remailer

An internet site that allows people to send anonymous E-MAIL. When an e-mail message is sent via a remailer, the remailer removes all the information that might identify the sender, such as name, e-mail address, ISP and IP ADDRESS, before forwarding it to the intended recipient.

Remailers are widely used by contributors to discussions in NEWSGROUPS who wish to remain anonymous for some reason, perhaps to hide personal problems from spouses and bosses or to discuss sensitive religious or political issues without fear of recrimination. Many PORNOGRAPHY distributors also rely on remailers to keep their identities secret, which has led authorities to concentrate on their activities. The most famous remailer, Finland-based ANON.PENET.FI, owned by Johan Helsingius, was subjected to great pressure from several sources, including the Church of Scientology, to reveal the identities of some of its 700,000 users. Police investigations and widespread media coverage followed, at least some of which was hysterical and inaccurate. All this resulted in anon.penet.fi's closure in 1996, but many remailers continue to operate worldwide, and are widely supported by internet privacy and free-speech campaigners.

Remote access

R

Access to a computer system or NETWORK from a distant location, usually by dialling in with a MODEM. A typical example of remote access is a dial-up connection to an ISP. Many workers now rely on remote access to stay in touch with their offices while travelling or working at home. By dialling into a remote access SERVER, which is usually equipped with a FIREWALL and other security devices, they can access network resources as if they were on a local machine.

RFC

Request For Comments, one of many numbered documents outlining specifications for proposed internet standards. Unlike proposals issued by traditional standards bodies such as ANSI (American National Standards Institute) and the ISO (International Standards Organisation), RFCs are generally the work of people or groups working independently. Because of the way it is administered, the RFC approach allows good ideas to be reviewed by the whole internet COMMUNITY rather than by a select few committee members.

Most of the internet's most widely used standards and PROTOCOLS have emerged from the RFC process, including IP, HTTP, URLS and the E-MAIL format standard (a full list is maintained by the IETF). Some are rather gnomic (see RFC 124, for example), but others are more expansive; a good example is RFC 1118, also known as the Hitchhiker's Guide to the Internet. Unwary researchers have occasionally been caught out by documents such as RFC 2324, which describes HTCPCP 1.0, a way of controlling coffee pots across internet connections. It is, of course, dated April 1st 1998.

> *There is coffee all over the world. Increasingly, in a world in which computing is ubiquitous, the computists want to make coffee. Coffee brewing is an art, but the distributed intelligence of the web-connected world transcends art. Thus there is a strong, dark, rich requirement for a protocol designed espressoly for the brewing of coffee. Coffee is brewed using coffee pots. Networked coffee pots require a control protocol if they are to be controlled.*
>
> Extract from RFC 2324

Rich media

An ADVERTISING term used to describe the latest generation of ONLINE marketing tools. Rich media advertising generally relies on the use of FLASH, JAVA or STREAMING MEDIA technologies to create advertisements that can contain sound, video and animations rather than just static images. Prompted by the decline in popularity and effectiveness of BANNERS, advertisers have turned to rich media in an attempt to boost flagging revenues and improve the efficiency of their campaigns. According to DoubleClick, an advertising research company, almost 25% of online adverts used some form of rich media in the third quarter of 2002, generating responses ten times greater than their traditional static counterparts.

Unlike banners and POP-UPS, which traditionally measure audience interest in terms of CLICKTHROUGHS to other WEB-SITES, rich media adverts are designed to intrigue and entertain as well as simply drive traffic. Some seek to imitate television advertising by displaying digital video clips and animations; others adopt an educational or interactive approach, allowing people to explore the advert at their own pace. One problem with rich media advertising is that it consumes considerably more BANDWIDTH than the simple GIF images that constitute banners. Users of dial-up internet connections routinely find that pages containing rich media take much longer to load, prompting some cynics to speculate that such advertising is the brainchild of ISPs determined to upgrade them to more expensive BROADBAND connections.

ROT13

A simple ENCRYPTION scheme for text messages, in which each letter of the alphabet is rotated with the one 13 places behind or ahead of it. The sentence "My hovercraft is full of eels" becomes "Zl ubirepensg vf shyy bs rryf" when thus encoded. Some USENET readers and E-MAIL clients include a ROT13 feature, which is often used to avoid offending readers in the more polite NEWSGROUPS or to reveal the secrets of computer games.

Rotation

A process used to display advertisements on web pages. Many WEBSITES use rotators to display different advertisers'

BANNERS sequentially or even at random, depending on how often each advertiser has paid to show them. So one page may display a different advertisement each time it is loaded, eventually cycling back to the beginning of the list.

Router

A device that decides how and where to send internet traffic. A router examines the address information carried by each PACKET as it arrives at a NETWORK and chooses the best route to send it to its final destination. Routers maintain their own records of available network pathways and the prevailing traffic conditions to help them decide on the most code-effective routes. Network GATEWAYS, POPS and some SWITCHES include routing functions.

RSA

A powerful ENCRYPTION scheme based on principles of PUBLIC KEY CRYPTOGRAPHY. Developed by Ron Rivest, Adi Shamir and Leonard Adelman (on whose names the abbreviation is based) at the Massachusetts Institute of Technology (MIT) in 1977, RSA is probably the most widely used security algorithm of its kind. It is included in many commercial products, including those developed by MICROSOFT, NETSCAPE and LOTUS.

The magic words are squeamish ossifrage.
Contents of the message encrypted in the first RSA Challenge, cracked in 1994 after 17 years

RSAC

Recreational Software Advisory Council (see ICRA).

RSS

Rich Site Summary, a relative of XML used to describe web CONTENT for distribution or syndication to other sites. RSS documents contain descriptions and locations of items such as news stories, discussion forum extracts or WEBLOG entries. Once an RSS document has been created by the publisher it is registered with a CONTENT AGGREGATOR or directory, from where it can be accessed by anyone with a web BROWSER or another program capable of understanding RSS.

RTFM

Read the .... manual, a suggestion often directed at NEWBIES asking obvious questions about technical subjects in NEWS-GROUPS.

Script

A simple program or sequence of instructions that is carried out by another program. All sorts of programs use scripts as a way of automating procedures or carrying out simple tasks. Many communications programs, for example, use scripts to control the LOGIN sequence by automatically sending a username and PASSWORD when prompted by the HOST computer.

The most common use of scripts in the web environment is to control web pages, either in the BROWSER or on the SERVER. Scripting languages such as JAVASCRIPT and JScript are designed to slot into standard HTML code and provide features beyond those of the mark-up language itself, such as checking the status of web forms or changing the appearance of some page elements when a button is pressed. The scripts that are written for these functions are interpreted directly by the browser, without any need to pass data back to the server for processing.

Script kiddie

A pejorative term for an aspiring HACKER or CRACKER, especially one who modifies VIRUSES and other harmful pieces of software with the intention of disrupting other people's computer systems. Script kiddies usually regard themselves as ingenious and daring, but they are generally treated with disdain by hardcore hackers and crackers, who consider them lazy, untalented and incapable of writing real software. Still, they are capable of wreaking considerable havoc. Many contemporary E-MAIL-hosted viruses, including 2000's disruptive I Love You and its variants, are the work of script kiddies, and much of the damage caused by TROJAN HORSE programs has been ascribed to their work.

SDMI

The Secure Digital Music Initiative, a scheme developed by a consortium of music industry heavyweights and technology companies to prevent the piracy of music on the internet. SDMI aims to counter the threat posed by MP3, a way of recording music from CDs that makes it easy to distribute electronically. It uses ENCRYPTION and watermarking techniques to discourage unauthorised copying and distribution. Many companies initially expressed support for SDMI's proposals, including manufacturers of portable music players that can store music in memory rather than on moving disks.

Believers in SDMI originally claimed that the technological advances in its core components, including new encoding techniques that deliver better sound quality than MP3, would gradually move people away from a format that is now well over ten years old. But SDMI suffered a blow in 2000 when its watermarking technology was cracked after it issued a challenge to HACKERS to try to break it. A group of academic researchers from the Department of Computer Science at Princeton University successfully met SDMI's challenge and broke its code, but was subsequently prevented from publishing the details of its technique following a threat of prosecution under the Digital Millennium Copyright Act. The ensuing lack of consensus within the music industry on the best way to protect its copyrighted CONTENT forced SDMI into retreat in 2001, and music companies continue to look for a better way to prevent piracy.

The difficulty seems to be, not so much that we publish unduly in view of the extent and variety of present-day interests, but rather that publication has been extended far beyond our present ability to make real use of the record. The summation of human experience is being expanded at a prodigious rate, and the means we use for threading through the consequent maze to the momentary important item is the same as was used in the days of square-rigged ships.

Vannevar Bush, *As We May Think*, 1945

S

Search engine

Software that finds things on the internet, usually a dedicated WEBSITE. One way or another, most web users eventually find their way to one of the big names, such as GOOGLE or YAHOO, because, though far from perfect, they are the only way of finding information in the vastness of the internet.

The reputation of search engines has been steadily diminishing almost from the day that they first appeared, as it has become clear they are not up to the immense job of indexing the web. This apparent shortcoming is not immediately obvious to users, who seem to have the opposite problem: too much information. Search engine indexes are now truly immense. Google, comfortably the leading example of the genre, boasted an index of over 3 billion pages at the beginning of 2003. Among all this data, even quite complex and detailed searches can yield vast lists of sites with little guidance on how useful each is likely to be. Most engines have no useful way of determining the relevance of each occurrence of a word, so they simply list them all according to the frequency with which they occur or how near the top of the document they are. There are variations on this theme. Google, for example, ranks sites according to how many others LINK to them, a good indication of the regard in which they are generally held. But even the best sites suffer from a plethora of broken and outdated links, which is a source of frustration for users.

Some of these problems can be solved by increased horsepower and improved application of information theory. One new line of investigation involves the use of P2P technology to canvas search results and BOOKMARKS from other users on the network as part of the page ranking process. But there are other problems to solve, too. Currently, many search engines now focus more on marketing, ADVERTISING and strategic partnerships than on the core technology. Most operate some sort of KEYWORD advertising scheme, in which adverts are displayed alongside the list of search results. Some sell rankings to companies that pay to appear at the top of the search list, raising doubts about their objectivity. Others exclude potentially useful sites on the basis that they are in some way competitive. Meanwhile, many companies now offer services to website owners offering to optimise their search engine rankings; and unscrupulous website owners and advertising networks have found a bewildering number of ways to skew search results and fool the engines into displaying lowly sites ahead of more popular or more useful ones, including techniques such as PAGEJACKING.

Consequently, an industry that started as a largely philanthropic movement has become fiercely commercial and competitive, and many of the original players have either vanished or been absorbed as part of a steady consolidation process. ALTAVISTA, the king of the search engines until 1999, was sold to rival Overture in early 2003 for a fraction of its value at the time of its previous sale to Digital.

> *Getting information off the internet is like*
> *taking a drink from a fire hydrant.*
> Mitchell Kapor

Server

A program that provides services to another program, often one running on a different computer. On the internet the most commonly encountered examples are web servers, which are programs that send HTML pages in response to a request from a client, in this case a BROWSER. Several different types of server software can run on a single computer at the same time. A web server, a DATABASE server and even a game server can theoretically all run on the same machine, although in practice the overheads imposed by each usually make this impractical. The term is also used to refer to a computer running a particular program, especially in the case of a FILE SERVER.

Server farm

A group of computers configured as SERVERS gathered together in a single location. Server farms may be used for several different reasons. A busy WEBSITE, such as a popular SEARCH ENGINE, may use a server farm to spread the load of user requests across several machines, improving the speed of response and managing data transfers more efficiently. The big search engines have server farms numbering tens, hundreds or even thousands of computers.

Servlet

A small JAVA program that runs on a SERVER; in essence, the server equivalent of an APPLET. Servlets have some advantages compared with similar programs written to the CGI specification, for example, because they can use technical features of the Java VIRTUAL MACHINE to run faster. Most web servers provide facilities to run servlets.

SETI@home

An initiative to enlist the aid of internet users in the Search for Extraterrestrial Intelligence. Instead of trying to make sense of the vast amount of information collected by SETI's radio telescopes by running it through the organisation's overtaxed computers, SETI@home parcels out the task to volunteers. Thus distributed to numerous computers, the job of looking for messages from alien civilisations becomes more manageable. A similar approach has been used to crack ENCRYPTION schemes such as DES. Unlike the DES effort, SETI@home has yet to yield positive results, although this is not for the want of trying: over 2m participants signed up for the project in its first year. In February 2003 there were over 4m SETI users, who contributed a total of 1.3m years of processing time to the project. (See GRID COMPUTING.)

Signature

A piece of standard text attached to the end of an E-MAIL message. Many people use signatures to automatically add their contact details to their communications. Some extend this idea by adding quotes, witticisms or company mottoes. Perhaps the best-known examples are corporate disclaimers, most of which are considerably longer than the messages to which they are appended. Many e-mail programs allow their users to create multiple signatures from which they can select the most appropriate at the time of sending their message, a feature which has got absent-minded communicators into trouble when attaching irreverent or indecent examples to bosses or family members. (See DIGITAL SIGNATURE.)

Silver surfer

A web-surfing enthusiast of advancing years. Older web users are becoming more interesting to advertisers and retailers. According to most surveys, they still constitute one of the fastest-growing demographic groups in the global internet market. In the UK, a 2002 survey by BMRB, a research organisation, found that 83% of retired people now spend more time ONLINE than pursuing other interests. Many other studies show that older people use the web more often, stay online longer and visit more WEBSITES than younger users, making them irresistible to advertisers. They also have more money and own more credit cards, and are thus good targets for sales of everything from high-tech gadgets to cars. E-MAIL is especially popular among silver surfers, and many CHAT systems now include rooms for the over-50s.

Smiley

See EMOTICON.

SMS

Short Messaging Service, a way for mobile phone users to send each other short text messages from the keypads of their GSM phones. Especially popular with teenagers, SMS is also used by many doctors, salespeople and other professionals as a cheap and easy way of sending and receiving time-critical information.

One study in late 2002 by Gartner, a research company, showed that more Europeans now use SMS than E-MAIL. Some companies offer SMS-to-e-mail GATEWAYS, allowing subscribers to send and receive internet e-mail while they are on the road.

SMS has surprised everyone in the mobile phone world, proving much more popular than clumsier and more complex technologies such as WAP. In the UK, over 2m SMS messages were sent every hour in September 2002 alone and monthly numbers are now well over 1 billion. The GSM Association estimates that in 2002, people around the world sent 360 billion SMS messages, dwarfing the number of other non-voice uses for mobile phones. In this context, SMS must be seen not just as an interesting toy for phone owners but also as a rich source of revenue for telecoms companies, which charge for every message sent. Many companies are now finding ways to extend the usefulness of SMS beyond mere personal messaging. One promising development is shopping, which can be done simply by sending an appropriately formatted message to a retailer without the need for a web BROWSER or even a computer. Many companies now view SMS as a more reliable marketing tool than direct mail or telesales.

SMTP

Simple Mail Transport Protocol, the standard way of transferring E-MAIL from one computer to another on the internet. ISPS typically maintain an SMTP server to which mail clients must connect when sending messages. SMTP generally works in tandem with mailbox management software based on POP3 or IMAP.

SOAP

Simple Access Object Protocol, designed to allow programs running on different kinds of computers or OPERATING SYSTEMS to exchange information. SOAP is tailored to work with standard HTTP transfers and XML-based messages, thus allowing programs to communicate with each other across the internet. One SERVER might ask another for the latest stock quotes, for example. SOAP would then handle the request and manage the conversation between them. (See WEB SERVICES.)

Source code

The original code of a computer program. Unlike executable binary code, which has been turned into the ones and zeros that computer processors can understand, source code can be read by humans, albeit rather specialised ones. The source code of commercial software products has traditionally been jealously guarded by its creators, who fear that competitors may use its secrets to copy their expensive new features. But this has been challenged by the OPEN SOURCE movement.

Spam

Junk E-MAIL. Spam causes problems for most internet users, whose mailboxes and favourite NEWSGROUPS fill up daily with advertisements for get-rich-quick schemes, cosmetic surgery procedures and pornographic websites. The senders of spam, who are called spammers, collect e-mail addresses from newsgroups, e-mail directories and third-party vendors to which they then send unsolicited messages.

The spam problem is growing incredibly fast, as spammers discover better ways of finding e-mail addresses and new ways of covering their tracks. A study in the United States by Ferris Research estimated that unsolicited email cost US companies nearly $9 billion in 2002 as a result of productivity losses, heavy technical support requirements and BANDWIDTH consumption. In the UK, spam accounted for 40% of all e-mail sent in December 2002, according to one survey, an increase of more than 30% in a single year. One reason for this sudden rise is the advent of the "dictionary harvest" attack against businesses, in which a spammer sends tens of thousands of common names to a corporate e-mail system. He then collects the names of those that are received normally rather than returned, indicating that they are live addresses.

Large ISPs have been hit particularly hard by spammers. In February 2003, AOL reported that its anti-spam technology was blocking 780m pieces of junk mail every day, an average of 22 pieces per member. In December 2002, the company was awarded $7m damages against a company that sent its members nearly 1 billion unsolicited e-mails advertising adult websites. Unfortunately for e-mail users, the regulation of spam has proved to be as difficult as any other kind of regulation of the internet. Because offenders can change their identities so fast ONLINE, they can usually stay one step ahead of the anti-spam police, almost always private companies rather than governments, which have been slow to pass legislation restricting the distribution of unwanted e-mail. But new filtering techniques, combined with frequent updates to directories of known spammers, are helping businesses and ISPs to counter the problem. One threat comes from a new generation of BOT programs that automatically create fake FREE-MAIL accounts from which to send their spam, and researchers are busily developing defences based on Turing tests to distinguish between bots and real human beings.

How spam came to be used in this context is obscure. Many people agree that it derives from a sketch by Monty Python, a group of British comedians, which features a large number of occurrences of the word "spam" in the script, the credits and a song inspired by a type of luncheon meat called Spam that has been on sale since 1937. The more literally minded have suggested that it stands for Self-Propelled Advertising Material.

Spammer

Someone who sends SPAM to people or NEWSGROUPS.

Splinternet

A term coined by Clyde Wayne Crews, director of technology

studies at the libertarian Cato Institute, to describe new, unregulated versions of the internet on which people can behave as they choose without fear of intervention. Rather than creating more regulations, he argues, we should create more internets, which would run as private, autonomous NETWORKS free from concerns about PORNOGRAPHY, gambling and COPYRIGHT issues, for example. Although the term itself is new, the idea is not: several companies have set up private, internet-like networks for special-interest groups, and the INTERNET2 initiative is based on its own private BACKBONE.

Spyware

Software that conceals itself in other programs and reports back to its creators on their usage. Coined by programming wizard Steve Gibson, the expression was originally used to describe a program that collected non-identifiable user information for ADVERTISING purposes without the user's knowledge, raising inevitable privacy concerns among web users. Many other programs have since been shown to have spyware characteristics. Some large companies have been criticised for collecting data without the user's permission, most notably Real Networks, whose RealJukebox program for recording from CDs on to hard disks reported details of its users' listening habits and music libraries back to corporate headquarters. Recent versions have had this feature removed. The problem appears to be growing, especially in the business world: one in three European companies' networks are now infected with spyware, according to a 2003 survey by Websense, a web management company, raising fears about the confidentiality of business information.

S

SSL

Secure Sockets Layer, a set of security PROTOCOLS invented by NETSCAPE for protecting electronic financial transactions. SSL is an open specification that includes ENCRYPTION software based on the RSA algorithm, and it is widely used by WEBSITES to prevent credit-card or other personal information being intercepted by snoopers. Although it is in itself extremely secure, SSL secures only the link between a user's computer and a SERVER at the end. Unlike a certificate signed with a DIGITAL SIGNATURE, it says nothing at all about who the user is actually connected to, a fact that has largely been concealed from the users themselves, who are regularly assured that any site featuring SSL encryption is safe. Some clever CRACKERS have managed to divert users invisibly away from bona-fide sites to a convincing SSL-enabled imitation, where they then proceed to steal their money in a secure but nonetheless illegal way.

Start-up

A new business venture. In the late 1990s it seemed almost obligatory for anyone under the age of 40 to have a start-up idea in the high-technology area, usually one which would survive as far as a profitable IPO. But the bursting of the DOTCOM bubble has made venture capitalists much more sceptical about such high-tech start-ups.

> *There's a term in business school now: "Doing a Google". That means raising a lot of money without having a clear business model.*
> Sergey Brin, co-founder of the Google search engine

S Stanford University

An academic institution of unrivalled influence in the high-tech world. Many of Silicon Valley's most successful companies were formed by Stanford graduates, including Hewlett-Packard, Cisco, SUN MICROSYSTEMS and YAHOO. Famous alumni include Vint Cerf, so-called father of the internet, and Jim Clark, founder of NETSCAPE.

Steganography

The science of communicating in a way which hides the existence of the communication. Unlike codes, which render communications unreadable but still potentially interceptable, steganography (from a Greek phrase meaning covered writing) relies on hiding messages where they would not be expected.

Steganographic tools such as invisible inks and microdots have long been used by espionage agencies. Now digital versions of these tools are creeping into the internet culture. Owners of digital images, for example, can encode a watermark within JPEG or GIF files to track pirate copies of their property. A casual observer will see nothing but the picture itself, but the creators of the watermark can detect its pattern. Such techniques are being extended to audio files, and form an important part of the SDMI anti-piracy initiative. Encrypted music samples can be played normally by appropriate hardware or software without the listener being aware of alterations to the signal. In theory, the ENCRYPTION cannot be removed without critically damaging the sound quality, but in 2000 researchers into SDMI's watermarking technology proved that this was not the case, a discovery that prompted legal action to prevent them publishing the details of their work.

Stickiness

A highly valued but generally unmeasurable quality of a WEBSITE that keeps its visitors hanging around or encourages them to come back often. Advertisers like stickiness, and what advertisers like, websites try hard to deliver. Quite how to obtain it is not well established as web audiences are notoriously fickle, but some favoured techniques include adding high-level CONTENT and STREAMING MEDIA samples, running competitions and providing extended features such as CHAT or discussion groups.

Streaming media

Audio, video and other CONTENT sequences that can be played as they arrive. Instead of downloading a whole file in one go and then playing it back, streaming media technologies such as those developed by Real Networks and MICROSOFT load the file into a memory buffer. Once a suitably large segment has downloaded (20 seconds worth, say) it starts to play, so viewers or listeners do not have to wait minutes or hours to experience their chosen clip. The makers of such software are adamant that audio and low-resolution video can be streamed efficiently across ordinary 56K dial-up connections to the net, although anyone who has tried the experience will probably think the claims are exaggerated.

There is intense competition in the streaming media market, especially between Real Networks and Microsoft, as more and more companies seek to include television-like features in their ONLINE presence, particularly in news, movie trailers and sports events, usually given away for free. But its evangelists have not done a good job of explaining how people can make money out of it in its current form. Although the technology is leaping ahead, consumers have been reluctant to pay for streamed media and the business case for using it remains far from clear. A 2002 study by IDC, a research company, found that only 13% of European companies use any kind of streaming media, and most of these use it solely for internal communications. But many employees routinely use their company BAND-WIDTH in the pursuit of more creative examples of its use, particularly movie trailers.

As bandwidth increases, the market for such features will surely grow. The increase in BROADBAND connections in people's homes, in particular, is already having an effect. A survey in 2002 by the Cable & Telecommunications Association for Marketing showed that 56% of internet users had listened to music or watched video or news clips online. Some people use streaming media technology to take VIRTUAL tours of houses for sale or to watch demonstrations of everything from fly-fishing to cooking. One hope for the future of streaming media is the forthcoming 3G data technology, which will theoretically allow owners of wireless PDAs and other portable devices to entertain themselves on the move.

Style sheet

A template attached to a web page that describes how it should look. The idea of style sheets was borrowed from early word processors and desktop publishing programs. They are used by designers to apply a consistent look and feel to their sites, by making sure that all headlines appear automatically in the same typefaces and colours, for example, and that all the body text is formatted correctly.

Sun Microsystems

The creator of JAVA and a major player in the development of new internet technologies. Founded by a group of STANFORD UNIVERSITY graduates, Sun's original strength was as a supplier of high-powered workstations built on its own SPARC microprocessors and running the UNIX operating system. But in the 1990s as MICROSOFT WINDOWS and Intel chips (known collectively as Wintel) became increasingly dominant and demand for Sun's products slowed. So the company turned to its talented engineers (including Bill Joy, who rewrote one version of Unix to include support for TCP/IP, among other things) to produce a system that could take the battle back to the Wintel giant. The eventual result was JAVA, a language designed to run on any computer and, by extension, remove people's dependence on WINDOWS and Pentium processors.

Java has been a tremendous success in the programming community but some of Sun's recent high-profile ventures have stalled, including the much vaunted but largely ignored JINI, a system for connecting electronic devices together intelligently. Sun still relies on sales of powerful workstations and SERVERS for the bulk of its revenue, but it is active in its pursuit of revenue from software sources, most notably WEB SERVICES, in which it remains a strong competitor to Microsoft.

Switch

A NETWORK device that moves data traffic between networks. Switches often incorporate some of the functions of a ROUTER but are generally simpler in operation, making decisions only about the next destination of a piece of data rather than planning complex routes. Most networks on the internet use PACKET-SWITCHING to move data around, although some, such as those based on ATM, are in part CIRCUIT-SWITCHED. The type of switch determines many of a network's fundamental characteristics and is the cause of much disagreement between BELLHEADS and NETHEADS.

3G

See page 240.

T1

See T-CARRIER.

T3

See T-CARRIER.

Tag

One of the defining elements of the HTML in which web pages are written. Tags, which are simple text expressions such as ‹FONT› or ‹B›, are used to describe how an element of a web page should look or behave. When a BROWSER loads the page it reads the tags and interprets their instructions accordingly. So a piece of HTML which reads

```
<FONT color=#00AA00 face="arial, helvetica, geneva, sans serif"
size=3><B>Essential Internet</B></FONT>
```

will display the words "Essential Internet" in bold type, the Arial typeface (by first preference) and a fetching shade of green.

The ways in which different browsers interpret tags vary, which is why a page that looks one way in NAVIGATOR may be almost unrecognisable in OPERA. For this and other reasons, many tags (including the <FONT> tag) are facing redundancy in the next version of HTML, which recommends other, more consistent ways of achieving the same effects. (See STYLE SHEET.)

T-carrier

A digital telecommunications system developed by Bell Labs in the 1960s. The most commonly used types of T-carrier connection are T1 and T3 lines. T1 lines, which typically carry data at 1.5MBPS (although speeds of 2mbps are possible), are commonly used by ISPS to supply corporate BANDWIDTH; 45mbps T3 lines are also in widespread use. T-carrier systems can use many kinds of transmission media, including TWISTED PAIR copper, coaxial cable, FIBRE OPTIC and even microwave.

In Europe a roughly parallel E-carrier system is used in which an E1 line, which carries data at 2.048mbps, is equivalent to an American T1. Thereafter the capacity of E-carrier lines is measured in straight multiples of the E1 capacity, so an E2 line has a capacity of 4.096mbps, an E3 6.144mbps, and so on.

TCP

Short for Transmission Control Protocol, software that manages the transfer of data across a NETWORK. TCP handles the complex job of breaking up data into discrete PACKETS, handing them across to another program to deliver them, making sure they have all arrived at the right destination and then reassembling them in the right order. The delivery part of this process is handled by IP, which is why the two are usually bracketed together. (See TCP/IP.)

T

TCP/IP

The software that makes the internet work. It is useful to think of TCP/IP as a kind of electronic removals outfit, which is used to ship data from one physical place to another. The TCP part of the outfit is responsible for the donkey-work of packing everything up individually and labelling it carefully. IP handles the driving of the digital van (or vans, which may all take different routes) and the map-reading. Once everything has arrived at the right address TCP then takes over again, unpacking everything and putting it back in its proper place.

The TCP/IP combination has triumphed over other PROTO-COLS because it works efficiently across disparate networks and many different kinds of computer PLATFORMS. Every major OPERATING SYSTEM now speaks TCP/IP (or can easily be made to); and although some network purists have argued that other alternatives are more robust or more secure, none has been able to find a cheap, fast, easy-to-use way of doing the same jobs.

Telnet

A program used to access a remote computer. Some internet PROTOCOLS such as HTTP allow you to access material on an internet site anonymously, but telnet requires you to LOGIN to a computer with a username and a PASSWORD. Once logged on, various facilities may be provided by the HOST computer, especially E-MAIL, as if you were actually sitting at the computer itself. Most OPERATING SYSTEMS include a telnet client as a standard part of the furniture. Telnet hosts usually run simple terminal-style, text-only interfaces with arcane command line interfaces, often running on top of variants of the UNIX operating system. Some ISPS provide a telnet interface to their mail SERVER, allowing subscribers to access their e-mail from any machine with a telnet program: that is, nearly all of them.

Thin client

T

A stripped-down INFORMATION APPLIANCE used to communicate with a central information source, often used as a synonym for NETWORK COMPUTER. The economic idea behind thin clients is a simple and attractive one: don't pay for features that you don't need. So computers of this kind have no CD-ROM drives, no hard disks and no sound cards. The only software they possess is that needed to connect to the mothership-like SERVER, which provides applications and services as they are required. So far the thinness of such devices has been more or less matched by that of the business being done by their manufacturers.

Thread

The trail of responses to a message posted in a NEWSGROUP or other electronic forum. Following the thread of a discussion is often difficult when there are many different simultaneous conversations going on, so some newsreaders, E-MAIL clients and SERVER-based discussion software provide a visual means of doing so. Threaded discussions usually appear as a series of hierarchically indented responses to the original message.

Thumbnail

A small version of a larger IMAGE. Many WEBSITES, especially those with collections of software screen shots or photographs, use thumbnails to display lots of miniaturised versions of their pictures. This speeds DOWNLOAD times and makes it easier for visitors to browse through the goods on offer before committing to a BANDWIDTH-intensive download.

Tiger team

A team of skilled security experts or HACKERS hired to probe a corporate NETWORK for weaknesses and reveal potentially disastrous security holes. Tiger teams resort to a wide variety of tactics to gain access to computer networks and company resources, some of a distinctly low-tech nature. Rifling through dustbins looking for valuable network information, cajoling PASSWORDS out of employees by phone, stealing security badges and breaking into vaulted SERVER rooms through the roof are all tried and tested techniques. Nevertheless, their technical exploits are legendary, and some commentators have noted that were these made public they would be regarded as some of

T

the most brilliant hacks in the history of computing. Some teams claim 100% success records, neatly demonstrating in the process that the strongest FIREWALLS and ENCRYPTION algorithms are only as tough as the weakest human or physical links.

Tiger teams have existed in the military and commercial worlds for years, being used to test the integrity of everything from banks to nuclear laboratories and weapons plants. Their arrival in the internet world is an inevitable consequence of fears about the security of E-COMMERCE transactions and privacy of customer information, as well as a certain paranoia among DOTCOMS that some of their less enviable business performance figures might be revealed.

> *Secure web servers are the equivalent of heavy armoured cars. The problem is, they are being used to transfer rolls of coins and checks written in crayon by people on park benches to merchants doing business in cardboard boxes from beneath highway bridges. Further, the roads are subject to random detours, anyone with a screwdriver can control the traffic lights, and there are no police.*
> Gene Spafford

TLA

Three-Letter Acronym, such as IMO (in my opinion). (See ACRONYM.)

TLD

Short for top-level domain. A TLD identifies the most general part of the DOMAIN name in an internet address, specifying either what sort of organisation owns that domain name or which country it is registered in. Generic top-level domains (GTLDS) include .com, which identifies a commercial organisa-tion; .edu, which indicates an educational establishment such as a school or university; and .mil, which is reserved for US military organisations. Country-code top-level domains (CCTLDS), such as .uk, .de and .fr, identify the country in which the domain resides.

Controversy surrounds the use and administration of TLDs, which may not always be what they seem. In 2000, a US company called DotTV agreed to pay $50m over 12 years for the right to register internet addresses with the .tv TLD, once the exclusive right of the island of Tuvalu in the south Pacific. Now anyone in the world can register a .tv address, much to the annoyance of internet purists, who insist that TLDs should be maintained for the good of a country's inhabitants. Others say that the deal has improved the economic fortunes of the island, whose government used its first $19m cheque to build roads and improve the education system.

In an attempt to provide a larger number of more meaningful internet addresses, ICANN finally ratified a new set of seven GTLDS - .aero, .biz, .coop, .info, .museum, .name and .pro - which were introduced in 2001 after much heated discussion. But many say that the changes do not go far enough and have advocated the introduction of lots of additional TLDs to make the purpose of particular sites more apparent to users. One suggestion that has been widely applauded is the introduction of a .sucks domain, which could be used by sites that wish to register their displeasure with the behaviour of a company or individual.

In the absence of co-operation from ICANN, support is growing for an alternate system to create and manage TLDs. One such organisation, the Open Root Server Confederation (ORSC), already maintains a network of name servers that allows people to access and register domains such as .web, .gallery, .faq and .xxx. Accessing these new domains generally requires the co-operation of an ISP, however, and as yet few people are even aware that they exist. ICANN outraged supporters of the alternative domain name server system with the introduction of the .biz TLD, which had been up and running on the alternative system since 1996.

Trojan horse

A malicious program or piece of code contained within an apparently harmless program. Trojan horses are often installed inadvertently by people receiving, for example, electronic greet-ings cards by E-MAIL. Some Trojans simply damage data on hard disks or perform various kinds of mischief, such as dis-playing odd messages on the computer screen. More sophisti-cated modern versions can open up a computer to attack from the internet, allowing a CRACKER or SCRIPT KIDDIE with the right software to effectively take over control of the machine. One famous Trojan horse program, Back Orifice, was created by a HACKER group, Cult of the Dead Cow, to illustrate security holes in MICROSOFT OPERATING SYSTEMS. Other common examples are Netbus and SubSeven. Many anti-VIRUS pro-grams now routinely scan for the well-known Trojans, and some personal FIREWALLS prevent them from advertising their presence to potential intruders.

Trusted third party

An organisation entrusted with the keeping of cryptographic keys. The apparent idea behind the appointment of trusted third parties (TTPs) is that by holding a copy of someone's public key they can provide independent confirmation of that person's identity to other parties in an E-COMMERCE deal. This is in itself not a bad idea, but governments are also keen to use TTP schemes to keep tabs on suspected criminals who are using strong cryptography. This process may or may not require a warrant, but recent amendments to legislation in many coun-tries now make it much easier to do.

Proposed TTP schemes all suffer from major flaws, which render them unusable in practical ways. The most obvious is that the sorts of people governments claim to be targeting with their proposals are unlikely to co-operate with authorities and turn over copies of their PRIVATE KEYS.

Supporters of cryptography point out that law-abiding citi-zens are at the greatest risk from such KEY ESCROW schemes. In particular, businesses seeking to get involved in e-commerce have had their confidence severely undermined by the looming threat of TTP. Their concerns are many and legitimate. All these schemes are open to abuse by government officials and security organisations, whose records in this area are not unblemished. Moreover, the third parties themselves are almost irresistible targets for malicious CRACKERS, for whom large-scale stores of private keys represent a playground of immense proportions. This inevitably makes TTPs horribly expensive to administer, as they require military-grade security to keep them closed to unauthorised visitors. (See also PUBLIC KEY CRYPTOGRAPHY and REGULATION OF INVESTIGATORY POWERS ACT.)

TTP

Short for TRUSTED THIRD PARTY.

Tunnelling

A technique used to create private NETWORKS on the public systems of the internet. Using tunnelling, companies can build their own VIRTUAL private networks (VPNs) without the need for expensive dedicated systems and LEASED LINES, by encapsulating a separate network PROTOCOL within standard TCP/IP PACKETS. The IETF is considering several proposals for a standard tunnelling protocol, including PPTP (Point-to-Point Tunnelling Protocol) from MICROSOFT and Layer 2 Forwarding from Cisco.

Twisted pair

The pair of copper wires that connect most people to the internet. Despite the invention of many newer and glitzier ways of transmitting data between two points, copper wire remains the cheapest and most convenient to use because it is installed in so many homes as part of the ordinary telephone system. Some new high-speed networks, such as those based on DSL technologies, can run happily across copper.

Typosquatting

The practice of buying up DOMAIN names carefully chosen to look like existing site names. Typosquatters register slight variations of well-known names in the hope that that users will mistype the names of URLs they are intending to visit and find themselves redirected to another site, often one where they will become victims of MOUSETRAPPING. Names like www-msn.com or aoll.com are used to "steal" legitimate traffic from MSN and AOL, passing the hapless and usually ignorant typist on to a series of sites, usually offering adult entertainment or gambling services. Typosquatting can generate revenue in several ways, principally by charging advertisers and clients on a per-visitor basis or for advertisements on PORTAL sites, which often disappear in a blizzard of BROWSER windows and are never seen by visitors.

Despite many efforts to stop typosquatting, most companies still have to rely on expensive litigation against its perpetrators to prevent the use of the domain names they register. Some companies have done a good job of obtaining these names for themselves, either legally or presciently – yahoo.com and yahooo.com are both owned by YAHOO, for example – but less powerful organisations have found that it can be extremely difficult to stop typosquatters unless trademark infringements are involved. John Zuccarini registered dozens of names designed to mimic sites belonging to Yahoo, Dow Jones, Encyclopedia Britannica and JoeCartoon.com among others, earning up to $1m dollars in the process. He was eventually stopped by the US courts, which relieved him of $1.9m in fines. Typosquatting is rare in Europe but widespread in the United States, where specific legislation called the Anti-Cybersquatting Consumer Protection Act has been introduced to prevent it. (See CYBERSQUATTING.)

T

UDDI

Universal Description, Discovery and Integration. UDDI promises to solve one of the biggest problems for businesses: making themselves properly visible to potential business partners on the web. At the same time, it provides tools to help sift useful data about other companies' products and services from the ever increasing mass of data ONLINE. In essence, it is simply a web-based registry in which businesses can list and describe their services on the internet in ways that make them easy to find and use. Using UDDI, a company looking for specific kinds of human-resources management services, for example, could search the registry and find offerings that matched its own technical and logistical criteria. The result of an initiative from IBM, Ariba and MICROSOFT, the UDDI project is now supported by hundreds of companies keen to ensure that their next-generation web offerings, especially WEB SERVICES, are visible to potential customers and interoperable with products from other vendors.

UDRP

Uniform Dispute Resolution Policy, a set of rules for determining who has the right to own a particular DOMAIN name. UDRP was developed by ICANN to help trademark holders protect their intellectual property rights and avoid expensive litigation against CYBERSQUATTERS. It has been criticised by trademark holders for being too narrowly focused and ineffectual, and by others who believe that UDRP gives trademark owners rights that extend beyond the scope of national laws and that it ignores the essentially stateless nature of the internet. ICANN's attempts to impose its dispute-resolution policy on countries administering TLDs have also attracted criticism from those who consider it tantamount to the "hijacking" of international trademark law.

UMTS

Universal Mobile Telecommunications System, a technical specification for high-speed mobile data services (see 3G).

Uniform resource locator

See URL.

Unix

An OPERATING SYSTEM, the inspiration behind much modern software and the code on which the internet was originally built. Unix was invented by Ken Thompson at AT&T's Bell Labs in 1969, and its original purpose was apparently to provide a way for its author to play games on his computer. It quickly turned into an enormously powerful and secure system capable of supporting big networks and now has users ranging from small academic institutions to huge ISPs.

This transformation of Unix can be largely ascribed to its continued development and fine-tuning by many different groups of people. AT&T's decision to release the SOURCE CODE to universities ensured that the system influenced lots of up-and-coming computer scientists and developers, whose freedom to tinker with the innards had both good and bad results. On the positive side, Unix has become a flexible and open development environment in which programmers can create powerful programs that do particular jobs extremely well. The prowess of some Unix tools, such as the EMACS text processor, is legendary. So influential was Unix that some of its elements can even be seen in the design of comparatively trivial operating systems such as MICROSOFT's DOS and WINDOWS.

U

Less positively, Unix has struggled to shake off its HACKER image and is still too difficult for ordinary folk to use in everyday computing. This has not been helped by the fragmentation of the system into competing flavours. Despite efforts by SUN MICROSYSTEMS, SCO (Santa Cruz Operation, a software company) and others to create friendlier versions of Unix that smooth over its many complexities and inconsistencies, the software has not been widely adopted by companies and has lost a great deal of ground to Microsoft's WINDOWS.

A light at the end of the tunnel is LINUX, a cousin of Unix, which has captured the imagination of the business world in a way that mainstream Unix never quite managed. As Sun focuses the bulk of its attention on JAVA, Linux may yet be the software that keeps the Unix spirit alive and in circulation on the internet.

> *If you have any trouble sounding condescending,*
> *find a Unix user to show you how it's done.*
> Scott Adams

Upload

To transfer information from a local computer to a remote one, such as a web SERVER, across a NETWORK or MODEM connection. When transferring files across an internet connection, the file transfer protocol (FTP) is generally used.

URI

Uniform Resource Identifier, a way of locating and finding a specific resource or piece of CONTENT on the internet, such as a page of text, an IMAGE file or a video sequence. There are several types of URI, of which by far the most important is the URL.

URL

Uniform Resource Locator, an internet address that describes the location of a specific site or document, usually on the WORLD WIDE WEB. A complete URL describes both the PROTOCOL used by the site in question (HTTP, FTP, GOPHER and so on) and a DOMAIN name (economist.com, for example). A machine name specifying the actual part of the domain where the document resides, such as www, is usually included (although this is not a necessity and many sites do without it). So the complete URL for *The Economist's* WEBSITE is:

http://www.economist.com

This example is easy for most web users to remember, but most are more complex and would take forever to type even if they were memorable. For the sake of greater simplicity, most URLS are listed without the protocol prefix and all web BROWSERS now assume that unless specified otherwise, they should use the HTTP protocol to download pages from the site to which a URL refers. But other means have been devised to make life easier still for web surfers. The simplest of these are further enhancements to the software browsers, which can now remember all the URLS visited in the recent past and even type them in for you. More ambitious was the REALNAMES project, which attempted to assign a memorable name to a web address rather than an incomprehensible string of characters. But RealNames faltered in the face of relentless indifference from the web's users, who have developed a tolerance (and some say a perverse liking) for the current system. Now resigned to the fact is that the internet is simply too big to provide memorable addresses for all its constituents, they adopt all sorts of ways to get to the URL they need, BOOKMARKS, directories and SEARCH ENGINES being the most common.

Usenet

U

Where NEWSGROUPS live. Usenet is home to over 40,000 of these discussion groups, each dedicated to a specific topic and each containing a bewildering range of conversations. All of human life can be found on Usenet, which attracts and repels potential visitors in more or less equal measure.

Usenet is in effect a vast, distributed BULLETIN BOARD system, running mainly on UNIX machines that communicate with each other through standard internet PROTOCOLS. First devised at the end of the 1970s as a way for computer enthusiasts to share information, Usenet's early growth was completely independent of the WORD WIDE WEB, which it predated by over a decade. In recent years, most of the traffic in the newsgroups has been generated by people with a dial-up internet connection, who regard it as just another internet service. This greatly annoys hardcore Usenetters.

Usenet is probably the largest widely available information source in existence, an extraordinary and daunting resource, but it is in danger of becoming unusable. The volume of traffic generated by its millions of users, now measured in multiple gigabytes every day across all the groups, inevitably includes a high proportion of noise. SPAMMERS proliferate, often posting their messages to hundreds of groups at a time, and the quality of debate is reckoned to have declined dramatically. The second big threat is CENSORSHIP. Although several well-publicised attempts to remove newsgroups from the feeds of some ISPs have failed, others have succeeded because they have been made covertly. Many universities and colleges now routinely ban some newsgroups, and others are sure to follow.

> We've heard that a million monkeys at a million keyboards could produce the Complete Works of Shakespeare; now, thanks to the internet, we know this is not true.
> Robert Wilensky

Uuencode

U A technique for encoding BINARY FILES and messages into a form that can be sent via E-MAIL. Because most e-mail systems cannot handle 8-BIT binary files reliably, ATTACHMENTS must be converted into 7-bit text-only form before sending. Many e-mail programs include uuencode (UUE) capabilities for doing just this. Like so many pieces of internet-related software, UUE began life as a UNIX program but has spread rapidly to all the other major OPERATING SYSTEMS. Some general-purpose COMPRESSION utilities such as Winzip can decode UUE files.

UWB

Short for ultra-wideband, a technology for transmitting large amounts of data wirelessly over short distances. Unlike other wireless technologies such as BLUETOOTH and WI-FI, which block off specific sections of radio spectrum for their own use, UWB broadcasts small PACKETS of data over a wide range of radio frequencies, reassembling them into their original data files at the receiving end. UWB has several advantages over its competitors. It allows data to be transmitted much faster, offering theoretical speeds of up to 100MBPS, nearly ten times faster than Wi-Fi. It also uses less power, making it ideal for use in mobile devices with limited battery life. Its critics, largely composed of telecoms companies, have voiced concerns about interference with other devices that use portions of the radio spectrum, although their complaints have lessened since it became clear that UWB might provide a way to generate money from their expensively acquired radio-spectrum licences. One potential drawback is its short range, limited to about 30 feet, which makes it much less flexible than Wi-Fi for providing ad hoc internet connections through fixed-line networks but ideal for transferring big files between MP3 players and computers, for example. Computer and consumer electronic devices with UWB capability were expected to appear in late 2003.

vBNS

The Very High Speed Backbone Network Service, a high-speed BACKBONE funded by the National Science Foundation that connects American supercomputer centres. VBNS is the successor to DARPANET and NSFNET, two of the original networks on which the internet was based.

VBScript

A program for creating SCRIPTS based on MICROSOFT's Visual Basic programming language. VBSCRIPT is the equivalent of NETSCAPE'S JAVASCRIPT, with one significant difference: Javascript works with Microsoft's BROWSER INTERNET EXPLORER, but VBscript does not work with Netscape's NAVIGATOR. This means that any code written in VBscript cannot be used by a large proportion of the browsing public. For this reason, the use of VBscript has so far been limited to INTRANET-based networks running only Internet Explorer.

Before you become too entranced with gorgeous gadgets and mesmerizing video displays, let me remind you that information is not knowledge, knowledge is not wisdom, and wisdom is not foresight. Each grows out of the other and we need them all.
Arthur C. Clarke

Videoconferencing

Long touted as the miracle technology that would bring people closer together without the need for them to meet physically, videoconferencing has yet to make its mark in most industries. However, despite being hamstrung by BANDWIDTH limitations and cultural obstacles, it is still alive and kicking, albeit somewhat feebly. The internet currently solves very few of its problems, as PACKET-based networks are generally unsuitable for delivering video reliably. STREAMING MEDIA technologies are also unsuitable for live video content. Despite all this, many companies continue to market hardware aimed at the video-conferencing market, and some companies that rely on large numbers of remote workers have invested in dedicated high-speed connections designed for video. Most videoconferencing currently takes place between individuals armed with WEBCAMS.

Viewser

A passive recipient of supposedly interactive CONTENT on WEBSITES, broadly analogous to a chatroom LURKER. Rather than registering for products and services or using the free features, viewsers simply pass by in the hope of finding something that catches their attention. Converting viewsers to users is a big challenge for sites already struggling to maximise the DWELL-TIME of their visitors.

Virtual

Describes something that exists in essence or effect, but not in any physical sense. This hackneyed term is often used to describe electronic phenomena, particularly those relating to a COMMUNITY or other kind of relationship. Virtual girlfriends, virtual worlds, virtual bands, virtual tourists, virtual libraries, virtual postcards and virtual seminars are among its many trite uses on the web. One legitimate use is VIRTUAL MACHINE.

Virtual community

See COMMUNITY.

V

Virtual machine

Software that acts an interpreter for JAVA programs. The virtual machine (or VM) is a critical part of SUN MICROSYSTEMS's strategy to make Java truly portable among different types of computers, because it is the one common factor across all PLAT-FORMS. Rather than having to understand the specifics of every kind of computer processor, a programmer writes just one version of a program, which is compiled into bytecode. This code is then fed to the virtual machine, which translates its instructions into terms the processor understands.

VMS are available for most types of processor and OPERATING SYSTEM combinations, theoretically enabling a Java program to run as advertised on most of the world's new computers. One problem with all of them is that the process of turning bytecode into native processor instructions is extremely labour-intensive. Much of the criticism of Java's sluggish performance on anything but the fastest computers can be attributed to poorly implemented VMS, but this situation is improving rapidly as computers get more powerful.

VMS have caused friction in the high-tech world, especially between Sun and MICROSOFT. Sun took legal action against Microsoft to try to force it to distribute a fully compatible version of the Java VM with the WINDOWS operating system, claiming that Microsoft's own implementation was flawed and represented a cynical attempt to kill the market for Java applications and control its distribution points. A judge upheld its action in late 2002.

Virus

A self-replicating piece of software designed to cause damage to computers or inconvenience to their users. Historically transmitted by floppy disks, the internet has greatly increased the threat posed by viruses as it provides a much-improved distribution NETWORK for infected files. Some imaginative virus writers have harnessed the internet features of business software to create especially awkward and intrusive programs.

The first widespread example was the Melissa virus, which achieved worldwide fame in early 1999 when it forced several companies, including MICROSOFT, to shut down their E-MAIL networks. Unlike many other types of virus, Melissa does not destroy data on a computer's hard disk; instead, it infects Microsoft Word documents with a macro written in Microsoft's Visual Basic language. When a curious recipient opens an infected document which arrives as an e-mail ATTACHMENT, the virus copies itself rapidly by hijacking the local Microsoft Outlook-based e-mail system and mailing itself to the first 50 entries it finds in the address book. What starts as a small ripple of outgoing messages quickly becomes an overwhelming flood, severely overloading mail SERVERS and, if traffic is heavy enough, causing them to fail.

Melissa's fame stemmed in part from prurient interest from newspapers and magazines, intrigued by the list of pornographic WEBSITES contained in the infected Word document. Less attention has been paid to the fact that anyone with an up-to-date copy of Microsoft Office (many tens of millions of people) and a modicum of programming talent can write similar viruses without any need for advanced development tools. They have inevitably done so. As many as 1 in 200 emails were infected with a virus of some kind in 2002, twice as many as in the preceding year. Melissa has inspired hundreds of more dangerous macro-based viruses, which have caused much trouble to individuals and businesses alike. In 2000, I Love You, a variation on the Melissa theme, destroyed music and graphics files on hard disks. A rash of other such viruses appeared shortly afterwards, most aiming to exploit security holes in the WINDOWS OPERATING SYSTEM in general and Microsoft Outlook in particular. Other examples include Klez, which spoofs e-mail addresses and is thus hard to trace, and Code Red, which attacked many thousands of web servers in 2001, causing widespread chaos.

Many companies now produce anti-virus software and most new PCs are sold with some sort of virus protection installed, but virus writers work hard to keep one step ahead. Virus protection software is well developed and most commercial products include databases of thousands of virus signatures (small fragments of code that uniquely identify each infective agent) which are checked against incoming files. But new viruses spread so quickly that it is difficult to keep these databases current. By the time a PC is up and running, many new viruses may already be active and widespread on the internet. The burden of responsibility for updating the software inevitably lies with the users, who do not always understand the need for rigorous downloading of updates and may leave their machines open to attack. In any case, the damage may be done long before the anti-virus companies are notified of a new threat. Many virus writers routinely build countermeasures into their creations, some of which can detect and disable anti-virus software before it has a chance to do its work.

> *I think computer viruses should count as life. I think it says something about human nature that the only form of life we have created so far is purely destructive. We've created life in our own image.*
> Stephen Hawking

VISP

Virtual Internet Service Provider, a company that resells the services of a "real" ISP under its own brand, negating the need for its own expensive equipment and fast connections to the wider internet. VISPs typically offer the same services as conventional ISPs, such as E-MAIL and web hosting, passing on a percentage of their revenue to the company actually providing the service. Many well-known companies all over the world have become VISPs, including banks, publishers and supermarket chains, using the strength of their brands and customer relationships to build new revenue sources.

VM

V   See VIRTUAL MACHINE.

Voice portal

A PORTAL system that lets people navigate the web by using their voices rather than their BROWSERS. Voice portals use speech-recognition technology to decipher verbal requests for information, and thus have the potential to provide access to the web's vast store of information without the need for anything more technically sophisticated than a telephone. Despite this promise, the enduringly primitive nature of speech-recognition technology is slowing development of voice portals, and most experts agree that it will be many years before they are widely used for anything except the most basic call-centre functions. The latest examples are based on VoiceXML, a variant of the widespread XML standard for exchanging data.

VOIP

Voice Over IP (see INTERNET TELEPHONY).

Vortal

A variation on the popular PORTAL theme, in which a WEBSITE provides access to information related to a specific industry or area of interest. Vortals are springing up in many guises and are widely expected to be hugely profitable. Many adopt an INFO-MEDIARY role, bringing buyers and sellers with shared interests together in a single, manageable place.

VPN

Virtual Private Network. VPNs help solve an expensive problem for companies that want to set up their own private data networks. Instead of relying on costly LEASED LINES to build their infrastructure, they use special ENCRYPTION protocols in conjunction with TUNNELLING protocols such as PPTP to broadcast data across public communications channels such as the internet. VPNs are now widely used by companies with lots of remote workers, who need to give employees secure access to data on corporate LANS across normal dial-up or BROADBAND connections.

VRML

Virtual Reality Modelling Language, originally created by Silicon Graphics to describe three-dimensional environments on the web. Like HTML, VRML (pronounced "vur-mal") code is interpreted by the BROWSER (or, often, a specialised plug-in) and turned into a visual scene. The latest version of this 3D technology, called VRML 97, includes sophisticated features such as animation and sound, aimed at aiding the creation of immersive environments in which people can interact and communicate easily. Despite this, few websites use it. The web is odd enough already, it seems, without subjecting people to ever more warped views of it.

V.90

The latest in the V series of MODEM standards. V.90 modems can theoretically transmit data downstream (that is, from a remote machine to the one in which the modem is installed) at 56KBPS. What sets them apart from other modems is that downstream data does not need to be modulated; it is instead passed as a bitstream encoded to use nearly all of a typical ISP's 64K digital line capacity.

W3C

The World Wide Web Consortium, a group devoted to the shep-herding of new technical standards for the web. Based at the Massachusetts Institute of Technology (MIT) and headed by Tim Berners-Lee (the inventor of HTML and HTTP, and thus of the web itself), the W3C oversees the development of exten-sions and additions to the underlying languages and technolo-gies currently propping up the web. A good example of what happens when academics are let loose with great technology is its WEBSITE, at www.w3.org.

WAP

Wireless Application Protocol, a set of specifications that de-scribes how portable wireless devices such as phones and PDAS should access the internet and communicate with each other. WAP was the first credible attempt to create standards for net access by such devices. The first WAP phones were launched with great fanfares in Europe in early 2000, offering access to basic news and other information. Many more advanced WAP services followed, characterised largely by the indifference of users towards them.

WAP uses its own local communications mechanisms but is designed to work closely with existing internet standards, speaking fluently to web transport PROTOCOLS such as HTTP and TCP/IP and reading many kinds of web CONTENT. WML, a language related to HTML that is designed for handheld wireless devices, makes the job of creating WAP-compatible versions of websites a comparatively easy one, but the limitations of the wireless technology and the physical shortcomings of the devices make it hard to replicate the advanced features of modern websites. In the short term, high-BANDWIDTH content such as video will be beyond WAP's reach, although the advent of 3G networks may eventually make access to it possible. But personal banking, games, timetables, cinema and restaurant bookings and so on are all within WAP's reach.

Despite a level of hype not seen since the early days of the web, few of the services on offer so far have proved to be useful, and studies show that as little as 3% of owners of WAP-enabled phones actually make use of them. This has led many one-time supporters of the technology to become its harshest critics. But much of their criticism is based on a misguided belief that high-speed services such as GPRS and UMTS are replacements for WAP, rather than complementary carriers for WAP-based content. It is true that WAP is currently slow and difficult to use, but its usefulness will become more apparent as bandwidth increases and the usability of mobile devices improves. Version 2 of the WAP specification was ratified in 2001 and is in use on most modern mobile phone handsets.

Warchalking

The practice of drawing a chalk symbol on a wall to mark the presence of a wireless networking NODE, usually one based on WI-FI. Anyone seeing such a symbol can fire up their laptop or PDA in the hope of connecting to the NETWORK via a standard 802.11b-compliant network card, thus obtaining free internet access. The idea of Matt Jones, a British technology expert, warchalking has proved controversial. GEEKS love it because it promises to help them find a fast (and free) internet connection almost anywhere in a city they happen to be. Computer systems administrators are alarmed by it because it potentially exposes them to CRACKERS.

Jones has argued that warchalking actually helps them by drawing attention to the fact that they have a potential problem and has devised three distinct symbols to identify open, closed and unavailable encrypted network nodes. The symbols are accompanied by ID codes which act as PASSWORDS to the node. If the status of the node changes, the chalk symbol can easily be modified. Warchalking iconography has been compared to the hobo sign language that evolved in the United States in the early 20th century; itinerants used it to mark places where free food and shelter were available.

W

Warez

Pirated software, generally distributed on USENET. The warez (pronounced wares) movement perfectly exemplifies the difficulties of regulating internet activity. Every day many hundreds of MEGABYTES of illegally copied software are uploaded to special NEWSGROUPS, from which anyone with an internet account can then DOWNLOAD it. The pirates themselves are anonymous and untraceable, as are the people who download the software. The elaborate copy-protection mechanisms used by the software's creators are no match for experienced warez CRACKERS, who routinely break them in days or even hours. A complex form of NETIQUETTE exists among serious warez traders: anyone regularly downloading software is expected to UPLOAD samples of their own.

WASP

Wireless Application Service Provider. WASPs are an important part of the emerging wireless internet world, as they not only connect users of mobile devices such as phones and PDAs to the internet but also provide applications for them to use. Typical services provided by a WASP might include corporate messaging and scheduling functions for mobile workforces, location-based services (such as tools for finding restaurants, bars or spare parking meters) and broader E-MAIL-based functions. WASPs may have a role to play in the rapidly emerging WI-FI marketplace. (See ASP.)

WDM

Wave-Division Multiplexing (see MULTIPLEXING).

W

Web

The common name for the WORLD WIDE WEB.

Web-Braille

A system enabling blind or partially sighted people to read books and other documents ONLINE. Developed by the US Library of Congress, Web-Braille documents can be read on-site or downloaded for later reading on a special Braille display or embosser attached to the computer. For copyright reasons, Web-Braille publications are currently available only to Americans from the US National Library Service WEBSITE and to eligible overseas citizens, although other countries have announced plans for similar services.

Web bug

A tiny graphic on a web page or in an E-MAIL message designed to track the behaviour and identity of the person reading it. Web bugs are GIF images 1 pixel × 1 pixel in size and are transparent rather than coloured, so they are almost never detected by readers unless they look at the source code that makes up the page or message. Although they sound innocuous, these "invisible dots" are powerful tools for advertisers and WEBSITE owners. This is because the act of viewing them reveals much useful information about the person or computer displaying them, in particular the IP address, the URL of the page that was viewed and the type of BROWSER being used. ADVERTISING networks use them to build a profile of web surfers over time, correlating identity information with lists of sites that they visit, thus helping them to display targeted advertising to web surfers based on their surfing habits.

Web bugs have more intrusive uses, particularly in conjunction with HTML-based e-mail messages. They can tell the sender if and when the message has been read and how often it is forwarded, because each viewing of each bug generates a request to the originating SERVER to send and display the image. They can also be synchronised with COOKIES, allowing websites to discover the e-mail identity of people who visit their sites. One frequently cited example of why this is a bad idea involves visitors to health sites, who may wish to obtain information about

W

serious illnesses without being identified. This aspect of web bug usage upsets privacy campaigners, some of whom have set up websites to expose offenders. Marketers and advertising networks predictably claim that the use of web bugs helps web surfers by making it easier to provide them with useful CONTENT and advertising.

Webcam

A camera hooked up to the WORLD WIDE WEB showing regularly updated pictures of the subject in focus. People have pointed webcams at all sorts of unusual things, including Coke machines, fishtanks, Antarctica, busy traffic routes and, most intriguingly, themselves. Jennifer Ringley, in particular, achieved worldwide fame with her Jennicam, which allows high-tech voyeurs to spy on her going about her unremarkable daily business. The prospect of watching her do this without any clothes on, a rare but nonetheless recorded event, is apparently enticing enough to persuade thousands of people to pay her $90 a year for the privilege. Anyone seeking to duplicate her achievement can buy a suitable camera for around $150, but they should consider that the amount of traffic needed to become profitable is substantial and the market is now flooded with Jennicam lookalikes. This is why just about the only businesses making money from webcams are PORNOGRAPHY sites.

Personal webcams have grown enormously popular in the last few years. Used principally for one-to-one conversations, especially in conjunction with INSTANT MESSAGING software, such cameras are now commonly supported by CHAT rooms and PORTALS run by companies such as YAHOO. They can also be used to create miniature versions of Jennicam-like public sites, although they are usually of limited quality and have BANDWIDTH restrictions attached. Some even double up as low-end digital cameras, adding to their all-round attraction. Manufacturers of personal webcams deny that their principal use is for encounters of the salacious kind, a claim that might be doubted by anyone interested enough to visit one of the many adult chat rooms that proliferate on the web.

W

Webcast

An audio or video broadcast on the web, usually of an event such as a concert, an interview or a sports fixture. Webcasting has become a popular way of increasing the STICKINESS of PORTAL sites, especially those run by ISPS, but it is widely used by traditional media as a way of disseminating material to a global audience. The improvement in STREAMING MEDIA technology has given webcasting some much-needed credibility with consumers, but it needs big increases in BANDWIDTH to become really effective. The use of MULTICASTING technology is becoming more widespread for webcast events on the MBONE. Some people use the term to describe PUSH MEDIA.

Web farm

See SERVER FARM.

Webification

Broadly, the conversion of CONTENT from its original format into a format capable of being displayed on the WORLD WIDE WEB. On a small scale, such a process is a fairly trivial matter; it is comparatively easy for web designers and producers to convert text documents into HTML or scanned images into JPEG and GIF files that can be displayed in web BROWSERS. But owners of large collections of content, especially media companies, have found that the process of transforming their archived materials into a form that can be easily accessed by internet users is a long and expensive one with dubious returns and many pitfalls relating to copyright laws. Visitor expectations of sites such as that run by the BBC are high, but it is unlikely that the full range of text, audio and video material held in the vaults of large organisations will ever see the light of day on the web.

The term is also used to describe the gradual evolution of conventional media into web-like entities composed of easily digested chunks with interactive components. Digital television is the best current example.

Webisode

An episode of a television show or video that is broadcast from a WEBSITE, using web-based technologies such as STREAMING MEDIA. Webisodes are often shortened previews or trailers for programs designed for promotional purposes, and there are several sites devoted exclusively to this phenomenon.

Weblog

A WEBSITE that records and analyses events, usually on a particular subject or containing items with a common theme. Now often known as blogs, in their simplest forms weblogs are not much more than ONLINE diaries of individual activities or ideas, but as their scope broadens they can become considerably more interesting and useful. Good weblogs are detailed and fascinating chronicles of their chosen subject, and typically include articles or analysis written by the website owner, LINKS to and comments on other websites and extensive contributions by the community of visitors to the site.

The weblog phenomenon has grown immensely in the last couple of years, and many companies now offer blogging software and hosting services, often for free. Cynics have suggested that bloggers, as they are known, are at best exhibitionists and at worst vanity publishers with, in the vast majority of cases, nothing remotely useful or interesting to say. This is yet another use of the web for pointless and self-indulgent purposes, they say. Bloggers claim that weblogs are a unique and valuable cultural resource that allows people's ideas and creativity to be expressed for all to see. Whatever the general truth of this, there are some exceptions that seem to have caught the imagination of a great many readers. Some weblogs have become rich and complex resources, and are visited by many thousands of people every day. Others are sufficiently quirky or interesting

W

to attract the attention of more mainstream media. An example is pepysdiary.com, a 21st-century manifestation of Samuel Pepys's diary.

> The newest computer can merely compound, at speed, the oldest problem in the relations between human beings, and in the end the communicator will be confronted with the old problem, of what to say and how to say it.
>
> Edward R. Murrow

Webmaster

Someone who builds, manages or administers a WEBSITE. Webmasters are much in demand, although definitions of what they do vary somewhat. In some organisations a webmaster is broadly the equivalent of a TV or radio producer and has a largely organisational or marketing function, whereas in others he or she may be configuring SERVERS, writing code and designing logos.

Web ring

A system for connecting together websites relating to a common theme or subject of interest. Web rings let visitors jump from one site to the next automatically, eventually ending up back where they started, although they can also choose to visit participating sites randomly. Such rings are popular with web surfers, because unlike SEARCH ENGINES and directories they more or less ensure that the information they contain is relevant to a particular user's sphere of interest. They are also of increasing interest to site owners and advertisers, who see much potential in a self-selecting user base of this kind. The concept was pioneered in 1995 by 17-year-old Sage Weil, who created www.webring.org, once the web's biggest collection of rings. Before vanishing into the noise at YAHOO, webring.org contained over 80,000 individual rings, consisting of over 1.3m individual sites. Web rings exist for every conceivable subject of interest to human beings, and some that many people may find inconceivable too. Someone who manages a web ring is known as a ringmaster.

Web services

A new generation of tools for delivering useful features and functions to WEBSITES and other web-enabled software. Web services fundamentally change the way in which people think about creating new products that run on computers, for both consumers and business users. Instead of having to create a new application from scratch with complicated programming tools and methodologies, web services let people simply subscribe to live services created by other people which they can then "plug in" to their new product. For example, a company that wanted to add an INSTANT MESSAGING feature to its customer-support service might simply subscribe to such a feature created by a third party without having to write a single line of code. Similarly, a company with a useful financial program could simply publish a web services-enabled version in a UDDI directory and generate revenue from subscribers.

By far the most important application of web services, though, is in the integration of programs and data across corporate networks. Because they are based on industry standards such as XML and SOAP, web services can theoretically help programs that know nothing about each other communicate in any number of ways. This solves one of business's oldest problems: how to make their expensive software investments more useful. By allowing a stock-control program to talk to an ordering system, for example, a retailer can manage its business much more efficiently, even if the two programs have different heritages or even run on different OPERATING SYSTEMS. Organisations undergoing mergers or acquisitions can use web services to quickly integrate their systems with those of their new partners, perhaps saving as much as 50% on the costs of integration, according to some estimates. Software vendors can provide their applications ONLINE and use web services to provide automatic, unsupervised upgrades and maintenance.

W

Despite their comparative youth, web services are already cropping up in all sorts of companies. Inevitably, there are arguments about exactly what a web service is and how it should be used, and some are concerned that the principal benefit, compatibility, is already being lost as people fight for their own piece of turf. For once, though, the industry's bigger players seem in broad agreement on how to make web services work. MICROSOFT in particular has entered the fray with its .NET strategy. Its earliest endeavours are centred on its Passport system, which millions of people use to LOGIN and authenticate themselves to websites such as Hotmail and Expedia, although it plans a core set of "foundation" services including instant messaging, E-MAIL, calendars, personal alerts and data storage. More critically, it is creating a base upon which other developers and service providers can build. Early adopters of the .NET program included EBAY, which hopes to provide subsets of its ONLINE AUCTION technology as web services. Predictably, there are worries that Microsoft's ability to disseminate hundreds of millions of copies of .NET-enabled software with the next version of its WINDOWS and Office products will give it an unbreakable hold on the web-services business. But other companies, notably SUN MICROSYSTEMS and IBM, are taking web services equally seriously and are doing plenty of business.

Website

A location on the WORLD WIDE WEB, identified by a web address such as www.economist.com. Websites consist of one or more pages of information and data encoded with HTML to make them readable by a web BROWSER. Some websites consist of a single home page belonging to an individual or a small company; big corporate sites may consist of thousands of pages. However large or small, it is now considered obligatory for businesses to have a website so as to retain credibility with an increasingly web-conscious customer base.

WebTone

Broadly, a Utopian web equivalent of dialtone: continuous, reliable, round-the-clock access to the internet. SUN MICROSYSTEMS's definition specifies that WebTone is always "on", like the telephone; that it provides services to business and consumers via a web-based NETWORK; and that it is available to a wide array of devices such as phones, PDAS and perhaps even kitchen implements, such as microwave ovens, at any time. Of these three stipulations, only the first is currently a reality, and then only to those who subscribe to an always-on service such as ADSL.

WebTV

A service incorporating access to both television and the internet. Founded by three ex-Apple employees and now owned by MICROSOFT, WebTV was the first company to try to provide these two seemingly incompatible services in one place. It uses a special set-top box (made by licensees such as Philips and Sony) to integrate the functions of an existing television set and a dial-up internet connection, and can even display both at the same time. Microsoft now claims 1m subscribers in the United States, but growth has been much slower than anticipated thanks to the inherent dissonance between television and the web. (See also CONVERGENCE.)

Web year

An expression coined in the mid-1990s to describe the apparent compression of time in the internet world; that is, the length of time it takes internet technologies to evolve to the same extent that other technologies might evolve in a calendar year. Tim Berners-Lee, creator of the WORLD WIDE WEB, once estimated a web year to be about three months in the real world. The expression has lost favour with those who deplore the bureaucracy and legal barriers that now stand in the way of developments. No longer,

W

they say, is it possible for people simply to write code and release products on a whim, and web years may now be even longer than real ones. (See INTERNET TIME.)

Well

Short for Whole Earth 'Lectronic Link. The Well was one of the first VIRTUAL communities, and it has built up a mythology of its own since its inception as a mutual support system for hippie commune founders. It is particularly noted for the quality of its debate and discussion, although its loftiness – said by some to be elitism in action – is not easily digested by everyone. Its value to the wider internet COMMUNITY is now mostly symbolic, although several members of the original Well community maintain a high profile in net cultural circles.

WEP

Wired Equivalent Privacy, a PROTOCOL designed to secure communications across WI-FI network connections. WEP uses advanced ENCRYPTION techniques to render such communications safe from intrusion by CRACKERS and other mischief makers, but its effectiveness has been called into question by several researchers. One group at the University of California, Berkeley, discovered major security flaws in WEP that might leave companies using Wi-Fi open to attack. A bigger problem is that most users of Wi-Fi equipment, especially domestic users, install and use it without even switching WEP protection on, much to the delight of DRIVE-BY HACKERS.

W   Whois

A program that tells you the owner of any second-level DOMAIN name. Whois programs run either on a web SERVER or from a local machine and provide a quick way of finding out how to contact the owners of a WEBSITE. Commercial organisations that register domain names provide whois GATEWAYS to determine whether or not a domain is still available for sale.

Wi-Fi

Wireless Fidelity, a wireless networking technology based on the IEEE 802.11b standard. Such terse descriptions do little to illustrate the explosion in interest in Wi-Fi as a way of accessing company NETWORKS and the wider internet. Wi-Fi lets users of portable devices such as laptops and PDAS connect to network resources without the need for cables, by means of a simple and cheap card that plugs into a slot on the device. Once a connection has been established to a base station on the main network, users can send and receive data at very high speeds over distances of several hundred feet, unencumbered by inconveniences such as walls or ceilings. This has made Wi-Fi popular with home users and businesses alike. The former can sit in the garden surfing the web and checking E-MAIL, and the latter can work anywhere within an office building without the need to be physically connected to a SERVER.

Wi-Fi is cheap and easy for consumers and businesses to set up, and as such represents a short-term threat to subscription-based high-speed data services such as GPRS and 3G. Armed with a suitably equipped laptop or PDA, anyone can walk into a coffee shop or office with a Wi-Fi node and connect to the internet, often for free, without the need to buy expensive new hardware or pay monthly subscriptions to telecoms companies. It also allows closely located people to share internet connections; for example, one household in a street might subscribe to a fast DSL connection from a local ISP and share it with its Wi-Fi-equipped neighbours. One well-known chain of coffee shops has installed Wi-Fi nodes in thousands of its outlets in the United States, and is extending trials in Europe. Many other organisations are busily setting up wireless hotspots at railway stations and airports throughout Europe, hoping to generate substantial revenues from itinerant business users tired of relying on slow, expensive MODEM connections. A new generation of wireless ISPs is emerging, providing branded access to

W

Wi-Fi services in hotels and other places where people might find themselves away from home with their laptop.

Analysts such as Cahners In-Stat expect the Wi-Fi market to grow to over $5 billion by 2005 even in the face of rapidly falling hardware prices (a simple installation can cost well under $200), with corresponding effects elsewhere in the digital economy. Some have noted that it makes home BROADBAND connections much more appealing, for example, because consumers can share them with other family members and be unconstrained by the location of the primary home PC.

Windows

The world's most widely used software. MICROSOFT's Windows started life in the mid-1980s as an unpromising competitor to Apple's Macintosh OPERATING SYSTEM. Designed principally as a glamorous front-end for Microsoft's lucrative MS-DOS, Windows failed to catch on until its third iteration appeared in 1990. A major cosmetic overhaul and some internal wizardry, which made it easier to install and configure, helped boost its popularity, but the real selling point was the huge amount of third-party software that Microsoft had persuaded people to write. The industry quickly adopted Windows 3.0 and its successor 3.1 as the new standard on which software was constructed, killing off IBM's competing OS/2 and severely damaging the MacOS in the process.

With no serious competition, Windows has grown ever stronger. Later versions, Windows 95 and Windows 98, proved to be easier and safer to use than their predecessors (although still fundamentally flawed, according to many critics). Nearly all commercial software is now written for the Windows PLATFORM. The biggest strides forward have been made in internet connectivity, which has been included in various forms since 1995. In particular, the addition of the INTERNET EXPLORER BROWSER to the standard Windows package has dramatically altered the internet landscape. With this unmatchable distribution mechanism, Microsoft has wrested the lion's share of the browser market from NETSCAPE. Such dominance of the browser market and Windows' power to exclude competitors from the marketplace led to the high-profile antitrust case brought by the US government against the company in 1999, followed by dozens of civil suits from competitors and American states.

Windows itself is still mutating rapidly and is gradually spreading to every device capable of hosting an operating system, whether it needs one or not. Windows XP, the latest version for desktop and laptop computers, includes many advanced features for internet users and built-in support for everything from BLUETOOTH devices to digital cameras. Various other flavours exist for the SERVER market, and these are slowly replacing Windows NT and Windows 2000 as the operating systems of choice for heavyweight commercial applications and web servers. A cut-down version, Windows CE, is widely used in PDAs, and new versions are planned for set-top boxes, smart cards and eventually even fridges and cookers, thus fulfilling Bill Gates's "Windows Everywhere" promise from the early 1990s.

The only thing that I'd rather own than Windows is English,
because then I could charge you two hundred and forty-nine dollars
for the right to speak it.
Scott McNealy

WMA

Windows Media Audio, MICROSOFT's answer to the dominance of the popular MP3 audio format. Microsoft says that WMA and its digital video cousin, WMV, are more efficient mechanisms for distributing digital content than the decade-old variants based on MPEG technology; its files are smaller, making them quicker to send and receive across the internet, and many claims have been made for their superior quality. None of this has impressed the world's amateur media enthusiasts, who continue to record and distribute MP3 files by the million in preference to anything that Microsoft has to offer.

W

WML

Wireless Mark-up Language, which allows text-based web information to be displayed on wireless devices such as mobile phones and PDAS. WML uses existing protocols such as GSM as its transport mechanism and is part of the WAP specification.

> *Every now and then, a technology or an idea comes along that is so profound, so powerful, so universal that its impact changes everything. The printing press. The incandescent light. The automobile. Manned flight. It doesn't happen often, but when it does, the world is changed forever.*
> Lou Gerstner, chairman of IBM

World Wide Web

The hypermedia technology that makes the internet usable by mere humans. The World Wide Web, or the web as it is now commonly known, was originally designed to help workers at CERN, a European particle physics laboratory near Geneva, share information among themselves using a single, unified interface. Soon the world realised that the web was of great importance not just to high-energy physicists but also to people in almost every other sphere of human activity. The web's subsequent growth can only be described as explosive. In mid-1993, when the first graphical web BROWSER was launched, there were about 150 WEBSITES holding a few thousand web pages. At the beginning of 1995, there were about 10,000 sites, a number that grew to 4.5m by mid-1999. In early 2003 a survey by Netcraft received responses from 35m websites worldwide, and thousands more sites go live every day.

W　　The technology underlying the web has not changed much since Tim Berners-Lee, often described as the father of the web, outlined the first versions of HTML and HTTP, the two fundamental building blocks of web technology. What has changed is people's ability to think of new things to do with it. In conjunction with other tools such as JAVA and DHTML, web pages have evolved from mere repositories for static information into busy, interactive environments where people can shop for gifts, exchange goods and services, watch films, learn French and communicate with friends or strangers. Those who predicted the decline of the web following the DOTCOM debacle are now eating their words; we may not all be using the web to order our groceries, but its momentum has if anything grown rather than declined. It may not yet be the "embodiment of human knowledge" envisaged by Berners-Lee, but at more than 3 billion pages, one for every second person on earth, it is getting there fast.

Worm

A self-replicating program which shares many characteristics of a VIRUS. Worms have become a serious problem in recent years, as CRACKERS and SCRIPT KIDDIES seek new ways to disrupt computers on the internet. Unlike viruses, which generally need a host of some kind such as a word-processing document or an executable program file to reproduce themselves, worms can copy themselves from one computer to the next almost invisibly. Many modern worms have exploited vulnerabilities in popular SERVER software created by MICROSOFT. Their danger lies in their ability to do this extremely quickly; the SQL Slammer worm, which was released in early 2003, flooded thousands of web servers with data within minutes of its release, forcing many companies and organisations to shut down their NETWORKS. Other recent examples include Code Red, which caused similarly widespread chaos in 2001.

The most famous worm in the internet's history was created by Robert Morris, a computer science graduate at Cornell University, in 1988. Although his program was intended to be completely benign, an unfortunate coding error caused it to become destructive and it eventually caused 6,000 machines to crash, at that time about 10% of all the computers on the internet.

W

WSDL

Web Services Description Language, a programming language
designed to help companies describe the WEB SERVICES they
create and to provide a way for other people to access them.
WSDL is closely related to an impressive number of other abbreviated technologies: it is based on XML, is derived from
SOAP and is an important part of UDDI.

WWW

Short for WORLD WIDE WEB.

Xanadu

An ambitious electronic data storage and retrieval system devised by Theodore Nelson in the 1960s and named after the mythical place in Coleridge's poem "Kubla Khan". Nelson is credited with coining the term HYPERTEXT to help describe his system, which he portrayed as "a universal instantaneous hypertext publishing network". Many of Xanadu's proposed features precede similar ones found in today's WORLD WIDE WEB, although it is a mistake to think of Xanadu as being web-like in any meaningful way; indeed, Nelson has been hypercritical of the web and modern software design generally. Instead, it concentrates on solving the problems of version management and rights management (both serious problems on the web) through the use of reusable but nonetheless COPYRIGHT hypermedia published from a central pool of CONTENT.

Nelson himself described Xanadu as being well known but poorly understood, a situation that was not improved by his tortuous descriptions of his work and his penchant for contrived words such as humber (a contraction of humungous number), xanalogical storage and the DOCUVERSE. No real implementation of Xanadu exists today, despite decades of effort by Nelson to realise his vision, although some of the underlying code was made available to the OPEN SOURCE COMMUNITY in 1999.

X-commerce

A term used to describe any type of commerce carried out electronically, in which "x" denotes the type of commerce in question. The most common varieties of relevance to internet users are E-COMMERCE and M-COMMERCE, although people are contriving all sorts of other values for x; t-commerce, for example, is sometimes used to describe commercial activity conducted via television sets. Visa has used the expression "u-commerce" to describe any transaction conducted via a ubiquitous device such as a mobile phone or a PDA. Some companies refer to themselves simply as x-commerce companies, without any apparent sign of the irony of such nomenclature.

XHTML

Extensible Hypertext Mark-up Language, effectively the latest version of HTML 4.0, the language used to describe web pages, which has been reformulated to include elements of XML. As its name suggests, XHTML's capabilities can be extended with the addition of new TAGS reflecting the use being made of the code, so web authors can customise sites and the way in which their CONTENT is managed without being hampered by the restrictions of plain HTML. XHTML also encourages a more structured way of thinking about content, helping WEBMASTERS to manage large or complex sites more efficiently.

XML

Extensible Mark-up Language, a way of describing and sharing data on NETWORKS. Like its cousin HTML, XML consists of a set of TAGS that describe a chunk of data. The resemblance more or less ends there. XML is designed to describe the CONTENT of a page in terms of the type of data it contains, rather than the way that data should look. So while an HTML tag such as ‹FONT› simply specifies that the following text should be displayed in a particular size and weight, an XML ‹FISH› tag might indicate that the following data describes a particular species of fish.

This characteristic of XML makes it easy for like-minded groups of people to share information, because they need only agree on a set of tags that meets their particular needs. Thus a global consortium of fishmongers might agree on a standard way of describing information about fish catches – the number landed, the average size of the fish, the different species – and use their own XML tags to actually store the data. An intelligent SEARCH ENGINE could then look for data types rather than just words: all the fishmongers who landed haddock of a particular size on a specified date, rather than just any WEBSITE containing the word haddock.

After a slow start, XML is now in widespread use. MICROSOFT's Channel Definition Format, for example, which describes how broadcast-like data channels should be interpreted by BROWSERS, is based on XML, and the language is being used to format everything from news feeds to search-engine results. All sorts of variants are appearing that are being used to solve a wide variety of problems: AIXML to create intelligent web BOTS, for example, and VoiceXML to create voice-enabled applications such as VOICE PORTALS and recognition systems. But the language's real importance in the future is in BUSINESS-TO-BUSINESS E-COMMERCE, where its ability to help companies share information will make the automation of many business processes much easier. Many of the web's most interesting developments such as WEB SERVICES are based on XML, and it is establishing itself in businesses and other organisations as they become ever keener to maximise the efficiency of their ONLINE operations.

XSL

Extensible Style-sheet Language, which tells a BROWSER how XML TAGS should look. XSL-based STYLE SHEETS are associated with specific XML documents to control the formatting of user-defined tags. XSL can specify where on a page XML data should be displayed and what sort of font it should use, for example. It is based on several other style sheet standards, including the W3C's CSS.

Yahoo

A searchable directory of WEBSITES, founded by David Filo and
Jerry Yang, two STANFORD UNIVERSITY graduates, in 1994. It
started life as a simple collection of their own BOOKMARKS, and
rapidly grew to become the massive resource it is today, with
hundreds of thousands of sites and millions of pages. Yahoo or-
ganises the web by category rather than search KEYWORD, using
teams of editors to sift through sites and put them in the appropriate boxes. The success of its approach is reflected in the phe-
nomenal traffic it generates. At the end of 2001 Yahoo's website
was generating over 1.3 billion page views every day, which is
one of the reasons it continues to be so attractive to advertisers.
Much of its traffic comes from people attracted by the PORTAL
facilities on offer, including CHAT, E-MAIL and AUCTIONS.

In contrast to many internet companies, Yahoo consistently
made a profit during the early years of the DOTCOM boom. But
in 2001 it suffered from the decline in ADVERTISING markets,
losing $93m and some of its lustre at the same time. Its multi-
tude of ADVERTISING and promotional deals has generated a
revenue stream that competitors such as Excite and LYCOS
have struggled to match. The company has been highly acquisi-
tive in recent years, successfully completing the purchase of the
Geocities ONLINE COMMUNITY and pursuing a buy-out of
broadcast.com, an aggregator of CONTENT based on STREAM-
ING MEDIA. More recently it bought Inktomi, one of the first
search-engine companies.

Filo and Yang are also unusual in that they have managed to
retain substantial stakes in the company they founded, and their
combined worth is regularly measured in billions of dollars.
Nevertheless, like all other internet companies Yahoo's value has
fluctuated considerably, and the company reported a flattening
of revenue in 2001 as the advertising market on which its
revenue depends slowed dramatically. Big staff lay-offs were
followed by the departure of CEO Tim Koogle, who was replaced by Terry Semel, a Hollywood veteran. But its cost-reduc-
ing strategy appears to have paid off. In combination with new
revenue sources such as customised and business e-mail, for
which the company now charges, it posted profits again in 2002.

Zip

A popular type of COMPRESSION, used to shrink PC files before transmission across a NETWORK or storage on disk. Many utilities for creating zip files exist, and they are a commonly used format for distributing software on the internet.

Zmodem

An error-correcting file transfer PROTOCOL, once widely used by PC communications software but now consigned to a life of leisure on the world's BULLETIN BOARD systems. Zmodem is considerably more efficient than its cousins Xmodem and Ymodem.

1.0

Pronounced "one point oh", a term denoting the first version or iteration of something, usually a piece of software but often extended to websites, new hardware devices and even companies or strategies.

The wireless telegraph is not difficult to understand. The ordinary telegraph is like a very long cat. You pull the tail in New York, and it meows in Los Angeles. The wireless is the same, only without the cat.
Albert Einstein

3G

Abbreviation for third-generation networks, a generic term for a forthcoming generation of mobile wireless communications systems. 3G networks promise to improve on existing wireless data communications by massively increasing the BAND-WIDTH available to small devices such as telephones and PDAS from the typical 9,600BPS in use today to 2MBPS, faster than the majority of today's internet connections. At such speeds, it will be possible to DOWNLOAD all sorts of things to mobile devices, including video, music and searchable, indexed text, thus transforming them from the comparatively dumb terminals they are today into potentially intelligent INFORMATION APPLIANCES.

Optimistic estimates of 3G rollout suggest that the new networks will replace existing wireless networks by around 2005. But so far the road to 3G has been a tortuous one, involving stops at intermediate technologies such as GPRS (general packet radio service) along the way and some real difficulties in persuading consumers and businesses that they need high-speed wireless services at all. The biggest barrier for most would-be 3G operators is the cost of developing and implementing the technology, which requires investment in widescale networks of new masts from which to broadcast the data. This will be a massive expense on top of the huge amounts that operators have already paid governments all over the world for their licences to operate 3G services. Cost is also a big issue for 3G users, who will have to pay for expensive new handsets and higher service rates.

Enthusiasm for 3G services generally has been so limited that some analysts, notably Datamonitor, have suggested that it may be more cost-effective for telecoms operators to shelve their plans altogether. This suggestion has been taken seriously in countries such as Sweden, where some operators have abandoned plans to introduce 3G for the foreseeable future. The prospects for 3G services have not been helped by the failure of the latest high-speed services to take off in Japan, where DoCoMo, the world's second largest mobile phone company and operator of the phenomenally successful I-MODE service, had persuaded only 4% of its user base to upgrade in January 2003.

> *How many webmasters does it take*
> *to change a lightbulb?*
> *404 (Not found).*

404 Not Found

An error message generated by a WEBSITE. 404 errors occur when a URL or a LINK from another web page is either wrong or has changed for some reason, and the page cannot then be found. The number itself is an HTTP status code, established by Tim Berners-Lee as part of the original HTTP specification. The 404 Not Found message has a special place in the hearts of web users because of its ubiquitous and often unforgiving nature. At its most prosaic, the message simply appears in text form. More imaginative site owners have embellished it to include an animation, a haiku or a philosophical treatise on the meaning of 404: not necessarily what you were looking for, but sometimes amusing nonetheless. Much to the consternation of web GEEKS everywhere, the future of 404 messages was threatened by the arrival of version 5 of Internet Explorer, which hijacked 404 pages and replaced them with its own useful but rather soulless advice. The latest version, Internet Explorer 6, performs the same trick, but this has not put off creative HACKERS who have

simply used Microsoft's prosaic alternative as a platform for
parody and irreverence.

802.11

A collection of specifications for connecting electronic devices
together wirelessly, particularly in LOCAL AREA NETWORKS
(LANs). This unfriendly term, an inevitable result of its origin
within the Institute of Electrical and Electronic Engineers, en-
compasses a family of technologies rapidly becoming accepted
as the best and cheapest way of networking computers without
the need for cables. The 802.11b standard in particular, better
known as WI-FI, has emerged as a popular technology within
homes and offices for connecting mobile devices such as
laptops and PDAs at high speeds over relatively short distances.
The latest incarnation, known as 802.11g, allows data to be
transferred between such devices at up to 54MBPS, nearly 1,000
times as fast as a typical dial-up MODEM.

Appendices

1 **A brief history of the internet**

Before the beginning

1858 The first telegraph cable is laid across the Atlantic between Valentia Harbour in Ireland and Trinity Bay in Newfoundland. The first communication across the cable is sent in August. A second cable is laid in 1866, allowing Queen Victoria and President Johnson to exchange messages. The first Royal telegraph message reads: "The Queen congratulates the President on the successful completion of an undertaking which she hopes may serve as an additional bond of Union between the United States and England."

1943 Alan Turing builds Colossus, the machine used to decipher German communications in the second world war, and one of the world's earliest programmable electronic computers.

1945 In a highly prescient article in the *The Atlantic Monthly*, entitled "As We May Think", Vannevar Bush, the first director of what eventually became the National Science Foundation, describes a machine he calls a memex. The microfilm-based memex would enable the user to link related pieces of information together for rapid retrieval. Almost 50 years before the web, the ideas were there.

1948 Claude Shannon, a mathematician at AT&T's Bell Labs, publishes *A Mathematical Theory of Communication*. His theory enables the calculation of the information-carrying capacity of any channel. Shannon's work, which included the introduction of the word "bit" to describe a piece of binary information, underpins all information theory and all modern communications systems, including the internet.

1958 Responding to the launch of Sputnik, the first Earth-orbiting satellite, President Dwight D. Eisenhower creates the Advanced Research Projects Agency (ARPA) to oversee the development of space and military programs. ARPA's brief includes the creation of new computer and communications systems.

1960 J.C.R. Licklider, a researcher at the Massachusetts Institute of Technology (MIT), publishes "Man-Computer Symbiosis", a paper describing ways in which men and machines might co-operate to make decisions and save valuable time in solving problems.

1961 Leonard Kleinrock, a researcher at MIT, publishes the first paper on packet-switching theory, alerting ARPA scientists to the possibility of treating communications links in terms of passing active packages of information around rather than shovelling them through fixed circuits.

1962 Paul Baran, a computer scientist at the Rand Corporation working on the survivability of communications networks under nuclear attack, describes a distributed computer network for the first time. His model, in which a network is built of a number of nodes, was revolutionary in its use of messages split up into blocks, each taking a different path to its final destination: in essence, a packet-based network.

1965 The word "packet" is used for the first time by Donald Davies, a British reseacher at the National Physical Laboratory (NPL), to describe a way of breaking up messages for transmission across new kinds of networks. Davies's work mirrored closely that of Paul Baran, although it focused on public communications networks rather military ones.

ARPA sponsors its first study of co-operatively networked computers, involving the connection of two machines in California and Massachusetts across a dedicated 2,000 bits per second telephone link.

Ted Nelson coins the term "hypertext".

1967 Larry Roberts, a computer scientist at ARPA, proposes a design for a fast, decentralised network built on dial-up telephone lines. In London, Donald Davies builds the National Physical Laboratory Data Network, an early experiment in packet-switching.

At the Association for Computing Machinery Symposium in October, Roberts presents the first paper on the proposed design for the "ARPA net" network.

Representatives of the three bodies researching packet networks (ARPA, RAND and NPL) meet for the first time.

1968 The contract to build the Interface Message Processors (IMPS) at at the core of the experimental ARPA network is awarded to Bolt, Beranek and Newman (BBN), a technical consulting firm in Cambridge, Massachusetts.

The Arpanet age

1969 The first four ARPA network hosts, located at Stanford University, the University of California at Los Angeles (UCLA), the University of California at Santa Barbara and the University of Utah, are connected across 50kbps lines provided by AT&T. The first recorded network crash occurs in October, as the letter G of LOGIN is entered when trying to access the Stanford computer from UCLA.

At Bell Labs, Ken Thompson and Dennis Ritchie invent Unix, the operating system destined to become the bedrock of the internet.

Compuserve starts life as a computer time-sharing service at an American insurance company.

Telnet, a program allowing people to log into and control computers from a remote terminal, is born.

1970 AlohaNet, a system for exchanging data between computers on four Hawaiian islands, is created by Norman Abramson.

1972 BBN's Ray Tomlinson writes the first e-mail program, and establishes the use of the @ sign in e-mail addresses. In July, Larry Roberts creates the first program which can list, forward and reply to messages – the first real e-mail client.

The first public demonstration of the ARPA network is held at the International Conference on Computer Communications in Washington's Hilton Hotel; 40 machines take part.

1973 The ARPA network goes global, connecting machines in the United States to hosts at University College in London and The Royal Radar Establishment in Norway.

At Harvard, a PhD student, Bob Metcalfe, outlines the idea for Ethernet, a new and fast way of networking computers. His invention is tested for the first time on computers at Xerox PARC in Palo Alto, California.

1974 BBN launches Telenet, the first commercial packet-switched networking service. Vint Cerf and Bob Kahn publish the first specifications for their Transmission Control Protocol (TCP), a new way of managing the transmission of data packets across networks.

1975 Microsoft is founded by Bill Gates and Paul Allen to produce software for microcomputers. TCP's capabilities are tested across satellite links from the United States to Hawaii and the UK. The first mailing list, MsgGroup, is born on Arpanet.

1976 Queen Elizabeth II sends the first royal e-mail from the Royal Signals and Radar Establishment at Malvern, UK.

At Bell Labs, researchers develop the Unix-to-Unix Copy program, which later forms the basis of Usenet.

Whitfield Diffie, a cryptographer and privacy advocate, and Martin Hellman, an electrical engineer, invent public-key cryptography.

1977 Three researchers at MIT, Ron Rivest, Adi Shamir and Len Adleman, invent the RSA algorithm (the abbreviation is based on their names), a public key method for encrypting messages.

1978 The TCP protocol is split into two parts, creating the new Internet Protocol (IP). Networks that make use of this protocol become known as internets; the aggregate of these internets constitutes the wider internet.

1979 Usenet is founded by Tom Truscott and Jim Ellis at Duke University and Steve Bellovin at the University of North Carolina.

Richard Bartle and Roy Trubshaw, of the University of Essex in England, create the first multiuser dungeon software for role-playing games.

1981 IBM launches the first personal computer (PC), reshaping the computing landscape. It is equipped with Microsoft's DOS operating system, the source of the company's early fortunes.

The National Science Foundation (NSF) builds the CSNET backbone, a new network for use by academics and researchers with no access to Arpanet.

The internet age

1982 EUNet, the European Unix Network, is created to provide e-mail and Usenet services between the UK, Denmark, Sweden and the Netherlands.

The Domain Name System (DNS) is established at the University of Wisconsin, bringing order to the previously chaotic addressing system on electronic networks. JANET, the UK's Joint Academic Network, is established.

Widespread development of PC-based local area networks begins.

The first smiley is used at Carnegie Mellon University. :-)

1983 TCP/IP is officially adopted by ARPA and the US Department of Defense as the core internet protocol.

1984 The term "cyberspace" first appears in William Gibson's novel *Neuromancer*.

The Well, one of the net's most famous communities, is started by Stewart Brand, Larry Brilliant and others. It quickly becomes an important forum for electronic discussion.

The first Macintosh computer appears.

1985 The NSF builds on its CSNET idea with the creation of NSFNET, a new high-speed backbone connecting five supercomputing centres in the United States. The arrival of NSFNET triggers an explosion of smaller networks.

America Online (AOL) begins life as Quantum Computer Services.

1986 The Internet Engineering Task Force (IETF) is created to co-ordinate technical developments on Arpanet and key internet gateway systems.

NNTP, the Network News Transport Protocol, arrives and begins to replace UUCP on Usenet as the standard way of exchanging newsgroup data.

1987 UUNET, a commercial organisation providing access to

Usenet and other network services, is founded.

Bill Atkinson writes Hypercard for the Apple Macintosh, the first tool for creating mass-market hypertext and hypermedia applications.

1988 Robert Morris, a computer science graduate at Cornell University, releases a self-replicating program on to the internet. This so-called worm eventually brings down 6,000 hosts, 10% of all the machines on the network.

Internet relay chat (IRC) is developed in Finland by Jarkko Oikarinen.

1989 In Germany, the Fraunhofer Institute patents the MP3 music compression algorithm.

The World (world.std.com), the first dial-up Internet Service Provider (ISP), is founded in Massachusetts.

1990 Arpanet officially ceases to be a research tool and becomes just another network.

In July, John Perry Barlow and Mitch Kapor found the Electronic Freedom Foundation (EFF).

1991 A team at CERN, Europe's particle physics laboratory, releases the first text-only "browser" for use with the HTML mark-up language and HTTP protocol that it has developed to allow far-flung researchers to collaborate. Tim Berners-Lee later posts the first public web software on the alt.hypertext newsgroup.

Linus Torvalds, a Finnish student, starts work on writing the operating system that will eventually become Linux.

The first version of Pretty Good Privacy (PGP), a software package that uses the RSA algorithm for encrypting the contents of messages, is released by Phil Zimmerman.

Commercial traffic is permitted to use the NSFNET backbone for the first time. By March, traffic passes 1 trillion bytes and 10 billion packets per month.

Gopher, a program for finding information on the web, is released by the University of Minnesota.

1992 CERN releases its World Wide Web software into the public domain.

The number of internet hosts passes 1m.

The web age

1993 The first graphical browser, Mosaic for X, written by Marc Andreessen, is released by the National Centre for Supercomputing Applications (NCSA). Traffic on the World Wide Web expands by over 300,000%; by contrast, Gopher usage grows at a mere 997%.

InterNIC is created by the National Science Foundation to direct the management of internet registration services.

CERN announces that the web and its supporting technology will be freely available to all.

1994 Marc Andreessen and Jim Clark start Netscape, releasing the first version of the Navigator browser in the autumn. Linus Torvalds unveils version 1.0 of the Linux kernel.

The World Wide Web Consortium is formed to steer the development of web technologies, with Tim Berners-Lee appointed as its director.

Laurence Canter and Martha Siegel, two American lawyers, become the most despised people in internet history after flooding Usenet with advertisements for their green card lottery services, thus becoming the first spammers.

Pizza Hut starts taking orders over the internet. The first internet bank, First Virtual, opens in the United States. Wasting no time, Vladimir Levin, a Russian computer expert, becomes the first internet bank robber, stealing millions of dollars from Citibank.

Traffic on the NSFNET backbone exceeds 10 trillion bytes per month.

1995 The web constitutes the bulk of internet traffic. Sun Microsystems unveils Java. The first version of the RealAudio audio streaming product appears. Compuserve and AOL, hitherto proprietary networks, provide dial-up access to the internet for the first time.

Netscape goes public after only 14 months of existence, offering 5m shares to the public on August 8th at an initial price of $28. Shares close at $58.25, valuing the company at over $2 billion and earning its co-founder, Jim Clark, $663m on the first day of trading. In December the share price hits $170.

Jeff Bezos opens his online bookstore at Amazon.com. The web-based eBay auction house accepts its first bids.

Digital launches its AltaVista search engine, the first serious attempt to index the web.

Microsoft releases Windows 95, the long-awaited upgrade to its popular Windows program. The first version of the company's web browser, Internet Explorer, is released; based on code licensed from Spyglass, it is sold as part of an add-on package for Windows 95.

NSFNET announces that it will no longer provide direct access to its backbone, farming out responsibility for managing access to private companies. Charging for domain names begins, with each costing $50 per year.

Compuserve removes access to 200 pornographic newsgroups after pressure from Bavarian government officials, attracting the ire of free-speech and anti-censorship campaigners.

1996 The browser wars begin in earnest as Microsoft and Netscape each launch the third version of their browser.

Despite widespread opposition the controversial US Communications Decency Act (CDA), designed to control the distribution of indecent material over the internet, becomes law in the United States.

Internet telephony, already well-known to researchers and academics but a new development in the commercial world, comes to the attention of US telecoms companies. The Carriers Telecommunication Association (ACTA) files a petition to the Federal Communications Commission (FCC) seeking to ban IP telephony products, arguing that they should be subject to regulation. The FCC disagrees.

1997 NASA's home page generates 46m hits in one day as people log in to watch the broadcast from the Pathfinder spacecraft on Mars.

.com and .net addresses disappear for several hours as human error at Network Solutions causes the DNS table for .com and .net domains to become corrupted, making millions of systems unreachable.

The DES private key encryption system is broken by the collaborative efforts of thousands of internet users who tested 18 quadrillion possible key combinations. The challenge, set by RSA Data Security, was to decrypt a message which was eventually found to read "Strong cryptography makes the world a safer place".

The Communications Decency Act is overturned by the US Supreme Court, which pronounces it unconstitutional.

Netscape launches version 4 of its browser just ahead of Microsoft. The US Justice Department files its first complaint against Microsoft on the grounds of breaching antitrust regulations with its browser distribution strategy.

1998 Netscape announces that it will give away not only its browser but the browser's source code as well, an unprecedented move by a software company. A separate division, Mozilla.org, is set up to create products based on the open source element of the business.

Network Solutions registers its 2 millionth domain.

The Microsoft antitrust trial begins in October. Originally predicted to last eight weeks, the proceedings continue into 1999 as the scope of the trial expands to cover Microsoft's broader exclusionary practices.

AOL and Netscape announce their intention to merge in a $4.2 billion deal, a move that web purists see as a betrayal of Netscape's ideals. Many Netscape employees resign.

The first portable MP3 players arrive, enabling people to play back pirated digital music. The Secure Digital Music Initiative (SDMI), designed to prevent this kind of music piracy, is announced by a consortium of music and technology companies.

Portals become big business on the web. Major search engines and ISPs re-engineer their sites to add customisation, chat and auction features.

1999   Day traders operating from home PCs seize
opportunities to capitalise on the boom in internet and
other stocks. Charles Schwab, an American stockbroker
specialising in electronic trading, sees its market
capitalisation rise to $25.5 billion at the end of the
financial year, valuing it more highly than many old-
style brokers such as Merrill Lynch.

The Melissa virus, carried in Microsoft Word
documents, attacks e-mail networks all over the world,
replicating itself in enormous numbers and swamping
mail servers.

AOL and Microsoft come to blows over chat
software, as AOL tries to prevent users of Microsoft's
product accessing its huge user base. Microsoft pushes
for open standards in the chat market.

Microsoft's web-based e-mail service, Hotmail, is
cracked, leaving its 40m accounts open to access
without a password.

In November, Judge Thomas Penfield Jackson rules
that Microsoft harmed consumer interests and distorted
competition in internet markets, fuelling speculation
about the future of the company and its strategy.

The number of internet users passes 200m.

2000   AOL announces a $150 billion takeover of entertainment
giant Time Warner, creating the world's biggest media
company and gaining access to over 100m subscribers.

The Iridium global satellite communications network
goes into liquidation after its failure to turn a $5 billion
investment into a viable business. Plans are made to pull
the company's 66 satellites out of orbit.

Some of the world's biggest websites, including
Yahoo, Amazon and eBay, suffer denial-of-service
attacks by malicious hackers, forcing them offline for
several hours and renewing concerns about the security
of internet businesses.

The NASDAQ index, the weathervane for high-tech
companies, reaches 5,000 for the first time as
enthusiasm for the new wave of internet companies
reaches its peak in March. In November, it undergoes its

worst slide in its history, 22.9%, as that enthusiasm evaporates.

The UK's Queen Elizabeth becomes the first royal dotcom millionaire following an investment in Getmapping.com, a site reproducing the Domesday Book with digital aerial photographs.

AT&T's wireless communications division raises $10.6 billion on the first day of public trading of its shares, setting a record for the biggest IPO in American history. The company's valuation hits $70 billion at the end of the day's trading.

Judge Jackson rules that Microsoft broke US antitrust laws, using "technological shackles" to prevent rivals from competing with its Internet Explorer browser, and orders that the company be split into two competing entities. The value of Microsoft shares plummets, causing a new wave of volatility in the valuation of high-tech stocks. Cisco's market capitalisation creeps ahead of Microsoft's, making it the world's most valuable company.

The Regulation of Investigatory Powers Act becomes law in the UK, allowing authorities to eavesdrop anonymously on any electronic conversation and to demand the electronic keys to encrypted messages and documents.

Metallica, a rock band, forces the Napster music distribution network to remove 300,000 users, which it says pirated its music using the MP3 format. An American federal judge rules that MP3.com broke copyright law by collating 45,000 commercial CDs into its database, prompting the site to shut down its popular MyMP3 web-based distribution service. In October, Napster is acquired by German media giant Bertelsmann, once a litigator against the company.

Despite the warnings given by 1999's Melissa virus, the "I Love You" virus causes havoc on computers worldwide, flooding e-mail networks and deleting users' music and graphics files. Microsoft is criticised for security holes in its Outlook e-mail program, said to be responsible for allowing the virus to propagate and destroy information.

President Clinton delivers the first presidential address to be broadcast on the web. In a somewhat grander display of the medium's growing significance, 9m people log on to MSN.com for a webcast concert by Madonna, a popular singer.

As interest in wireless communications technology grows, the UK government auctions off "third-generation" wide-spectrum bandwidth licences to mobile operators, raising £22.5 billion. Germany announces plans to follow suit.

Academics from Princeton University successfully crack the copyright protection developed by the SDMI, raising doubts about its ability to prevent the widespread illicit copying of digital music.

Boo.com, one of Europe's highest-profile online retailers, goes into liquidation after its widely criticised marketing strategy and complex design fail to create a profitable market for its sportswear and fashion goods. Valuations of European e-commerce companies fall rapidly as confidence among high-tech investors evaporates. In the United States, the number of staff lay-offs at dotcom companies approaches 30,000.

The total number of web pages reaches 1 billion.

2001 The internet economy gets off to a bad start as Amazon and Yahoo both lay off substantial percentages of their staff. Cisco, once the world's most valuable company, announces its first ever quarterly losses, which total $2.69 billion. eToys, once one of the darlings of the internet retailing world, closes down as the market slumps and funding dries up.

Yahoo bans the sale of Nazi memorabilia from all its websites, following an order by a French judge that the company must take steps to prevent French users from accessing sites that sell such material.

The FBI reports that over 1m credit-card numbers have been stolen by east European crackers, most of whom exploited security holes in Microsoft's Windows NT product. Over 40 companies in 20 American states are affected, with many reporting extortion attempts.

Tom Waits, Randy Newman and other musicians sue online music distribution site MP3.com for $40m in an attempt to recover allegedly lost revenue from music piracy.

The Taliban, Afghanistan's ruling party, bans access to the internet in an attempt to control "things that are wrong, obscene, immoral and against Islam".

In July, the Code Red worm attacks networks all over the world, exploiting a vulnerability in Microsoft's Windows server software. Hundreds of thousands of machines are affected within a week of its emergence. It continues to infect unprotected networks for months afterwards, forcing companies to shut down their networks and costing businesses billions of dollars in downtime. Infected machines bombard the White House website with traffic for a week. The Sircam virus strikes at around the same time, emailing copies of itself from the infected PCs with random documents attached, sometimes with embarrassing results.

Dmitry Sklyarov, a Russian programmer, becomes the first person to be jailed under the provisions of the Digital Millennium Copyright Act, America's widely-criticised intellectual property legislation. Arrested for creating a program that allegedly circumvented security on Adobe's eBook digital document format, allowing documents to be freely transported between computers, Sklyarov is allowed to return to Russia in December after widespread protests from free-speech campaigners.

ICANN ratifies a set of generic additions to the domain name system, creating seven new domain types: .aero, .biz, .coop, .info, .museum, .name and .pro. Critics express great displeasure at ICANN's apparent hijacking of .biz, which had been operational on an alternative domain name system for some time.

The US Court of Appeal rules that Microsoft broke antitrust laws to maintain its software monopoly, but reverses Judge Jackson's ruling that the company should be broken up. Dozens of states and private companies file private antitrust suits against the company; final rulings on the government litigation run on into 2002.

The US Congress passes the USA Patriot Act in the wake of the World Trade Centre attacks, giving intelligence agencies new powers to conduct surveillance on American citizens. The new law grants investigators powers to demand information from ISPs on everything from web searches to visited sites, as well as new "wiretapping" powers to eavesdrop on electronic communications without the need for court orders.

Six years after its launch, book retailer Amazon.com records its first ever operating profit, reporting a net income of $5m on its fourth-quarter sales. The company cites an 81% rise in international business and greatly reduced marketing costs as the principal reasons for its success.

Thousands of dotcoms close their doors as cash reserves dry up and investors cut their losses. The internet industry's flagship news resource, the *Industry Standard*, closes as its advertisers and sponsors disappear from the economy.

The total number of web pages reaches 3 billion, three times the figure reported in early 2000.

2002 The Napster music distribution network is finally forced to close after months of negotiation with the recording industry and attempts to re-engineer the service for legal use. Many new networks based on peer-to-peer (P2P) technology emerge to fill the gap, creating a much bigger problem for the music industry owing to their decentralised and ungovernable nature.

Microsoft settles its antitrust battle with the US government after three years of bitter wrangling. Many criticise the government's rulings as too lenient.

Australia's Supreme Court rules that Joe Gutnick, a gold-mining magnate, can sue Dow Jones for libel in Melbourne over money-laundering allegations on one of its websites, despite the fact that the site is based in the United States. The decision prompts widespread criticism from net campaigners and media companies, who fear that it undermines the internet's foundation as a platform for free speech and will cause a global flood of litigation.

Investors in Amazon at the beginning of the year more than double their money by the end of it as it becomes the best-performing company of the NASDAQ 100.

Despite the success of a handful of high-profile internet companies, high-tech economies continue to decline as stockmarkets crash all over the world. Telecoms firms are reported to have run up combined debts of over $1 trillion dollars globally. Hundreds of thousands of technology workers are laid off as companies struggle for survival.

US investigators discover the identities of 75,000 subscribers to a child pornography website based in Texas, subsequently releasing the names of over 7,000 subscribers to the UK police. More than 1,200 people are arrested as part of Operation Ore, the largest UK-based investigation into paedophilia, including doctors, teachers, care workers and policemen.

More than 300 Spanish website operators take their sites offline in protest at legislation designed to regulate online content. It requires companies to register all websites with the Spanish government and obliges ISPs to monitor sites for illicit content, citing concerns about privacy and censorship.

An unknown cracker attacks the computers at the heart of the internet, launching the first large-scale denial-of-service attack designed to cripple the name servers managing global internet traffic. Although several of the 13 servers are forced offline, the system recovers rapidly and traffic disruption is minimal.

2003 AOL announces a loss of $99 billion for fiscal 2002, the biggest annual loss in US corporate history. Steve Case, the company's founder, steps down from the chairmanship following a 60% drop in share price under his stewardship.

Microsoft agrees to pay $1.1 billion to settle class-action lawsuits brought against it by Californians, who claimed that the company used its power to unfairly restrict competition and skew prices in its favour. Over 13m businesses stand to gain from the settlement.

The SQL Slammer worm spreads rapidly through the internet, exploiting a vulnerability in Microsoft's SQL server software. The fastest-spreading computer infection ever seen, it floods thousands of networks with data within minutes of its release, causing computers to crash all over the world, including some of Microsoft's own. Websites, banking systems and ISPS are hit particularly hard, many experiencing complete shutdown.

AltaVista, one of the web's first search engines, is sold to rival Overture for $140m. Once valued at nearly $3 billion, the company was sold at a $2 billion loss by CMGI, its owner, following an ill-fated attempt to become a general-interest portal and the rise of more powerful search engines such as Google.

2 **Abbreviations**

ADSL	Asynchronous Digital Subscriber Line
AOL	America Online
ASP	Application Service Provider
ATM	Asynchronous Transfer Mode or Adobe Type Manager
BBS	Bulletin Board System
BCC	Blind Carbon Copy
BPS	Bits Per Second
BRI	Basic Rate Interface
CAD	Computer Aided Design
CC	Carbon Copy
CCS	Cascading Style Sheet
CDA	Communications Decency Act
CDF	Channel Definition Format
CGI	Common Gateway Interface
COM	Component Object Model
CORBA	Common Object Request Broker Architecture
DCOM	Distributed Component Object Model
DES	Data Encryption Standard
DHCP	Dynamic Host Configuration Protocol
DHTML	Dynamic Hypertext Mark-up Language
DOM	Document Object Model
DNS	Domain Name System
DSL	Digital Subscriber Line (or Loop)
EDI	Electronic Data Interchange
EFF	Electronic Frontier Foundation
FAQ	Frequently Asked Questions
FDM	Frequency-Division Multiplexing
FSF	Free Software Foundation
FTP	File Transfer Protocol
GIF	Graphics Interchange Format
GPRS	General Packet Radio Service
GSM	Global System for Mobile Communications
GUI	Graphical User Interface
HDML	Handheld Devices Mark-up Language
HTCPCP	Hyper Text Coffee Pot Control Protocol

HTML	Hypertext Mark-up Language
HTTP	Hypertext Transfer Protocol
IAB	Internet Architecture Board
IANA	Internet Assigned Names Authority
ICANN	Internet Corporation for Assigned Names and Numbers
ICQ	I Seek You
IETF	Internet Engineering Task Force
IM	Instant Messaging
IMAP	Internet Message Access Protocol
IOTP	Internet Open Trading Protocol
IP	Internet Protocol
IPO	Initial Public Offering
IRC	Internet Relay Chat
IRL	In Real Life
ISDN	Integrated Services Digital Network
ISP	Internet Service Provider
JANET	Joint Academic Network
JIT	Just In Time
JPEG	Joint Picture Experts Group (or JPG)
Kbps	Kilobits per second
LAN	Local Area Network
LDAP	Lightweight Directory Access Protocol
LINX	London Internet Exchange
MANAP	Manchester Network Access Point
Mbps	Millions of bits per second
Mbone	Multicast Backbone
MIME	Multipurpose Internet Mail Extensions
MOO	MUD Object Oriented
MSN	Microsoft Network
MPEG	Motion Picture Experts Group
MUD	Multi-user Dungeon
NAP	Network Access Point
NASDAQ	National Association of Securities Dealers Automated Quotation system
NC	Network Computer
NCSA	National Centre For Supercomputing Applications
NNTP	Network News Transport Protocol
OPS	Open Profiling Standard

ORB	Object Request Broker
OS	Operating System
OSI	Open Source Initiative
PANS	Public Access Network Services
PCS	Personal Communications Service
PDA	Personal Digital Assistant
PDF	Portable Document Format
PGP	Pretty Good Privacy
PKI	Public Key Infrastructure
PICS	Platform for Internet Content Selection
POP	Point of Presence
POP3	Post Office Protocol (latest version)
POTS	Plain Old Telephone Service
PPP	Point-to-Point Protocol
PRI	Primary Rate Interface
PVC	Permanent Virtual Circuit
QoS	Quality of Service
RFC	Request For Comments
RSAC	Recreational Software Advisory Council
SDMI	Secure Digital Music Initiative
SET	Secure Electronic Transactions
SMS	Short Messaging Service
SMTP	Simple Mail Transport Protocol
SOAP	Simple Object Access Protocol
SQL	Structured Query Language
SSL	Secure Sockets Layer
TCP	Transmission Control Protocol
TCP/IP	Transmission Control Protocol/Internet Protocol
TDM	Time-Division Multiplexing
TLA	Three-Letter Acronym
TLD	Top-level domain
TTP	Trusted Third Party
UDDI	Universal Description, Discovery and Integration
URI	Uniform Resource Identifier
URL	Uniform Resource Locator
UUCP	Unix-to-Unix Copy Protocol
vBNS	Very High Speed Backbone Network Service
VM	Virtual Machine
VOIP	Voice Over IP

VPN	Virtual Private Network
VRML	Virtual Reality Modelling Language
W3C	World Wide Web Consortium
WAP	Wireless Application Protocol
WASP	Wireless Application Service Provider
WDM	Wavelength-Division Multiplexing
WELL	Whole Earth 'Lectronic Link
WIPO	World Intellectual Property Organisation
WML	Wireless Mark-up Language
WSDL	Web Services Description Language
XHTML	Extensible Hypertext Mark-up Language
XML	Extensible Mark-up Language
XSL	Extensible Stylesheet Language
XTLA	Extended Three-Letter Acronym

3 **Recommended websites**

Books (second-hand, other)

the-tech.mit.edu/Shakespeare
The Bard's complete works

www.abebooks.co.uk
Excellent site specialising in rare, second-hand and out-of-print books

www.bibliofind.com
A searchable collection of used and rare books, periodicals and ephemera for sale

www.bibliomania.com
Collection of classic novels, poetry, drama, dictionaries and study guides

www.bookcrossing.com
Interesting book-sharing system based on the liberation of books into the wild

www.canterburytales.org
Chaucer's *Canterbury Tales*, in both original and translated versions

www.lrb.co.uk
London Review of Books online, complete with legendary personal ads

www.nybooks.com
The New York Review of Books

www.promo.net/pg
Official site of Project Gutenberg, aimed at making texts available free to the public online

Bookshops (new)

www.amazon.com
The web's most famous bookstore, with British (www.amazon.co.uk), German (www.amazon.de), French (www.amazon.fr) and Japanese (www.amazon.co.jp) subsidiaries

www.bn.com
Barnes & Noble, a US bookselling giant

www.bol.com
German media giant Bertelsmann's bookstore, catering for the
European market

www.books.co.uk
Directory and descriptions of the UK's online booksellers

www.bookshop.co.uk
UK bookshop

Business

adage.com
Advertising Age, a worldwide marketing and advertising
industry newspaper

cbs.marketwatch.com
Rich source of market and economic news for investors from
the CBS stable

forbes.com
In-depth business news and analysis for business leaders

strategis.ic.gc.ca
Canadian business information site, featuring company
directories, trade and investment resources and economic
analysis

www.acca.co.uk
Worldwide Association of Chartered Certified Accountants
site, listing many accounting resources

www.accountingweb.co.uk
UK accountants' community

www.bcentral.com
Microsoft's resource for small businesses seeking to get started
online

www.bnet.co.uk
A source of practical management information for UK
businesses

www.businessdailyreview.com
News and opinion with a business slant, daily

www.carol.co.uk
Company annual reports and other investor information

www.ceoexpress.com

Huge list of well-organised links to business, internet, media, finance and many other resources

www.edgar-online.com

Company SEC filings, annual reports and more

www.eiu.com

Global business information and analysis from the Economist Intelligence Unit, part of The Economist Group

www.europebusinessdaily.com

European business news, with many excellent links and other resources

www.ft.com

The *Financial Times*, an excellent source for international business news (the FT is part-owner of *The Economist*)

www.gbn.org

Home of the Global Business Network, with a forum for members' exchanges

www.globalsources.com

Product and trade information and links for volume buyers of consumer, business and industrial goods

www.hoovers.com

Global company directory and market intelligence source with financial data, company news and links to other relevant sites

www.iisg.nl/~w3vl

The World Wide Web Virtual Library's guide to the history of labour and business

www.mastercard.com

Mastercard's international site, with links to local resources

www.mckinseyquarterly.com

Library of articles and research from the McKinsey management consultancy

www.propertymall.co.uk

News and property information portal for the UK commercial property industry

www.smartmoney.com

The *Wall Street Journal*'s magazine of personal investment and finance, including a customisable portfolio tracker

www.strategy-business.com

Community site for business leaders encouraging the exchange

of new business ideas, including articles and book reviews
www.thebiz.co.uk
Business-to-business directory and database with a strong UK
focus
www.thomasregister.com
Searchable database of brand names, products and services
from the Thomas Register of US manufacturers
www.visa.com
Visa's international site, with links to local resources
www.wsj.com
The *Wall Street Journal*'s Europe, US and Asia editions,
available on a subscription basis

Central banks

www.bankofcanada.ca/en
Bank of Canada
www.bankofengland.co.uk
The Bank of England
www.bis.org
The Bank for International Settlements, the central bank of
central banks
www.bis.org./cbanks.htm
Links to central banks around the world
www.boj.or.jp/en
The Bank of Japan
www.bundesbank.de
The Bundesbank
www.ecb.int
The European Central Bank
www.federalreserve.gov
US Federal Reserve
www.patriot.net/users/bernkopf
A central-banking resource centre, with good links to
international central banks

Current affairs: Africa

allafrica.com
News index with wide geographical and topical coverage
polyglot.lss.wisc.edu/afrst/links.html
The University of Wisconsin's catalogue of Africa links
www.afbis.com/analysis/index.htm
Articles on business and investment from UK-based charity
Africa Economic Analysis
www.mbendi.co.za
Pan-African business encyclopedia
www.mg.co.za
Daily Mail and Guardian newspaper, covering news from all
African countries
www.north-africa.com
The *North Africa Journal*, a weekly monitor of current affairs
in Algeria, Morocco, Tunisia and other North African countries
www.irinnews.org/
The Integrated Regional Information Network (IRIN), a UN-
affiliated agency providing geographically organised news
from all over Africa

Current affairs: Asia

www.apecsec.org.sg
Asia Pacific Economic Co-operation, a regional grouping, with
news and economic data about member states
www.asiamedia.ucla.edu
News, views and links from the Asia Pacific Media Network

Current affairs: East Asia

business-times.asia1.com.sg
The *Business Times* of Singapore, a leading business daily with
coverage throughout South-East Asia
ce.cei.gov.cn
The China Economic Information website
coombs.anu.edu.au/WWWVL-AsianStudies.html
World Wide Web Virtual Library site on Asian studies, with
coverage of China, Hong Kong, Taiwan, Singapore and other

Asian countries

straitstimes.asia1.com.sg

The *Straits Times* online, based in Singapore but with coverage throughout Asia

www.bangkokpost.co.th

The *Bangkok Post*

www.fijilive.com

Rolling news from Fiji

www.fmprc.gov.cn/eng

China's Ministry of Foreign Affairs

www.insidechina.com

Inside China Today, news on China from the European Internet Network

www.japanecho.co.jp

A bi-monthly journal featuring English translations of essays, interviews and discussions on Japanese politics and economics

www.japantimes.co.jp

The *Japan Times*

www.mofa.go.jp

Japan's Ministry of Foreign Affairs

www.mofa.gov.tw/newmofa/emofa/index.htm

Taiwan's Ministry of Foreign Affairs

www.nni.nikkei.co.jp

The Nikkei Net Interactive, 24-hour business and financial news from Japan available by subscription

www.philippineupdate.com

Compilation of Western news articles on the Philippines

www.scmp.com

The *South China Morning Post*, including extensive news coverage of Hong Kong, China and Asia

www.taiwansecurity.org

Taiwanese news and current affairs, with a military slant

Current affairs: South Asia

indiaworld.com

Indian national and political news and current affairs

www.cmie.com

The Centre for Monitoring Indian Economy

www.dawn.com
Pakistan's English-language newspaper
www.economictimes.com
India's *Economic Times*, covering companies, industry,
economics and politics
www.timesofindia.com
The *Times of India*

Current affairs: US and Canada

canada.gc.ca
The Canadian government website
movingideas.org
Economics and social policy recommendations from the
Electronic Policy Network, allied with the US *Prospect*
magazine
msn.slate.com
Microsoft's *Slate* magazine, containing analysis of national
media coverage and its own acerbic views of the world
www.abcnews.com
ABC News
www.cato.org
The Cato Institute, a site devoted to US public policy debate
www.cnn.com
CNN
www.drudgereport.com
Famous and sometimes newsbreaking site, with links to many
others
www.firstgov.gov
The US government's official web portal
www.fpif.org
Foreign Policy in Focus, a site devoted to discussion of US
foreign policy
www.globeandmail.ca
The *Globe and Mail*, Canada's national newspaper
www.house.gov
The official site of the US House of Representatives
www.ipl.org/ref/POTUS
Presidents of the United States site, containing background

information on every president to date, election results, cabinet members and notable events

www.iwpr.org
The Institute for Women's Policy Research

www.latimes.com
The *Los Angeles Times*

www.motherjones.com
Witty and well-researched news for sceptical citizens, with a focus on social justice

www.nationalpost.com
Canadian newspaper

www.nytimes.com
The *New York Times*

www.public-policy.org
Centre for Public Policy site with links to US and Canadian members' websites

www.rollcall.com
Roll Call, the Capitol Hill watchdog of The Economist Group

www.senate.gov
The US Senate

www.theatlantic.com
Online version of *The Atlantic Monthly* magazine

www.wsj.com
The *Wall Street Journal* online, for subscribers only

www.usatoday.com
USA Today

www.washingtonpost.com
The *Washington Post*

www.whitehouse.gov
The US White House

Current affairs: UK

www.fco.gov.uk
The UK's Foreign & Commonwealth Office

www.faxyourmp.com
Send faxes to your local MP, with a postcode-based MP finder

www.guardian.co.uk
Guardian Unlimited, the web version of the *Guardian*, a left-

leaning daily

www.independent.co.uk

The *Independent*, a centre-left news daily

www.ippr.org.uk

Independent policy research think-tank, based in the UK

www.number-10.gov.uk

News and broadcasts from 10 Downing Street

www.open.gov.uk

Links to government and public-sector information and
services in the UK

www.parliament.uk

The UK Parliament, including sections for the House of Lords
and the House of Commons and the text of *Hansard*,
Parliament's daily journal

www.telegraph.co.uk

The Electronic Telegraph, the online version of the
conservative *Daily Telegraph*

www.the-times.co.uk

The Times, a UK daily in the political centre

Current affairs: Europe

europa.eu.int

The European Union's official site, including statistics and links
to the Parliament, Court of Justice and other EU sites

www.angloinfo.com

Information service for British ex-pats in France

www.austria.org

Austrian press and information service from Washington, DC

www.ce-review.org

Central European affairs, as covered by the Central and East
European New Media Initiative (CEENMI)

www.ecmi.de

European Centre for Minority Issues, which promotes
interdisciplinary research on minority–majority relations in
Europe

www.einmedia.com

European Internet Network hub site, with links to online news
resources from over 250 countries and US states

www.european-voice.com
A weekly newspaper on EU affairs, published by The Economist Group

www.handelsblatt.com
Germany's business and financial daily, in German with some English summaries

www.moscowtimes.ru
The *Moscow Times*, in English

www.nato.int
The North Atlantic Treaty Organisation, complete with news and an archive of all official NATO documents

www.osce.org
The Organisation for Security and Co-operation in Europe

www.praguereport.com
Daily English-language news from the Czech Republic

www.rferl.org
News coverage and analysis of central and eastern Europe and the former Soviet Union from Radio Free Europe/Radio Liberty

www.russiajournal.com
Russian business and news journal in English, with a special focus on foreign trade, investment and markets

www.spiegel.de
German current affairs, from *Der Spiegel*

www.swissinfo.org
Swiss news and current affairs in nine languages, from Swiss Radio International

www.times.spb.ru
The *St Petersburg Times*, affiliated with the *Moscow Times*

Current affairs: Middle East

gulf2000.columbia.edu
Treasure-trove of information on the eight countries of the Persian Gulf region

www.a7.org
The independent Arutz Sheva Israeli national radio station

www.arabia.com
Arabia Online, including current affairs, business news and cultural coverage from the Arab world

www.ariga.com
Site dedicated to coverage of the various peace movements in the Middle East

www.fas.harvard.edu/~mideast/inMEres/inMEres.html
Harvard's vast library of links to Middle East websites

www.haaretzdaily.com
English-language version of the *Haaretz* daily

www.israelnn.com
Israel National News, daily news from Israel in English

www.jpost.com
Internet edition of the *Jerusalem Post*, Israel's main English-language daily

www.mfa.gov.il
Israel's Ministry of Foreign Affairs site, providing detailed information on the Israeli government and its policies

Current affairs: Oceania

theage.com.au
The Age, Melbourne's daily newspaper

www.abc.net.au
Australian Broadcasting Corporation online

www.nzherald.co.nz
The *New Zealand Herald*, with news from Auckland and the country

www.scoop.co.nz/mason
Rolling news from New Zealand's Parliament Press Gallery

www.smh.com.au
The *Sydney Morning Herald*

Current affairs: South and Central America

lanic.utexas.edu
The Latin American Network Information Center, providing a well-organised encyclopedia of links broken down by category and by country

lcweb2.loc.gov/hlas/hlashome.html
The *Handbook of Latin American Studies*, with a searchable bibliography of scholarly works on Latin America published

by the Library of Congress and links to the Library's Hispanic
Reading Room
lib.nmsu.edu/subject/bord/laguia
Internet Resources for Latin America, a directory of
organisations, news sources and scholarly resources addressing
Latin American issues
www.brazzil.com
Monthly Brazilian magazine focusing on current affairs
www.cidac.org
Center for Research and Development, with analysis of
Mexico's politics and economy
www.latinfinance.com
A monthly magazine of investment news from Latin America
www.latinnews.com
General news from Latin America

Current affairs: World

aldaily.com
Arts and Letters Daily, a collection of literature, criticism,
philosophy, language and ideas with a useful directory of
online journals
lcweb2.loc.gov/frd/cs
Good but not always up-to-date country-by-country
information from the Library of Congress
news.bbc.co.uk
BBC news
news.google.com
Up-to-the-minute news from the web's best search engine
nobelprizes.com/nobel
Biographical information on Nobel Prize winners current and
past, with good links
stratfor.com
Geopolitical intelligence, news and analysis
www.1stheadlines.com
News headlines from key global media, including business,
sports and technology sections
www.crisisweb.org
The International Crisis Group, a think-tank with

comprehensive analysis and reports on conflicts all over the world

www.csmonitor.com

The *Christian Science Monitor* online

www.economist.com

The Economist online. Highlights include city and country briefings, a humorous diversions section and a useful data bank of market and financial information

www.economist.com/countries

Comprehensive country coverage from Economist.com, with the Economist Intelligence Unit

www.g7.utoronto.ca

G8 summit information centre

www.gksoft.com/govt/en

Centralised resource for linking to individual countries' government sites

www.hrw.org

News and reports from Human Rights Watch

www.icrc.org

The International Committee of the Red Cross

www.iea.org

International Energy Agency site, including statistics and world energy outlook

www.iht.com

The *International Herald Tribune*

www.imf.org

The International Monetary Fund

www.klipsan.com/calendar.htm

World elections calendar

www.onlinenewspapers.com

Links to thousands of newspaper websites worldwide

www.newsdirectory.com

Links to English-language newspapers and magazines around the world, from Botswana to Micronesia

www.politicalresources.net

A meta-directory for national political resources on the web

www.psr.keele.ac.uk

Political science resources, from Richard Kimber; especially strong on the UK

www.publist.com
Large directory of journals and periodicals
www.salon.com
News, politics, opinion, books, life and everything else, from one of the web's smartest publications
www.un.org
The UN

Economics

csf.colorado.edu/pkt
Archive of post-Keynesian thought
epinet.org
Economic issues and trends discussed by the Economic Policy Institute
utip.gov.utexas.edu
Inequality indicators and analysis from the University of Texas
www.bea.doc.gov
Economic data and analysis compiled by the Bureau of Economic Analysis, part of the US Department of Commerce
www.brook.edu
The Brookings Institution, an independent research body and think-tank
www.businesscycle.com
The Economic Cycle Research Institute's website, with discussions and explanations of economic trends
www.economy.com/dismal
The *Dismal Scientist*, a review and analysis of current economic news and trends
www.diw-berlin.de
The German Institute for Economic Research
www.economy.com
Economic, industrial and financial research
www.fao.org
The UN Food and Agriculture Organisation
www.fmcenter.org
Information, research and analysis of the Federal Reserve and financial markets from the non-profit Financial Markets Center

www.helsinki.fi/WebEc/journals.html
Huge list of links to economics journals on the web

www.heritage.org
Policy research and analysis from The Heritage Foundation, a Conservative US think-tank

www.iie.com
The Institute for International Economics

www.ilo.org
The International Labour Organization

www.imf.org
The International Monetary Fund

www.levy.org
The Levy Economics Institute, with papers on economic policy analysis

www.marxists.org
The Marxists Internet Archive in 29 languages, from Arabic to Vietnamese

www.nabe.com
The National Association for Business Economists

www.nber.org
The National Bureau of Economic Research

www.oecd.org
The Organisation for Economic Co-operation and Development

www.res.org.uk
The UK's Royal Economic Society

www.tutor2u.com
An online economics tutor, covering everything from game theory to congestion charging, with revision notes and quizzes

www.vanderbilt.edu/AEA
The American Economic Association's website

www.worldbank.org
The World Bank

www.wws.princeton.edu/~pkrugman
Princeton professor Paul Krugman's view of the economic world

www.wto.org
The World Trade Organization

www.wz-berlin.de/default.en.asp
The WZB, a German research institute with papers on Europe's variety of capitalist models
www1.ifs.org.uk
The UK's Institute for Fiscal Studies

Employment

hotjobs.yahoo.com
Mass job board from the Yahoo stable
jobasia.com
Large Asian recruitment website
www.adecco.com
Job-finding site from one of the world's largest recruitment companies, with a UK branch at www.adecco.co.uk
www.careerbuilder.com
Generalised jobs site with advice on résumés and job-seeking
www.careerjournal.com
The *Wall Street Journal*'s careers section
www.cityjobs.co.uk
Well-organised site for banking, finance, accountancy and legal jobs in the UK
www.craigslist.org
Popular San Francisco jobs and classified advertising site
www.dice.com
Large job board for technical experts
www.economist.com/globalexecutive
Careers site for senior executives (a partnership between the Whitehead Mann Group and Economist.com)
www.guru.com
Network for professionals and independent contractors looking for work, and for the companies that want them
www.latpro.com
Latin American professional recruitment website, for Spanish and Portuguese speakers
www.monster.com
World's largest online recruitment site, with offshoot sites in many countries

www.monstertrak.com
MonsterTrak, a job-seeking board for college graduates and students
www.techies.com
Jobs for techies
www.vaultreports.com
Careers information and employment research site
www.workopolis.com
Workopolis, a Canadian careers site in French and English
www.workthing.com
Careers website from the *Guardian*, a UK newspaper

Entertainment

dpsinfo.com
Home of the famous Dead People Server, with ancillary sites including AwardWeb and a genealogy resource
launch.yahoo.com
Vast assemblage of music videos, audio, concert listings and artist features covering all music genres
windowsmedia.com
Film, music and general entertainment portal from Microsoft, with lots of samples
www.apple.com/trailers
All the current and upcoming film trailers in Apple's QuickTime format
www.atomfilms.com
Short entertainment e-hub, with films and trailers lasting from 30 seconds to 30 minutes
www.bored.com
Links to online esoterica
www.boxofficeguru.com
Site focusing on the success or otherwise of the latest Hollywood films
www.eonline.com
The standard-bearer for US entertainment reporting
www.ifilm.com
Film portal with downloadable videos, reviews, links, news and more

www.imdb.com
Vast and justly famous film resource, now owned by Amazon
www.real.com
Streaming media from Real Networks, including news, film
clips, live music and live radio
www.station.sony.com
Sony's game site, featuring versions of Jeopardy, Wheel of
Fortune, Trivial Pursuit and Everquest
www.thesmokinggun.com
Documentation of the bizarre: uncensored court documents,
FBI files and more on extraneous or important subjects
www.timeout.com
Indispensable guide to shopping and travel in more than
30 cities
www.variety.com
The scoop, and the numbers, on the entertainment industry

Finance

finance.yahoo.com
Yahoo's excellent financial data and resource centre
www.bloomberg.com
Financial market updates and analysis from Bloomberg
www.briefing.com
Live stockmarket analysis
www.ebrd.com
The European Bank for Reconstruction and Development,
specialising in east and central European and Asian investment
www.fiafii.org
The Futures Industry Association
www.globalfindata.com
Huge current and historical financial data resource
www.hedgeindex.com
Statistical database on hedge fund performance, from Credit
Suisse First Boston/Tremont
www.ifc.org
The International Finance Corporation
www.marhedge.com
News bulletins and information on alternative investments

www.napf.co.uk
The UK's National Association of Pension Funds, representing the occupational pensions movement
www.reuters.com
Financial updates from Reuters
www.sec.gov
The Securities and Exchange Commission
www.stockcharts.com
Free stock charting, market analysis and financial tools
www.thestreet.com
Detailed reports and analysis from Wall Street
www.usatrade.gov
Guides to investment in different countries, compiled by US embassy staff

Health

bmj.com
The *British Medical Journal*
dir.yahoo.com/health
Yahoo's directory of health sites
jama.ama-assn.org
The *Journal of the American Medical Association*
www.cdc.gov
The US Center for Disease Control, with information for international travellers
www.cred.be
Centre for Research on the Epidemiology of Disasters, an excellent database of international disasters and related statistics
www.healthfinder.org
Gateway to consumer health and human services information, provided by the US Department of Health and Human Services
www.healthgate.com
Health and lifestyle recommendations and news
www.nih.gov
The US National Institutes for Health

www.nlm.nih.gov
US National Library of Medicine site, with a link to the
Medline database of health information
www.omni.ac.uk
Organising Medical Networked Information, a UK gateway to
biomedical internet resources
www.who.org
The World Health Organisation
www.yourcancerrisk.harvard.edu
Calculate your risk for different forms of cancer

Humour and satire

www.darwinawards.com
A celebration of Darwin, recognising those who improve the
gene pool by removing themselves from it in interesting ways
www.dilbert.com
Scott Adams' course in people management skills, or lack
thereof
www.doonesbury.com
Online home of the famous political cartoon, from Garry
Trudeau
www.improb.com
A look at brand new ways to waste research funds, including
the Ig Noble awards
www.mcsweeneys.net
Short fiction and humour from some of America's young lions
www.modernhumorist.com
Current events satire and analysis
www.private-eye.co.uk
UK political satire
www.satirewire.com
Excellent archive of satirical humour
www.straightdope.com
Questions on everything, answered by the acerbic Cecil
Adams
www.theonion.com
Satirical newspaper poking fun at politics, media and anything
newsworthy

www.thismodernworld.com
Left-wing cartoonist Tom Tomorrow hits more often than he misses
www.urbanlegends.com
Self-explanatory modern mythology site

Internet

download.cnet.com
Source of free and try-before-you-buy software on the web
java.sun.com
Cradle of Sun's ground-breaking web technology, and the web's most comprehensive Java resource
verisign-grs.com/whois
Global domain name finder, for discovering owners of registered domains
www.alertbox.com
Jakob Nielsen's respected bi-weekly analysis of website design and navigability
www.business2.com/webguide
Business 2.0 magazine's excellent directory of web information and resources, organised by subject
www.clickz.com
Online resource for web marketers
www.cnet.com/internet
CNET's hub for internet services, including guides to new broadband services
www.commerce.net
The e-commerce industry association's site, with a range of interesting resources, a research centre and the latest e-commerce news
www.eff.org
Organisation devoted to the protection of civil liberties on the internet, with lots of articles on privacy, censorship, free speech and government legislation
www.icra.org
The Internet Content Rating Organisation, helping parents and others to filter unwanted information form the web. Includes details of the PICS standard

www.ietf.org
The Internet Engineering Task Force
www.internet.com
Massive site providing well-organised links to thousands of
other internet resources, news and reviews
www.internetstats.com
Internet statistics and links to online survey information
www.isoc.org
Home of the Internet Society, with news and discussion of
internet standards
www.linux.org
Home to Linux, a rare Windows competitor, with links,
software, events, explanations, shopping and more
www.mozilla.org
Home of the Mozilla open source browser
www.opensource.org
Site offering different views of the open-source software
movement, with links to relevant resources
www.opera.com
Home of the Opera browser
www.sdmi.org
The Secure Digital Music Initiative's website
www.searchenginewatch.com
Lots of information on search engines, including performance
comparisons and tips for users
www.w3.org
Home of the World Wide Web Consortium, the standards
body for the web run by Tim Berners-Lee, its co-creator.
Includes news, discussion and a vast technical resource

Law

www.abanet.org
The American Bar Association
www.abanet.org/ceeli
The American Bar Association's Central and East European
Law Initiative
www.americanlawyer.com
The *American Lawyer*, the leading US monthly on law

www.asil.org
American Society of International Law
www.clubi.ie/competition
Site for *Competition*, a journal specialising in EU antitrust law
and the regulation of utilities, with antitrust law links
www.european-patent-office.org
The European Patent Office
www.hg.org
HierosGamos, a vast legal resource compiled by the UN with
comprehensive sections on the world's legal associations,
international law and much else
www.lawsoc.org.uk
The Law Society of England and Wales
www.uspto.gov
The US Patent and Trade Office

Personal finance

investor.cnet.com
Personal investment advice from CNet
moneycentral.msn.com/home.asp
Personal finance resource for American users, with sections on
saving and spending, retirement, wills, tax and much more
news.ft.com/yourmoney
High-quality information from the *Financial Times*, covering
saving, investing, mortgages, tax, insurance and more
www.euroland.com
Reports, analysis, investment advice and stock prices from
major European markets
www.fool.com
Legendary, irreverent investment and financial resource, with
a comprehensive UK section
www.moneyextra.com
Good advice for savers and investors in the UK
www.oft.gov.uk/Consumer/default.htm
Consumer advice from the UK's Office of Fair Trading,
including a section on money and credit
www.quicken.com
Personal finance news and tools from Intuit

www.thisismoney.co.uk
Personal finance in the UK, from the *Evening Standard* and
Daily Mail newspapers

Reference

4maps.4anything.com
Masses of maps from the 4anything network of websites
mappoint.msn.com
Excellent global mapping and travelling directions service from
Microsoft
www.about.com
Expert guides on thousands of subjects, each with dozens of
links and other web resources
www.atomica.com
Useful dictionary tool for checking words on web pages or
other documents
www.britannica.com
More than just the Encyclopedia Britannica
www.bt.com/directory-enquiries/dq_home.jsp
BT's telephone directory
www.dictionary.com
Online dictionary and thesaurus
www.encyclopedia.com
14,000 well-organised free entries from the *Concise Columbia
Electronic Encyclopedia*
www.framed.usps.com/ncsc/lookups/lookup_zip+4.html
Zip-code directory from the US Postal Service
www.gourmetsleuth.com/conversions.htm
Conversions for cooking measures and much more
www.infoplease.com
An almanac of almanacs, with a vast range of searchable
subjects
www.istockphoto.com
Free stock photography online
www.mapquest.com
Extensive global mapping and travel service
www.oanda.com
Olsen and Associates' currency and foreign exchange resource,

including forecasts, historical tables and converters
www.odci.gov/cia/publications/factbook
The *CIA World Factbook*, with vital statistics and information
on every country
www.radio-locator.com
Global radio station finder
www.refdesk.com
Lots of reference titbits
www.reporter.org
Useful resource for reporters and would-be reporters
www.streetmap.co.uk
Site displaying the UK's street maps by area or postcode,
including street maps of Greater London and road atlas maps
of mainland UK
www.timeanddate.com/worldclock
The right time, everywhere in the world
www.whatsonwhen.com
Upcoming events and entertainment around the world,
complete with travel services
www.wikipedia.org
Free encyclopedia with over 100,000 articles in the English
version, and a collaborative project to create a complete
encyclopedia in every language
www.worldwidewords.org
Excellent reference site for word enthusiasts
www.xe.com
The best of the currency converters and information sources
www.xrefer.com
Excellent umbrella reference source for searching many online
reference sources simultaneously

Science

scicentral.com
Reports and daily news from all areas of scientific research
www.astronomynow.com
Popular British astronomy magazine
www.chemsoc.org
The Royal Society of Chemistry's site

www.cid.harvard.edu/cidbiotech/links.htm
Biotechnology links from Harvard's Center for International
Development

www.earthsky.com
Science radio series based in the US, with tools for teachers
and projects for kids. Archives of programmes include short
explanatory blurbs for each topic

www.esa.int
European Space Agency site, with regular updates on European
developments

www.howstuffworks.com
How Stuff Works, a self-explanatory site covering everything
from computers to caffeine

www.inconstantmoon.com
Daily updates of images of the moon

www.mars2030.net
The Mars Millennium project, challenging students to design a
Mars-based community

www.nasa.gov
Home to NASA, the US space program

www.nature.com/nsu
Nature's research news site, updated daily

www.newscientist.com
Science news from the *New Scientist* in the UK

www.newshub.com/science
Science headlines from the world's premier news sources

www.noaa.gov
The National Oceanographic and Atmospheric Administration,
with information on the climate and atmosphere

www.nytimes.com/yr/mo/day/national/index-science.html
Daily science and health coverage from the *New York Times*

www.sciam.com
Scientific American

www.sciencedaily.com/index.htm
Daily news site specialising in research

www.sciencenews.org
Weekly science news magazine

www.skypub.com
Home to *Sky and Telescope*, a popular US astronomy magazine

with news updates and features
www.space.com
A space resource unparalleled in range and accessibility,
though probably not the best for breaking news
www.techreview.com
MIT's alumni magazine, recently expanded to include all sorts
of technological innovations
www.usno.navy.mil
The US Naval Observatory's website, detailing activities from
measuring the positions and motions of celestial objects to
measuring the Earth's rotation
www.whyfiles.org
The science behind topical news stories

Search engines

groups.google.gom
Usenet news groups, indexed by the mighty Google
search.netscape.com
Netscape
www.alexa.com
Alexa, a well-presented search resource including analysis of
site traffic
www.alltheweb.com
Fast and comprehensive search site, with useful tools for
researching behind the scenes at websites and features for
finding multimedia content
www.altavista.com
One of the web's first search engines, still a useful resource
www.askjeeves.com
Question and answer service
www.google.com
The web's biggest, fastest and most famous search engine,
with many advanced features including newsgroup and image
searching
www.hotbot.com
Powerful and flexible search engine, now part of the Lycos
network

www.lycos.com
Lycos
www.northernlight.com
Northern Light
www.yahoo.com
Vast directory resource with good search functions

Shopping

shopping.com
Huge US shopping portal
shopping.yahoo.com
Huge shopping portal from Yahoo, with reviews, ratings and hints for shopping online
www.ebay.com
Auction-format trading site for an endless variety of items, with a UK branch
www.lastminute.com
Famous UK-based site for last-minute bookings – travel, entertainment, restaurants and gifts – with sites in 11 countries including Australia and New Zealand
www.letsbuyit.com
Aggregate buying system for consumer and domestic goods, with several European subsidiaries
www.priceline.com
Name-your-own-price site for flights, hotels and more, with links to international sites
www.walmart.com
US retail giant

Sport

cbs.sportsline.com
Mammoth site devoted principally to US sports
espn.go.com
The Microsoft-hosted sporting monolith's vast website, for followers of US sports
news.bbc.co.uk/sport/default.stm
World sports coverage from the BBC

news.ft.com/culture/sport
The business of sport from the *Financial Times*
www.cricket.org
Cricket site with ball-by-ball coverage of international games,
extensive player information and many interviews and articles
www.cricket365.com
Huge cricket site, with comprehensive statistics and reports
www.sportal.com
Major sports hub, with an emphasis on European football
www.uefa.com
Union of European Football Associations

Statistics

europa.eu.int/comm/eurostat
The European Union's list of statistics agencies worldwide
www.abs.gov.au
The Australian Bureau of Statistics
www.cbs.gov.il/engindex.htm
Israel's Central Bureau of Statistics
www.cbs.nl/en/
Dutch social statistics and economic indicators
www.cso.ie
Ireland's Central Statistics Office
www.dst.dk
Denmark's statistical site, with an English version
www.fedstats.gov
One-stop shop for US federal statistics, from over 70 US agencies
www.ine.es
Spain's National Statistical Institute
www.ine.pt
Portugal's statistics institute
www.insee.fr/va/index.htm
France's National Institute of Statistics and Economic Studies
www.singstat.gov.sg
Statistics Singapore
www.ssb.no/english
Norwegian central store for national statistics and economic
indicators

www.stat.go.jp/english/index.htm
Japan's Statistics Bureau and Statistics Centre
www.statbel.fgov.be/home_en.htm
Belgium's National Institute of Statistics
www.statice.is
Statistics Iceland
www.statistics.gov.uk
The UK's Office for National Statistics
www.statistik.admin.ch/eindex.htm
Swiss Federal Statistical Office
www.statistik-bund.de
Germany's Federal Statistical Office
www.statssa.gov.za
Statistics South Africa
www.un.org/depts/unsd
The UN's statistics department

Stock exchanges

deutsche-boerse.com
The Deutsche Börse exchange in Frankfurt
www.euronext.com
Euronext, a merger of the Paris, Brussels and Amsterdam
exchanges, with links to the three local sites
www.liffe.com
London International Financial Futures and Options Exchange
www.lme.co.uk
The London Metal Exchange
www.londonstockexchange.com
The London Stock Exchange
www.nasdaq.com
The National Association of Securities Dealers Automated
Quotation (NASDAQ), home of the world's high-tech stocks
www.nyse.com
The New York Stock Exchange
www.tse.or.jp
The Tokyo Stock Exchange
www.world-exchanges.org
The International Federation of Stock Exchanges, with links to

member exchanges

Technology and new media

tornado-insider.com
Magazine for entrepreneurs and investors in business and technology
www.business2.com
Home for *Business* 2.0, the tech industry's business bible
www.herring.com
Business news, technology and research for investors and consumers
www.iwantmedia.com
Media news and resources
www.inside.com
E-zine focusing on media and technology
www.kuro5hin.org
A slightly more serious cousin of Slashdot
www.news.com
Daily technology news from CNET
www.ntk.net
Incisive, irreverent and usually caustic technology snippets from the UK
www.salon.com/tech
News, analysis and reviews from *Salon*, a stylish internet magazine
www.slashdot.org
News for nerds in the know
www.theregister.co.uk
Cynical tech news, with a focus on the UK
www.wired.com
Daily tech news and culture, with links to the original net culture magazine
www.zdnet.com
ZDNet, with tech news, reviews, resources, advice and more

Trade association directories

ca.yahoo.com/Regional/Countries/Canada/Business_and_Economy/
Organizations/Trade_Associations
Yahoo's directory of Canadian trade associations
dir.yahoo.com/Business_and_Economy/Organizations/Trade_Associations
US and worldwide trade associations from Yahoo
www.taforum.org
The UK's Trade Associations Forum, which provides a meeting
site for trade associations and A–Z links

Weblogs

blogdex.media.mit.edu
Huge collection of weblog snippets from Cameron Marlow at
MIT's Media Lab
portal.eatonweb.com
Huge directory of links to weblogs
www.blogger.com
Home of the most popular weblog service, with thousands of
links to user sites
www.moveabletype.org/spotlight-full.shtml
Links to weblogs based on Moveable Type's weblog system